COPYRIGHT LAW

European Community Law Series
Series Editor: Professor D Lasok, QC (University of Exeter)

European Community Law will have an important impact upon the law of the United Kingdom and other countries concerned with EC legislation. This new series will provide authoritative and up-to-date accounts of specific topics and areas. The volumes are addressed to legal practitioners, in-house lawyers, businessmen and to all those who need to communicate with lawyers in this field.

Volumes will include:

Rosa Greaves, *Transport Law of the European Community*

Friedl Weiss, *Public Supply and Public Works Contracts in European Community Law*

Philippe Bourin, *The European Investment Bank*

Frank Wooldridge, *European Company Law*

Julian Currall and Christopher Docksey, *Sex Discrimination in European Community Law*

David Freestone, *Environmental Protection in the European Community*

S K Chatterjee, *Legal Aspects of Drug Control and Treatment within the European Community*

European Community Law Series

1

COPYRIGHT LAW
in the United Kingdom and the European Community

Peter Stone

THE ATHLONE PRESS
London & Atlantic Highlands, NJ

First published 1990 by The Athlone Press Ltd
1 Park Drive, London NW11 7SG
and 171 First Avenue, Atlantic Highlands, NJ 07716

British Library Cataloguing in Publication Data
Stone, Peter
  Copyright law in the United Kingdom and the European
  Community. (European community law series)
  1. Great Britain. Copyright. Law
  I. Title II. Series
  344.1064821

  ISBN 0–485–70004–2

Library of Congress Cataloging in Publication Data
Stone, Peter, *1947–*
    Copyright law in the United Kingdom and the European Community/
  Peter Stone.
        p.   cm. — (European Community law series; bk. 1)
    Includes bibliographical references.
    ISBN 0–485–70004–2
    1. Copyright—Great Britain. 2. Copyright— European Economic
  Community countries. I. Title. II. Series.
  KJE2655.S76   1990
  346.4104′82—dc20
  [344.106482]

Typeset by J&L Composition Ltd, Filey, North Yorkshire
Printed in Great Britain by Billings and Sons Ltd, Worcester

Contents

Series Preface

West European integration has become an irreversible and ever-expanding process affecting directly not only the Member States of the European Community but also business interests and individuals in all walks of life. The prediction that, in time, 80% of the national legislation will eventually emanate from Brussels may not be accurate but the volume of regulations and directives so far produced in the Community has already assumed formidable dimensions. Consequently textbooks, commentaries and source publications have grown in size to the point of being too voluminous to be handled by anyone interested in a particular area. Moreover, in view of the abundance of material, large publications cannot always do justice to every topic which merits a treatment in depth.

In response to this challenge, the Athlone Press had launched a European Community Law Series addressed mainly to legal practice and the business world and also to students of law. The Series consists of concise and relatively short monographs designed to break new ground and fill the gaps in the existing literature. In monographs unencumbered with general information but still within the context of the integrative process, the Series offers guidance to the practitioner and businessman.

Volumes in the Series will take more or less self-contained subjects, and the Series will eventually compose a specialist library.

D Lasok

Series Editor

Volume Preface

Copyright provides the principal mechanism by which legal support is given to creative endeavour in the non-technological sphere. It also plays a lesser role in the technological sphere. While territorial in scope, it has long been the subject of international agreements designed to establish reciprocity and minimum standards of protection. In the United Kingdom the process of thorough review and reform, which seems to take place in forty-year cycles, has just been completed with the enactment of the Copyright, Designs and Patents Act 1988, which received the royal assent on 15 November 1988, and for the most part entered into force on 1 August 1989.

Meanwhile the constantly expanding activities of the European Community have increasingly affected copyright. Initially Community law was concerned primarily to limit the extent to which copyright could be used so as to impede trade between Member States, and to subject the activities of copyright collecting societies to controls designed to secure a measure of competition.

More recently, however, the European Commission has adopted a much more positive attitude to copyright, recognizing the importance of creative endeavour to the European economy. While complete unification is not envisaged in this sphere, the Commission now contemplates the harmonization of the copyright laws of the Member States by Community Directives on important questions where the traditional international treaties have failed to establish adequate solutions. It is clear that the Commission's views published in its Green Paper of 1988, have had substantial influence on the new British legislation.

This volume seeks both to expound the new British law of

copyright under the 1988 Act, much of which reflects the Berne Copyright Convention, to which all the Community countries are parties; and to examine, in the context of the various issues, the relevant existing rules of Community law and the policies on harmonization announced by the Commission in its Green Paper. It will be seen that British Law already accords better with the Commission's policies than those of many of the Member States, and that the envisaged Directives are unlikely to cause major upheaval in the United Kingdom. Rather, the development of harmonization at Community level may be seen as extending throughout the Community a level of protection for creative effort which for the most part has already been achieved in the United Kingdom.

The volume is aimed, not at the specialist practitioner in intellectual-property law, but at the law student who is approaching the subject for the first time, and at the lawyer or businessman who has some legal or commercial training or experience and is seeking a concise but accurate introduction to the matters in question.

Peter Stone,
Exeter

1
Introduction

THE NATURE OF COPYRIGHT

Copyright gives protection to the creators of a wide variety of types of subject-matter. At international level, the Berne Copyright Convention,[1] to which all the Member States of the European Community (and many other countries) are parties, provides for reciprocity and minimum standards of protection for authors of literary and artistic works (and their successors in title). These are defined by Art. 2(1) as including 'every production in the literary, scientific and artistic domain, ... such as books, pamphlets and other writings; lectures, addresses, sermons and other works of the same nature; dramatic or dramatico-musical works; choreographic works and entertainments in dumb show; musical compositions with or without words; cinematographic works [including] works expressed by a process analogous to cinematography; works of drawing, painting, architecture, sculpture, engraving and lithography; photographic works [including] works expressed by a process analogous to photography; works of applied art; illustrations, maps, plans, sketches and three-dimensional works relative to geography, topography, architecture or science'. Also included as original works are translations, adaptations, arrangements of music and other alterations of a literary or artistic work;[2] and collections of literary or artistic works, such as encyclopedias and anthologies, which, by reason of the selection and arrangement of their contents, constitute intellectual creations.[3]

The Berne and Universal Copyright Conventions do not, however, provide for protection in respect of sound recordings, broadcasts or cable transmissions as such (as distinct from 'primary' works, such as dramatic or musical works, which may be contained therein). Hence further treaties have been found necessary; these include: the Rome Convention for the Protection of Performers, Producers of Phonograms and Broadcasting Organizations (1961),[4] parties to which include the United Kingdom, France, West Germany, Italy, Luxembourg, Denmark and Ireland; the Geneva Convention for the Protection of Producers of Phonograms against Unauthorized Duplication of their Phonograms (1971),[5] parties to which include the United Kingdom, France, West Germany, Italy, Luxembourg, Denmark and Spain; and the European Agreement on the Protection of Television Broadcasts, Strasbourg (1960), parties to which include the United Kingdom, France, West Germany, Belgium, Denmark and Spain.

In the United Kingdom the types of work which receive copyright protection are now listed in s. 1(1) of the Copyright, Designs and Patents Act 1988 and further defined in ss. 3–8. The types of protected work are: (a) original literary, dramatic, musical or artistic works; (b) sound recordings, films, broadcasts and cable programmes; and (c) the typographical arrangement of published editions. Formerly, under the Copyright Act 1956, which is now replaced by the 1988 Act, only original literary, dramatic, musical or artistic works, which received protection under Part I of the 1956 Act, were referred to as 'works', and other types of subject-matter, such as sound recordings and cinemato- graph films, which received protection under Part II of the 1956 Act, were referred to as 'matters'. But now all types of protected subject-matter are referred to in the British legislation as 'works'.

In broad terms, copyright confers protection, by way of exclu- sive rights, in respect of two kinds of activity: (i) the making of, and the dealing with, physical copies of the protected work; and (ii) the giving or making of public performances, broadcasts and cable transmissions of the work. So it is convenient to speak of the 'physical' rights and the 'performing' rights. The protection con- ferred by copyright does not amount to a full monopoly, such as is conferred by a patent, but is limited to derivative activity. In other words, for there to be infringement, the defendant's article or performance must be actually copied (directly or indirectly) from the plaintiff's work.

The duration of copyright varies according to the type of work, but in most cases is much longer than the maximum term of twenty years now applicable to patents under the European Patent Convention (1973)[6] and the (British) Patents Act 1977. Thus the copyright in a literary work lasts until the end of the fiftieth year after that of the author's death.[7] Moreover, in countries belonging to the Berne Union, copyright (unlike patents) arises automatically from the creation or publication of a work, without any official grant or registration.[8] Copyright belongs to the author of the work, or his employer, or a successor in title.

The various copyrights are cumulative, so that, for example, one who for commercial purposes video-records a television broadcast of a film may, by his single act of copying, commit infringement of each of the following copyrights: (i) the copyright in the television broadcast itself: (ii) the copyright in the film which is being broadcast; (iii) the copyright in the screen-play, as an original dramatic work; (iv) the copyright in the film-score, as an original musical work; (v) the copyright in the novel on which the film is based, as an original literary work – with the result that the owner of each of these copyrights may take proceedings for infringement against the copyist.

THE BRITISH LEGISLATION

Until recently copyright was governed in the United Kingdom by the Copyright Act 1956 (hereafter 'the 1956 Act'), together with subsequent enactments (such as the Design Copyright Act 1968 and the Copyright (Computer Software) Amendment Act 1985), to the exclusion of the common law.[9] The 1956 Act entered into force on 1 June 1957. Transitional provisions, which applied to works and matters created before its commencement date, were contained in s. 50 and Schs. 7 and 8 of the 1956 Act.

Copyright is now governed by Part I of the Copyright, Designs and Patents Act 1988 (hereafter 'the 1988 Act' or 'the new Act'),[10] which replaces the 1956 Act and the subsequent amending Acts.[11] The 1988 Act followed a lengthy period of official consideration,[12] which culminated in a White Paper on *Intellectual Property and Innovation* (1986).[13] The new Act implements proposals contained in the 1986 White Paper, as well as making other changes proposed during its passage through Parliament, and consolidates the statutory law on copyright. Part I of the Act is organized as follows:

(i) Chapter I (ss. 1–15) deals with the subsistence, ownership and duration of copyright.[14]

(ii) Chapter II (ss. 16–27) specifies the acts which normally infringe copyright, and Chapter III (ss. 28–76) the exceptional cases where an otherwise infringing act is permissible.[15]

(iv) Chapter IV (ss. 77–89) introduces 'moral' rights of authors.[16]

(v) Chapter V (ss. 90–95) concerns dealings, such as assignments and licences.[17]

(vi) Chapter VI (ss. 96–115) deals with remedies for infringement.[18]

(vii) Chapter VII (ss. 116–44) regulates licensing schemes, and Chapter VIII (ss. 145–52) deals with the Copyright Tribunal.[19]

(ix) Chapter IX (ss. 153–62) deals with connecting factors and territorial scope.[20]

(x) Chapter X (ss. 163–79) deals with such matters as Crown copyright, transitional provisions and interpretation.

Part II (ss. 180–212) of the new Act replaces the Performers' Protection Acts 1958–72[21] and confers a right akin to copyright in respect of 'live' performances by artistes.[22] Part III (ss. 213–64) creates a new unregistered design right, akin to copyright but of short duration, in respect of industrial designs. Part IV (ss. 265–73) amends the Registered Designs Act 1949, and Sch. 4 contains the 1949 Act as amended.[23]

Transitional provisions
In relation to Part I of the 1988 Act, transitional provisions are introduced by s. 170 and specified in Sch. 1. The following general principles are laid down by the Schedule:[24]

(i) The new Act applies to existing works (i.e. works made before the commencement date) as well as future works (made after that date).[25]

(ii) With a view to securing continuity insofar as the new Act re-enacts earlier legislation, unless otherwise provided:

(a) references in other enactments, instruments or documents to copyright, or to copyright works or matters, under the 1956 Act, or to provisions of the 1956 Act, are to be construed as including references to copyright, or to copyright works, under, or to the corresponding provisions of, the new Act;

(b) references in the new Act or in other enactments or documents to the new provisions are to be construed as including references to the corresponding earlier provisions; and

(c) subordinate legislation made and other things done under earlier copyright legislation have effect under the corresponding provisions of the new Act.[26]

(iii) Copyright subsists, after the commencement date, in an existing work only if copyright subsisted in it immediately before that date.[27]

(iv) Authorship and first ownership of an existing work is determined in accordance with the law in force when the work was created.[28]

(v) The new provisions on infringement or remedies apply only to acts done after the commencement date, and the provisions of the 1956 Act continue to apply to acts done before that date.[29]

By s. 171, subject to certain savings, no copyright or similar right subsists otherwise than by virtue of the new Act. The savings relate to rights under other legislation which is not expressly repealed, amended or modified by the new Act; prerogative rights of the Crown and privileges of Parliament (otherwise than in relation to Bills and Acts); forfeiture under the law of customs and excise; and equitable rules on breach of trust or confidence.

By s. 172, provisions of the new Act corresponding to provisions of the previous legislation are not to be construed as departing from the previous law merely because of a change of expression, and decisions under the previous law may be referred to for the purpose of establishing departure or otherwise interpreting the new Act.

HARMONIZATION AT COMMUNITY LEVEL

The EC Commission has recently issued a *Green Paper on Copyright and the Challenge of Technology – Copyright Issues requiring Immediate Action*.[30] The issues identified by the Commission as requiring immediate attention at Community level in relation to the internal market are the following: (i) commercial piracy; (ii) home copying of sound recordings and films; (iii) rental rights in respect of sound recordings and films; and (iv) protection of computer programs and computerized databases.[31] It is evident that, even before publication of the Green Paper, the Commission's thinking was made known to the British government, and has been taken into account in the Copyright, Designs and Patents Act 1988.

The Commission's Green Paper emphasizes not only the effects of copyright on the internal market, and differences in national laws as a barrier to trade, but also technological advances, and the needs of users of technology, as well as the need to encourage creativity and innovation. Anxiety is expressed about excessive protection of industrial designs and computer programs.

As regards ordinary commercial piracy, the Commission emphasizes its significance in relation to video and sound recordings and computer software. It proposes improved co-operation at the external international level, and internally it contemplates extending the 1986 Regulation on measures to prohibit the release for free circulation of counterfeit goods[32] (i.e. goods which infringe trade marks) to cover pirate goods (i.e. goods which infringe copyright). It supports the availability of remedies by way of damages and injunctions, and proposes the extended availability of remedies by way of confiscation of infringing articles and of equipment used to produce them. It also favours the existence of criminal penalties, including imprisonment for serious or repeated offences. It looks with favour on associations of copyright owners designed to act against piracy, especially associations which include different interest groups. It also encourages the use of technical measures to facilitate enforcement, e.g. by the marking of films.

As regards the home copying of ordinary (i.e. analogue as distinct from digital) sound recordings,[33] there appears to have been disagreement within the Commission as to the possible introduction of a harmonized levy on blank tape and equipment, some Commissioners wishing to leave it to each Member State to decide whether to impose such levies, while others favoured the introduction of a harmonized levy at Community level, and yet others were opposed to such levies. Since, however, the level of such levies now existing or contemplated in various Member States was not substantially different, and systematic controls at borders were not involved, the Green Paper ultimately reached a provisional conclusion rejecting harmonization at Community level. Instead the Commission envisages reliance on technical obstacles to copying; the introduction of a rental right for audiovisual works; and that the Member States should be left free to decide whether or not to maintain or introduce levies.

The Commission also proposes the introduction of a rental right in all Member States in respect of sound and video recordings, to be conferred on authors of works recorded, producers of recordings and performers whose performances are recorded. This would be a right to refuse permission, and not merely to receive a fair payment. Thus the owners could take into account the effect of hiring on sales. A directive under Art. 100A of the EEC Treaty is contemplated.

In addition to its examination of problems relating to the market within the Community, the Commission indicates its concern to ensure that adequate protection of copyright works originating within the Community should exist in non-member States. Thus in Chapter 7 of the Green Paper, it reviews Community action in the context of various international bodies, such as the World International Property Organization (WIPO) and the General Agreement on Tariffs and Trade (GATT), and also draws attention to the possibility of the Community using its new 'trade policy instrument', created by Reg. 2641/84 on the Strengthening of the Common Commercial Policy with regard in particular to Protection against Illicit Commercial Practices,[34] for the purpose of imposing trade sanctions against third countries which disregard the Berne or Universal Copyright Conventions to the disadvantage of copyright owners belonging to the Community, even where the third country is not a party to these Conventions. In this context it refers to an apparently successful procedure of this kind in which Indonesia was induced to grant national treatment on a reciprocal basis to Community nationals in respect of copyright in sound recordings.

Perhaps the most significant feature of the Green Paper is the considerable sympathy evinced by the Commission for the interests of copyright owners. Hitherto Community law has to a large extent seemed more antagonistic than helpful to owners of intellectual property. Their rights have been restricted by the doctrines of Community-wide exhaustion and of common origin which have been established by the European Court in the interest of freedom of trade between Member States, and their licensing agreements have been scrutinized by the Commission under its powers to ensure freedom of competition, while legislation or proposals designed to create Community-wide patents or trade marks have not reached fruition. The Green Paper may mark a turning-point in attitudes, and indicate that the encouragement of creative intellectual effort through the intellectual-property system has now become an important policy of the Community.

Shortly after issuing its Green Paper, the Commission adopted proposals on the protection of intellectual property to be put forward on behalf of the Community in the Uruguay round of the GATT negotiations at Geneva.[35] These involve, *inter alia*, that all Contracting States to the GATT should accede to the Paris Convention for the Protection of Industrial Property and the Berne Copyright Convention; that provision should be made for a copyright in sound recordings, performances and radio broadcasts, to exist without formalities and last for twenty years; and in computer programs, to last at least twenty-five years.[36] The Commission also favours the protection of original or novel industrial designs for at least ten years, and of semiconductor topography, as well as the protection of trade or industrial secrets against disclosure and dishonest use.

2

Subsistence

In this chapter we shall consider the conditions required for copyright to exist. This involves examination of the types of work which receive protection; authorship and ownership; connecting factors; and duration.

In general the new British Act applies to existing works (i.e. works made before the commencement date) as well as future works (made after that date), [1] but copyright subsists, after the commencement date, in an existing work only if copyright subsisted in it immediately before that date,[2] and authorship and first ownership of existing works is determined in accordance with the law in force when the work was created.[3]

ORIGINAL LITERARY, DRAMATIC, MUSICAL AND ARTISTIC WORKS

Sections 1(1)(a), 3 and 4 of the 1988 Act[4] define and confer protection on original literary, dramatic, musical or artistic works. In general the Act subjects literary, dramatic and musical works to similar rules, but artistic works are subjected to somewhat different rules from the other three types of original work. We shall deal first with issues common to all four types – the requirements relating to fixation, effort and originality; and then with the characteristics of each type of original work.

The concept of 'an original ... work'

Fixation
It has long been required that there must be a physical embodiment (or fixation) of the work, e.g. in writing or on a canvas. As

regards artistic works, s. 4 of the new Act follows s. 3 of the 1956 Act in specifying the types of work protected in terms of physical objects such as paintings, drawings, engravings and photographs.

As regards literary, dramatic or musical works, s. 49(4) of the 1956 Act provided that such a work was made when it was first reduced to writing[5] or some other material form,[6] and s. 2 of the Copyright (Computer Software) Amendment Act 1985 added that the storage of a work in a computer should be treated as its reduction to a material form. The 1986 White Paper proposed legislation making clear that copyright subsists in works fixed in any form from which they can in principle be reproduced.[7] Accordingly s. 3(2) of the new Act specifies that copyright does not subsist in a literary, dramatic or musical work unless and until it has been recorded, in writing or otherwise, and that such a work is regarded as made at the time when it is so recorded, while s. 3(3) adds that it is immaterial whether the work is recorded by or with the permission of the author. For good measure s. 178 defines 'writing' as including any form of notation or code, whether by hand or otherwise, and regardless of the method by which, or the medium in or on which, it is recorded.

As regards fixation by storage or recording in a computer, it seems reasonably clear that some degree of permanence is required, and thus that a file which is contained merely in the transient memory of a computer, so that it would be lost if the power failed or the machine were switched off, is not yet stored or recorded, but a file which has been saved onto an electro-magnetic disk has been stored or recorded.[8]

Owing to the absence of a fixation or recording, transient extempore performances, e.g. by jazz musicians who improvise, do not give rise to copyright. 'Live' performances of certain types have, however, long received some protection under the Performers' Protection Acts 1958–72 or their predecessors, and this protection has now been extended by Part II of the 1988 Act, which replaces the Performers' Protection Acts.[9] The protection now conferred on certain 'live' performances by Part II of the new Act is equivalent to copyright in all but name.

In pursuance of the Berne Copyright Convention, since 1911 the existence of British copyright in a literary, dramatic, musical or artistic work has required no special formalities, such as registration or the endorsement of a notice claiming copyright on published copies of the work. Rather, copyright arises automatically upon the creation (in recorded form) or publication of the work. The commonly seen copyright notice, '(c), [owner's name], [year of first publication]', is without significance in British law, and is used in order to obtain protection in countries which are parties to the Universal Copyright Convention, but not to the Berne Convention.[10]

Authorial effort
For there to be an original work attracting copyright protection, the author must have exercised sufficient, i.e. more than minimal, effort, by way of skill and/or labour, in creating the work. The amount of creative effort required is not great, but it must be more than minimal. Moreover, the work itself must be more than negligible in size.

Thus copyright has been held not to exist in a simple card-index system, consisting of cards marked 'name', 'address' etc.;[11] or in a selection of commonplace tables in a diary;[12] or in a mere selection of local services from a general railway timetable.[13] Again, there is no separate copyright in the title of a work, and the title is not a sufficiently substantial part of the whole work to make copying it infringement of the copyright in the work itself.[14] Similarly, a single invented word, devised, albeit with considerable effort, for use as a trade mark, is too slight a creation to constitute a literary work.[15]

In general there cannot be an original work without a human author, for it is to the author or his employer that the copyright normally belongs,[16] and it is the author's lifetime which measures its duration.[17] Thus a 'painting', however beautiful, which is produced by a duck accidentally walking across a canvas, is not a 'work of authorship' and cannot receive protection as an original work.[18] But under the new Act it is now possible for copyright to exist in a literary, dramatic, musical or artistic work which is generated by a computer in circumstances such that there is (in the normal sense) no human author,[19] for ss. 9(3) and 12(3) provide that in such a case the person by whom the arrangements necessary for the creation of the work were undertaken is to be treated as the author,[20] and the copyright is to expire at the end of the fiftieth calendar year after the year in which the work was made. In some cases an object-code version of a computer program might be regarded as a computer-generated work. In the case of

11

computer-generated programs, the European Commission inclines to the view that the user of the generating computer should become the first owner of the copyright.[21]

Originality

Like ss. 2 and 3 of the 1956 Act, s. 1(1) (a) of the new Act requires that, to obtain protection, a literary, dramatic, musical or artistic work must be 'original'. This means that the work must not be copied from another work in the same form. As Peterson J. explained in *University of London Press v. University Tutorial Press*,[22] in a passage later approved by Privy Council per Lord Atkinson, in *Macmillan v. Cooper*,[23] the requisite originality, in the case of a literary work, relates to the expression of the thought, rather than to the thought itself; moreover the expression need not be in an original or novel form; rather, the requirement is merely that the work must not be copied from another work, that it should originate from the author.

The objection that the work is not original because it is merely copied from another work does not, however, apply where substantial skill and/or labour is used in converting a work from one form to another. Thus a selection of passages from an earlier literary work, even with the insertion of linking notes, will not normally attract copyright.[24] On the other hand, a translation of a literary work from one language to another will attract its own copyright,[25] as will a photograph of a drawing, painting or engraving,[26] an engraving derived from a photograph,[27] or a drawing of a carved head.[28] Similarly, an engineering drawing made from a prototype of an industrial product, such as a piece of 'knock-down' furniture, will probably attract copyright despite its derivative character.[29]

On the other hand, as was recognized recently by the Privy Council in *Interlego AG v. Tyco Industries Inc.*,[30] a drawing which is simply copied from another drawing is not original, however great the skill and labour applied in making the copy. In the absence of a change from one form of work to another, skill and labour merely in the process of copying cannot confer originality; rather, there must be some, qualitatively significant, element of material alteration or embellishment.

Literary, dramatic or musical works

For an original work, satisfying the requirements of fixation, effort and originality considered above, to qualify for copyright protection under s. 1(1)(a) of the new Act, the work must also be a literary, dramatic, musical or artistic work as defined by ss. 3(1) and 4.

Section 3(1) of the new Act defines:

> 'literary work' as any work, other than a dramatic or musical work, which is written, spoken or sung, and adds that the concept includes a table or compilation[31] and a computer program;[32]
> 'dramatic work' as including a work of dance or mime;[33]
> 'musical work' as a work consisting of music, exclusive of any words or action intended to be sung, spoken or performed with the music.[34]

As the definition makes clear, the lyric and the music of a song are treated as separate works and thus attract literary and musical copyrights respectively, which may be in different ownership and of different duration.

Little difficulty has arisen concerning the concepts of dramatic or musical works,[35] but the concept of a literary work has given rise to substantial case-law. Apart from the requirements for all types of original work, and the exclusion of dramatic and musical works, it seems that the concept of a literary work involves merely that the work should consist of words, numbers or some analogous code, and should express ideas, emotions or information intelligible to human beings, or instructions intelligible to a computer. Some assistance may be gained from s. 101 of the American Copyright Act 1976 as amended,[36] which defines 'literary works' as works expressed in words, numbers, or other verbal or numerical symbols or indicia. Again, in view of the failure of the British legislation to define a 'compilation', a persuasive analogy may be found in the American Copyright Act, which defines a 'compilation' as a work formed by the collection and assembling of pre-existing materials or of data which are selected, co-ordinated, or arranged in such a way that the resulting work as a whole constitutes an original work of authorship. For a work to be 'literary', the appeal must, however, be intellectual rather than visual.[37]

Certainly the concept of a literary work is not limited to works which would interest a literary critic. As Peterson J. explained in *University of London Press v. University Tutorial Press*,[38] 'literary work' is not confined to works such as novels, which have 'literary' style, but covers such things as a list of registered bills of sale, a list of foxhounds and hunting days, and trade catalogues. It covers work which is expressed in print or writing, regardless of whether the quality or style is high. 'Literary' is used in the same sense as when one speaks of political or electioneering literature, and refers to written or printed matter. Thus the category has been held to include: examination question-papers;[39] railway timetable guides;[40] simple price-lists[41] and more complex trade-catalogues;[42] an area directory of residents;[43] a football fixture-list,[43] a fixed-odds betting coupon,[45] and a racing information service.[46]

Moreover, secondary work on existing sources may create copyright, as in the case of translation from one 'human' language to another,[47] or from one computer language or code to another,[48] or of substantial editing,[49] or of the addition of *explanatory* notes.[50] Again, copyright may be acquired by compilation, whether of an anthology of poems,[51] or of a chronological list of football fixtures from a club's list,[52] or of a selection of wagers in the form of a fixed-odds betting coupon.[53] It may also be acquired by true abridgement or summary.[54] Similarly secondary work may create a copyright musical work, e.g. a piano reduction of an opera score.[55] Moreover, the necessary effort may consist in the exercise of commercial, rather than literary, judgement – as in compiling the most commercially advantageous list of football fixtures or in selecting the most profitable and attractive wagers for a fixed-odds coupon – provided that the preparation of the document was one of the objects of the exercise of commercial judgement.[56]

In Chapter 6 of its Green Paper,[57] the EC Commission favours the recognition of a copyright in a computerized database, as a compilation of works, belonging to its operator, at least where the database consists of works which themselves receive copyright protection. It is less clear as to the desirability of protecting a database as a compilation where it consists of non-copyright material. There is no reason to doubt that under present British law a computerized database is protected as a compilation, whether or not its constituent items of data themselves are sufficiently substantial to qualify as literary works.

Computer programs
As regards the existence of copyright in computer programs, the key provision is now s. 3(1) of the 1988 Act, which replaces a similar provision contained in s. 1(1) of the Copyright (Computer

Software) Amendment Act 1985[58] and defines 'literary work' as including a computer program. This reflects the view, now generally accepted internationally, that copyright, rather than patents, offers the appropriate form of protection for computer programs, at any rate in most circumstances.[59] The same technique has been adopted in Germany, where an Act of 24 June 1985 explicitly assimilates computer programs to literary works for copyright purposes. As will be seen below,[60] there is also the possibility that the screen-output generated by a computer program may receive separate copyright protection as a 'film'.

The British copyright legislation has made no attempt to define a 'computer program', but the definition given in the American copyright legislation, viz. 'a set of statements or instructions to be used directly or indirectly in a computer in order to bring about a certain result',[61] offers a persuasive analogy. A program may be expressed in the form of source code, written either in a high-level language such as Basic or Pascal, or in a low-level language such as the assembly language for a particular processor. Source code (whether in a high- or low-level language) is intelligible without much difficulty by a competent programmer, but a program will only 'run', i.e. operate, if the source code is translated into object code, intelligible to the computer, by means of another program known as an interpreter or compiler. An interpreter carries out the translation on each occasion on which the program is run, whereas a compiler creates a permanent version of the program in object code, which can then be run directly from the computer's operating system. Object code is difficult, though not impossible, to understand, even by the foremost experts. In common parlance 'software' refers to a program (whether in the form of source or object code), together with any accompanying documentation, such as a printed manual. Such documentation, however, is regarded as a separate and 'ordinary' literary work, analogous to a manual for a car or washing-machine.

Section 3(1) must be read in the light of ss. 21(3) and (4) of the 1988 Act, which replaces a similar provision of s. 1(2) of the 1985 Act and specifies that (for purposes of infringement) a version of a computer program, in which it is converted into or out of a computer language or code or into a different computer language or code, otherwise than incidentally in the course of running the program, constitutes a translation and an adaptation of the program.[62] Read together, it is clear that references in ss. 3(1) and 21 to a 'computer program' and to a 'version' of a computer program cover equally an embodiment of a program in the form of source code and an embodiment in the form of object code.

English decisions before the 1985 Act had shown willingness to recognize at least that a program in source code was a literary work, and that a version in object code was an adaptation of the version in source code from which it was derived, so that a defendant who copied the plaintiff's object code would infringe copyright in his source code. Such an approach received support from Goulding J. in *Sega Enterprises Ltd. v. Richards*,[63] which involved a game, FROGGER; from Megarry V.-C. in *Thrustcode Ltd. v. W.W. Computing Ltd.*,[64] which involved a program for controlling industrial production; and from Mason and Wilson JJ., dissenting, in the High Court of Australia in *Computer Edge Pty. Ltd. v. Apple Computer Inc.*,[65] which involved the operating system for the APPLE II computer. Elsewhere in Europe copyright protection was accorded to computer programs in advance of specific legislation in France,[66] Germany,[67] Italy[68] and the Netherlands.[69]

Within the European Community there is now legislation specifically providing for copyright protection of computer programs in France (by an Act of 3 July 1985), in Germany (by an act of 24 June 1985) and in Spain (by an Act of 11 November 1987), as well as in the United Kingdom. It is only in Greece that there seems to be reluctance to protect software in this way. Moreover the EC Commission, in its recent *Green Paper on Copyright and the Challenge of Technology – Copyright Issues requiring Immediate Attention*,[70] envisaged the adoption of a directive under Article 100A of the EEC Treaty, designed to harmonize the laws of the Member States in relation to the protection of computer programs within the framework of copyright,[71] and in January 1989 the Commission filed with the Council a proposal for such a directive.[72]

As we have seen,[73] s. 3(2) of the 1988 Act provides that copyright does not subsist in a literary work (including a computer program) unless and until it is recorded, in writing or otherwise, and that a work is regarded as made at the time at which it is so recorded.[74] It seems clear, however, that a program (or other work) created in electronic form will not attract copyright merely from its existence in the transient memory of a computer. It will not be 'recorded' (or, formerly, 'reduced' or 'stored') until a permanent fixation is made, in the sense that it is embodied in a tangible object so that its existence there is independent of the continuance of the power supply to a computer. Such recording will occur when the program is 'saved' onto a floppy disk or a hard disk or a tape, or it is 'burnt' into the circuitry of a silicon chip, or it is printed out on paper, perhaps in hexadecimal notation. In its Green Paper the EC Commission emphasized the desirability of copyright legislation in all the Member States specifying that the form in which a program is 'fixed' or embodied, e.g. on a magnetic disk or silicon chip, should be immaterial to the existence of copyright protection,[75] and accordingly Art. 1(3) of the proposed Directive[76] confers protection on 'the expression in any form' of a computer program.

In relation to computer programs, the German Federal Supreme Court has ruled that, for a program to receive full copyright protection, its creation should involve the application of above-average programming skill.[77] But such an approach has been rejected in France[78] and would certainly be rejected in the United Kingdom. In its Green Paper the EC Commission considered that it might be desirable for the contemplated directive on harmonization to define the requirement of originality for programs as merely requiring that the program must be the result of the creator's own intellectual effort, and must not consist merely of elements which, even in the relevant combination, are common-place in the industry,[79] but in the result Art. 1(4)(a) of its proposed Directive[80] merely specifies that the same conditions as regards originality should apply to computer programs as apply to other literary works.

At least as regards allegedly infringing acts (or alleged offences) committed since the entry into force of the Copyright (Computer Software) Amendment Act 1985 on 16 September 1985,[81] the following propositions can be confidently asserted as established rules of British law:

(i) Copyright exists in the United Kingdom in a 'recorded' version of a computer program, as a literary work, even if the program was created before the last-mentioned date,[82] unless the version is merely a substantially unaltered copy of an earlier program in the same form.

(ii) It is immaterial to the existence of the copyright whether the version was recorded in electronic form (whether on disk, tape or chip) or on paper.

(iii) It is also immaterial to the existence of the copyright whether the 'recorded' version in question was expressed in source code[83] or in object code[84] or even in a human language.[85]

(iv) It is also immaterial to the existence of copyright whether the program is part of the operating system of a computer or is an application program.[86]

In Chapter 5 of its Green Paper,[87] the EC Commission stated its intention of submitting to the Council, as a matter of urgency, a proposal for a directive under Art. 18 of the Single European Act, amending Art. 100 of the EEC Treaty, designed to harmonize the laws of the Member States in respect of the protection of computer programs within the framework of copyright, and in January 1989 it submitted such a proposal to the Council.[88] In its Green Paper the Commission adopted the view, generally accepted in all the Member States other than Greece, that copyright provides the principal form of protection appropriate for computer programs, and considered that Community legislation was desirable to ensure that such protection is accorded by explicit legislation in all Member States. It rejected suggestions for the creation of a full monopoly in new algorithms on the ground that this would constitute an excessive interference with competition, and conversely rejected suggestions for the exclusion of copyright protection from some features of software, such as access protocols, on the grounds that there was not yet sufficient experience of the problem of possibly excessive protection to justify such exclusions, and that solutions to difficulties of this kind could eventually be found either by case-law determining the scope of copyright protection, or by application of competition law, or by provisions for compulsory licensing.

Departing, however, from the Green Paper, Art. 2(3) of the Proposal of January 1989 specifies that copyright protection is not to extend to the ideas, principles, logic, algorithms, or programming languages underlying a program, and that this exclusion extends to 'the specification of interfaces' in so far as this constitutes ideas and principles which underlie a program. Some light is thrown on the concept of 'interface' by the Preamble to the Proposal, which refers to the principles describing any means of logical or physical interconnection and interaction which are required to permit elements of hardware and software to work with other software and hardware and with users in the ways they are intended to function. Thus it seems that only features of interface which are essential in terms of function will be caught by the exclusion.

In most respects at least, the harmonization proposed by the Commission will no doubt be welcomed in the United Kingdom, since it will not involve major change in British law but will improve the protection available to British software houses in other Member States.

Artistic works
Section 4 of the new Act, replacing s. 3(1) of the 1956 Act, defines 'artistic work' as comprising each of the following:

A graphic work, photograph, sculpture or collage[89]
These are explicitly protected 'irrespective of quality'.[90] 'Graphic work' is defined as including: (i) any painting, drawing, diagram, map, chart or plan; and (ii) any engraving, etching, lithograph, woodcut or similar work.[91] 'Photograph' is defined as a recording of light or other radiation on any medium on which an image is produced or from which an image may by any means be produced, and which is not part of a (moving) film; and 'sculpture' is defined as including a cast or model made for purposes of sculpture.[92]

As regards 'drawings', copyright has been held to extend to a simple drawing of a hand holding a pencil and marking a cross on a ballot paper, designed to assist illiterate voters, though in view of its simplicity it would only be protected against exact copying and copying with only microscopic variations.[93] Similarly, copyright has been recognized in a design used on the side of a tin of sweets,[94] and in a label for parcels.[95] In *Solar Thomson v. Barton*,[96] the Court of Appeal left open whether a drawing consisting of three concentric circles could constitute an artistic work, it being a full-size scale engineer's working drawing of a rubber ring for a pulley, drawn to precise measurements.[97]

Prior to the new Act it was copyright in technical drawings which formed the basis for the wide-ranging operation of copyright in the sphere of industrial designs and which came to have great importance after the decision of the Court of Appeal in *Dorling v.*

Honnor Marine[98] and the enactment of the Design Copyright Act 1968. But such use of ordinary copyright is now eliminated by s. 51 of the new Act, and replaced by a more limited unregistered design right created by Part III of the Act.[99]

A work of architecture, being a building or a model for a building;[100] and a work of artistic craftsmanship[101]

In these cases there is no provision for artistic quality to be ignored and the decision of the House of Lords in *George Hensher Ltd. v. Restawhile Upholstery (Lancs.) Ltd.*,[102] albeit confused, establishes in effect that a 'work of artistic craftsmanship' must be hand-made and not mass-produced, and that a three-dimensional prototype for an industrial product will not qualify.

The case involved a prototype for a drawing-room suite of a settee and chairs. The prototype was made by taking an existing suite and replacing the legs by a box or plinth and castors. It was too flimsy to be sat on, but it served as a model for production suites, and was destroyed after production had begun.

The House of Lords unanimously ruled that the prototype was not a 'work of artistic craftsmanship', but the five speeches took a variety of views on the meaning of the concept. There was, however, agreement that distinctive and original features of shape having eye-appeal, such as would satisfy the requirements of the Registered Designs Act 1949, are insufficient to make an object a 'work of artistic craftsmanship', and that some greater degree of aesthetic intention or achievement is necessary.

Lord Reid envisaged a durable, hand-made object, whether of practical utility or not, which its owner and a substantial, even if unsophisticated, section of the public would value because of its artistic quality – i.e. because they obtained emotional or intellectual pleasure, satisfaction or uplift from contemplating it; and thus excluded an object which was only intended for use as a step in a commercial operation. He denied, however, that the object need be a 'work of art'; this would set too high a standard.

Lord Morris, on the other hand, emphasized the value of the views of art critics, and explained that an artist is one who cultivates one of the fine arts which please by perfection of execution; and concluded that the object must be judged objectively for artistry by reference to ideas of beauty, taste, pleasure and aesthetic appeal. Similarly, Lord Dilhorne emphasized that a work of artistic craftsmanship had to be hand-made and not mass-produced, that expert evidence was admissible, and the object had to amount to a work of art. Again, Lord Kilbrandon required that the author be consciously concerned to produce a work of art, a thing of intrinsic beauty which would have an artistic justification for its existence.

Perhaps most interestingly, Lord Simon explained that in adding this category in 1911 Parliament had been influenced by the Arts and Crafts movement. A 'work of craftsmanship' presupposed special training, skill and knowledge for its production, and 'craftsmanship' implied a manifestation of pride in sound work-manship, a rejection of the shoddy, meretricious or facile. But it was the craftsmanship, rather than the work itself, which had to be artistic. Thus the category excluded the works of cobblers, dental mechanics, pattern-makers, boiler-makers, plumbers, wheel-wrights and thatchers; but included hand-painted tiles, stained-glass windows, wrought-iron gates made by blacksmiths, and some of the work of woodworkers, printers, bookbinders, cutlers, needleworkers, weavers and furniture-makers. He added that a gimmick is almost the negation of a work of art, since it appeals not to demands for the contemplation of beauty but to desire for change, modishness or prestige. On the other hand, an antithesis between utility and beauty, between function and art, was especially false in the context of the Arts and Crafts movement. The test was not the merit of the work, but whether the object was the work of an artist-craftsman, and should be decided on the evidence of acknowledged artist-craftsmen, or their trainers.

Subsequently in *Merlet v. Mothercare*[103] Walton J. held that a prototype of a cape for a baby did not qualify as a work of artistic craftsmanship, since the object had to be judged for artistic appeal in itself, without reference to its application (in this case as holding a baby and attached to the mother), and had to amount to a work of art. This point was not considered on appeal.[104]

OTHER WORKS

Sections 1(1)(b) and (c) and 5–8 of the new Act, replacing Part II of the 1956 Act (as amended), confer protection on: (i) sound recordings; (ii) (moving) films;[105] (iii) (television and radio) broadcasts;[106] (iv) cable programmes; and (v) the typographical arrangement of published editions of literary, dramatic or musical works. As in the case of literary, dramatic, musical or artistic works, there are no formalities required to create copyright in these other works.

Sound recordings

Section 5(1) of the new Act defines 'sound recording' as: (a) a recording of sounds, from which sounds may be reproduced; or (b) a recording of the whole or any part of a literary, dramatic or musical work, from which sounds reproducing the work may be produced; and specifies that the medium on which the recording is made, and the method by which the sounds are reproduced or produced, are immaterial.[107] By s. 5(2), copyright does not subsist in a sound recording which is, or to the extent that it is, a copy taken from a previous sound recording.

Formerly, by s. 12(6) of the 1956 Act, a provision unique in British law, copyright in a sound recording was effectively lost if records of the recording were issued to the public in this country by or with the licence of the owner without bearing a mark indicating the year of first publication, unless he had taken all reasonable steps for preventing such an occurrence. But the new Act does not retain any such provision.

Films

Section 5(1) of the new Act defines 'film' as a recording on any medium from which a moving image may by any means be produced.[108] Formerly, by s. 13(9) of the 1956 Act, the sounds embodied in a sound-track associated with the visual images were treated as part of the film, but now they obtain their independent copyright as a sound recording.[109] By s. 5(2), copyright does not subsist in a film which is, or to the extent that it is, a copy taken from a previous film.

There is some ground for argument that the screen displays generated by a computer program may attract a separate copyright as a film. In the United States the corresponding copyright is in 'audiovisual works', which are defined by s. 101 of the Copyright Act as works which consist of a series of related images which are intrinsically intended to be shown by the use of machines or devices, such as projectors, viewers or electronic equipment, together with any accompanying sounds, regardless of the nature of the material objects, such as films or tapes, in which the works are embodied.

In the United States a number of cases involving video-games, such as *Stern Electronics Inc. v. Kaufman*,[110] have established that the copyright in a computer program as such is not infringed by merely copying its screen displays, but have recognized a separate copyright in graphic-type screen displays as audiovisual works. It has been held that such an 'audiovisual' copyright in graphic-type screens generated by a program may extend to text-type displays produced by the same program, even if they are displayed at a different moment from the graphics,[111] but the practice of the American Copyright Office is to confine registrations of 'audiovisual works' to pictorial or graphic images, thus excluding text-based screens. After some vacillation, however, it seems that the American Copyright Office has now confirmed its practice of allowing registration of text-based screens as 'compilations of program terms'.

The recent case of *Digital Communications Associates Inc. v. Softklone Distributing Corp.*[112] involved a leading IBM–PC communications program, CROSSTALK, and a 'clone', MIRROR, which used an almost identical text-based status screen. In a judgment of major importance, the Federal District Court for the Northern District of Georgia held that a text-based screen display may attract a separate copyright, as a compilation of program terms, from the copyright in the program itself, and that the defendant had infringed copyright in the plaintiff's status screen, but not in its program as such. Infringement was established by reference to similarities in the arrangement and design of the parties' status screens – in the arrangement and highlighting on screen of the commands and their parameters. On the other hand, the court ruled that copyright would not protect the ideas of using a status screen, a command-driven program, or two-character commands; nor even the particular two-character commands chosen, i.e. the plaintiff's command-language.

Earlier, in *Broderbund Software Inc. v. Unison World Inc.*,[113] which involved PRINT SHOP, a menu-driven program for printing greeting cards, signs, banners and posters, running on an APPLE computer, and PRINTMASTER, a similar program for an IBM PC, infringement of audiovisual copyright was found by another Federal District Court on the basis of the 'eerie resemblance' between the screen displays of the two programs – their sequence and the choices offered, their layout, and the method of feedback to the user. In *Digital Communications v. Softklone* the court rejected any suggestion in *Broderbund* that copying of screen displays could establish infringement of copyright in a program of itself, but accepted the ruling of the Federal Court of Appeals for the Third Circuit in *Whelan Associates v. Jaslow Dental Laboratories*[114] that such copying could indirectly evidence such infringement.

In the United Kingdom, the existence of a separate copyright in screen displays produced by a computer program has not yet been considered by the courts. It seems difficult to envisage the recognition in this country of text-based screens as a separate compilation, for a compilation, like a program, is a type of literary work, and there is no record of the compilation separate from the program itself. On the other hand, the new definition of a film, in s. 5(1) of the 1988 Act, as a recording on any medium from which a moving image may by any means be produced, seems capable of being construed, if the courts can be persuaded that it would be beneficial to do so, as including screen output produced by a computer program, whether the screens displayed are primarily graphic-based or text-based. The former definition of a cinematograph film, in s. 13 of the 1956 Act, perhaps implied that the images must be of something existing before they were recorded. If so, the new definition appears to be wider. The argument likely to be most persuasive towards a holding that screen displays generated by a computer program count as a film, apart from the basic idea underlying copyright law that what is worth copying is generally worth protecting, is that such an approach would greatly facilitate proof of infringement. The courts could instinctively compare screen displays, while comparison of code or program structure necessitates consideration of expert evidence and puts the court to considerable intellectual effort. Moreover the very short commercial life of most programs could attract the court's sympathy to their authors.

Broadcasts and cable programmes
Section 6(1) of the new Act[115] defines 'broadcast' as a transmission by wireless telegraphy[116] of visual images, sounds or other information which either: (a) is capable of being lawfully received by

members of the public;[117] or (b) is transmitted for presentation to members of the public. But copyright does not subsist in a broadcast insofar as it infringes the copyright in another broadcast or in a cable programme.[118]

Section 7 of the new Act replaces s. 14A of the 1956 Act, which was added by s. 22 of the Cable and Broadcasting Act 1984. Section 7(1) defines 'cable programme' as any item included in a cable programme service, and 'cable programme service' as a service which consists wholly or mainly in sending visual images, sounds or other information by means of a telecommunications system,[119] otherwise than by wireless telegraphy, either (i) for reception at two or more places, whether simultaneously or at different times in response to requests by different users, or (ii) for presentation to members of the public, and which is not an excepted service under the section.

The excepted services, which are elaborately defined by s. 7(2), are: (a) interactive services;[120] (b) services internal to a business;[121] (c) domestic services of an individual;[122] (d) services confined to premises in single occupation;[123] and (e) ancillary services.[124] The exceptions, whose rationale is obscure to the present writer, may be amended by order of the Secretary of State of which a draft has been approved by both Houses of Parliament.[125] Copyright does not exist in a programme which is included in a cable service by reception and immediate retransmission of a broadcast, nor in a programme insofar as it infringes copyright in another cable programme or a broadcast.[126]

When a broadcast or cable transmission repeats a previous broadcast or transmission, a fresh copyright is created, but it expires at the expiry of the copyright in the original broadcast or transmission.[127]

Broadcasts and cable programmes are unique in receiving protection despite their transitory character and the possible absence of any fixation; e.g. in the case of live broadcasts of sporting events. Indeed it is in such cases that these copyrights have particular significance.

Published editions

The copyright in the typographical arrangement of a published edition of the whole or any part of one or more literary, dramatic or musical works[128] only protects against making a facsimile copy of the arrangement.[129] Copyright does not attach to an edition which reproduces the typographical arrangement of a previous edition.[130]

AUTHORSHIP AND OWNERSHIP

Authorship

The new Act speaks of the 'author' of works of all types,[131] but defines 'author' differently in relation to the various types of work. In the case of a literary, dramatic, musical or artistic work, ss. 9(1) and (3) and 178 specify that the author is the person who creates the work in question, or, if the work is generated by computer in circumstances such that there is no human creator, the person by whom the arrangements necessary for the creation of the work are undertaken. For this purpose it is well established that a person who dictates a letter or other document to his secretary, who takes it down in shorthand, is the author;[132] and that a ghost-writer, who puts information or stories supplied by another into a particular form of language, and not the supplier of the raw data, is the author of the resulting work;[133] and that a person who writes or draws, supposedly under spiritualistic influence, is still the author of his writing or drawing.[134] Similarly in *Tate v. Thomas*[135] a person who suggested the name for a play, many incidents to be included, and a few catch-lines, was held to have obtained no share in the copyright, since his contributions to the printable and publishable matter were insignificant.

In *Walter v. Lane*,[136] the House of Lords held, over Lord Robertson's powerful dissent, that a newspaper reporter who took down in shorthand for publication verbatim in his newspaper a public speech given by a politician was the author of and entitled to copyright in his report. But at that time the relevant legislation did not require originality, and in *Roberton v. Lewis*[137] Cross J. suggested that *Walter v. Lane* had ceased to be law, or at any rate that it did not apply if the speech or tune had already been fixed in a material form prior to the making of the fixation for which copyright was claimed. Moreover the 1988 Act not only defines 'author' as creator, but specifies (in s. 3(3)) that copyright subsists in a recorded literary, dramatic or musical work even if the record was made without the permission of the author.[138] It is submitted that, at any rate under the new Act, the principle so eloquently advocated in Lord Robertson's dissent in *Walter* will prevail: for authorship of an original literary, dramatic, musical or artistic work, there must be some element of composition or arrangement; an author is one who can claim the work as embodying his own thought (or other *intellectual* effort).

As regards other types of work, the 1988 Act defines 'author' as follows:

(i) In the case of a sound recording or film, the person by whom the arrangements necessary for the making of the recording or film are undertaken is treated as the author.[139]

(ii) In the case of a broadcast the person making the broadcast (or in the case of a broadcast which relays another broadcast by reception and immediate retransmission, the maker of the original broadcast) is treated as the author. Both the person who transmits a programme or item, if he has any responsibility for its contents, and any person who provides the programme and makes with the person who transmits it the arrangements necessary for its transmission, are treated as making the broadcast; and where more than one person is treated as making a broadcast, it becomes a work of joint authorship.[140]

(iii) In the case of a cable programme, the person providing the cable programme service in which the programme is included is treated as the author.[141]

(iv) In the case of the typographical arrangement of a published edition, the publisher is treated as the author.[142]

Initial ownership[143]

The general rule, laid down by s. 11(1) of the new Act, is that the author of a work is the first owner of the copyright in the work. In the case of a work of joint authorship (i.e. a work produced by the collaboration of two or more authors in which the contribution of each author is not distinct from that of the other author or authors, or a broadcast made by more than one person), the copyright normally belongs to all the co-authors jointly.[144] In the case of a published work of unknown authorship,[145] there is in some cases a presumption that the person named on the first-published copies as the publisher was the owner of the copyright at the time of such publication.[146] By Sch. 1, paras. 10 and 11, of the new Act, the authorship and the first ownership of a work created before its commencement is determined in accordance with the law in force at its creation.

The rule that the author is the first owner is, however, subject to the following exceptions:

Works made by employees

Where a literary, dramatic, musical or artistic work is made by an employee in the course of his employment (under a contract of service or apprenticeship), his employer is the first owner of the copyright, subject to any contrary agreement.[147] Such a contrary agreement need not be in writing and may even be implied.

Crown copyright

Where a work is made by the Crown, or by an officer or servant of the Crown in the course of his duties, copyright subsists in the work and the Crown is the first owner of the copyright.[148] 'The Crown' refers, not only to the Crown in right of the government of the United Kingdom, but also to the Crown in right of the government of Northern Ireland or of any dependent territory to which the Act extends.[149] Moreover Crown copyright exists also in Acts of Parliament and Measures of the General Synod of the Church of England.[150] The existence of copyright in the text of legislative measures is open to criticism as an obstacle to the performance of every citizen's duty to ascertain and comply with the directions of the legislature.

Parliamentary copyright

Where a work is made by or under the direction or control of the House of Commons or the House of Lords, copyright subsists in the work and the House in question is the first owner of the copyright.[151] This provision covers works made by officers or employees of a House in the course of their duties, and also applies to sound recordings, films, and live broadcasts or cable transmissions of the proceedings of a House, but not works which were merely commissioned by a House.[152] Subject to any modifications which may be made by Order in Council, the position is similar in the case of works made by or under the direction or control of a legislative body of a British dependent territory to which the Act extends.[153] Parliamentary copyright applies also to

Bills introduced into Parliament, though this copyright ceases when the Bill receives the Royal Assent or is lost.[154]

International organizations

Where an original literary, dramatic, musical or artistic work is made by an officer or employee of, or is published by, an international organization[155] designated for this purpose by Order in Council, and the work does not qualify for copyright protection by reference to the author's nationality, domicile or residence, nor to the place of first publication,[156] then copyright nevertheless subsists and the organization is the first owner.[157] At present the United Nations, the specialized Agencies of the United Nations, and the Organization of American States have been designated for this purpose.[158]

Works created or published in breach of confidence

In *Attorney-General v. Guardian Newspapers*[159] the House of Lords expressed sympathy for the view that where a work is created and published in breach of a binding obligation to respect confidence, the copyright will be held on a constructive trust for the person to whom the confidence obligation is owed. There is nothing in the new Act which would abolish any such rule.

The former rules (under ss. 4(3), 12(4) and 48(1) of the 1956 Act) that in the case of a photograph, the owner of the negative at the time of the taking of the photograph was treated as the author, and that a person who commissioned the taking of a photograph, or the painting or drawing of a portrait, or the making of an engraving, or the making of a sound recording, for money or money's worth, was entitled to the resulting copyright, have not been retained. But by Sch. 1, para. 11 of the new Act, they continue to apply to works created before the commencement of the new Act, and also, as regards the provisions on commissioned works, to works commissioned before but created after the commencement date.

As regards computer programs, in its Green Paper[160] the European Commission contemplates that the Member States should be required to adopt clear provisions on first ownership of copyright in a program (e.g. as between employer and employee, or commissioner and author), which would apply in the absence of contrary agreement between the parties involved, though each Member State could be left free to choose its own particular solution. Presumably it would regard the present state of British law as satisfying such needs. As regards programs which are themselves generated by computer, the Commission is inclined to regard the user of the generating computer as the appropriate first owner.

CONNECTING FACTORS

Like other intellectual-property rights, copyright is territorial, in the sense that it is infringed by acts done within the territory of the country by the law of which it is granted, and not by acts done elsewhere.[161] It is not, however, limited to works of authors who belong to the country by whose law it is granted, for both the Berne Copyright Convention[162] and the Universal Copyright Convention,[163] to both of which the United Kingdom is a party, prohibit discrimination in a Contracting State against authors from or works published in another Contracting State to the Convention in question. Accordingly Chapter IX (ss. 153–62) of the 1988 Act[164] requires that, for British copyright to exist in a work, the work must be connected, by means of the nationality, domicile or residence of the author or the place of the first publication of the work, with a qualifying country.

The following are the qualifying countries:

(i) The United Kingdom itself (including its territorial waters; structures or vessels exploring or exploiting its continental shelf; and ships, hovercraft and aircraft registered in the United Kingdom).[165]

(ii) Certain territories dependent or formerly dependent on the United Kingdom, to which the British copyright legislation has been extended, mainly by Order in Council under s. 31 of the 1956 Act or s. 157 of the new Act.[166] By s. 157(5) and Sch. 1, para. 36(2) and (4), of the 1988 Act, an Order in Council in force at the commencement of the 1988 Act extending the 1956 Act to a dependent territory remains in force in that territory until an Order is made extending the 1988 Act to that territory, and meanwhile such a territory is treated in the United Kingdom as a territory to which the 1988 Act has been extended; and similar provision is made for dependent territories, such as the Channel Islands, in which the 1911 Act was still in force at the commencement of the 1988 Act.[167] By para. 37 of Sch. 1 of the new Act, formerly dependent territories to which the 1956 Act extended, or to which the 1911 Act extended and the 1956 Act was therefore treated as extending, are treated in the United Kingdom as extended territories for the purposes of the 1988 Act until the territory is designated as a reciprocating country under s. 159. The benefits of being treated as an extended territory may be withdrawn by Order under s. 158(3) and Sch. 1, paras. 36(3) and (5) and 37(2), of the new Act.

(iii) Reciprocating countries, i.e. countries designated by Order in Council under s. 32 of the 1956 Act or s. 159 of the new Act.[168] To be designated under s. 159, a country must be either a Member State of the European Communities;[169] or a party to an international convention on copyright to which the United Kingdom is a party (e.g. the Berne Copyright Convention or the Universal Copyright Convention); or must otherwise give adequate protection to British works. For most purposes there are over 100 countries on which such advantages have been conferred, so that the requirement of a connecting factor is seldom an obstacle in practice.[170] But sound recordings (other than soundtracks of films) which qualify by virtue of a connection with a reciprocating country obtain performing and broadcasting rights only in the case of certain of such countries;[171] and only a small number of countries qualify for the purposes of protection of broadcasts or cable transmissions.[172] The requirement of a connecting-factor will usually be fulfilled in the case of computer programs, since they are treated in the United Kingdom as literary works, they are usually of American origin, and the United States is now a party to both the Berne and the Universal Copyright Conventions. In its Green Paper no firm view was taken by the EC Commission as to the appropriate connecting-factors for computer programs,[173] but Art. 3(1) of the 1989 Proposal for a Directive[174] adopts the national rules applicable to literary works.

The following are 'qualifying persons':

(a) An individual who either:
   (i) is a British citizen, a British Dependent Territories citizen, a British National (Overseas), a British Overseas citizen, a British subject or a British protected person under the British Nationality Act 1981;[175] or

      (ii) is a national of a reciprocating country;[176] or

      (iii) is domiciled or resident in the United Kingdom, a relevant British dependent (or formerly dependent) territory or a reciprocating country.[177]

  (b) A company which is incorporated under the law of a part of the United Kingdom, a relevant British dependent (or formerly dependent) territory or a reciprocating country.[178]

In broad terms, a work qualifies for copyright protection if either (i) the author is a qualifying person at the material time, or (ii) the work is first published in a qualifying country. In the case of joint authorship, it is enough that one of the authors qualifies; but if the work qualifies for protection only on this basis, only those of the authors who are qualifying persons become entitled to the copyright, and only their lives affect its duration.[179] For the purpose of qualification by reference to the place of first publication, one may rely on a publication as the first publication despite its having been preceded by a publication elsewhere within the previous thirty days.[180] The detailed rules for particular types of work are as follows:

(i) As regards a literary, dramatic, musical or artistic work which has not been published, copyright exists if the author was a qualifying person at the time when, or for a substantial part of the period during which, the work was made.[181]

(ii) In the case of a literary, dramatic, musical or artistic work which has been published, the requirement is that the author should have been a qualifying person at the time of its first publication or of his earlier death;[182] or alternatively that the first publication of the work should have taken place in a qualifying country.[183] Similarly, as regards typographical arrangements of published editions, the requirement is either that the publisher should have been a qualifying person at the date of the first publication of the edition, or that the first publication should have taken place in a qualifying country.[184]

(iii) As regards sound recordings and films, the requirement is that either: (a) the author was a qualifying person when the recording or film was made;[185] or (b) the recording or film has been published and its first publication took place in a qualifying country.[186] But sound recordings which qualify by virtue of a connection with a reciprocating country obtain performing and broadcasting rights only in the case of certain countries.[187]

(iv) Under the new Act, copyright subsists in a broadcast or a cable programme if the author was a qualifying person at the time when the broadcast was made or the programme was transmitted, or if the broadcast or programme was made or sent from a qualifying country.[188] But the number of qualifying countries is much smaller for these purposes than in other cases.[189]

(v) An alternatively sufficient connecting-factor is for the work to be made by the Crown (in right of the government of the United Kingdom, or of Northern Ireland, or of a British dependent territory to which the Act extends), or by a Crown officer or servant in the course of his duties, or made by or under the direction or control of a House of Parliament, or a legislative body of a relevant British dependent territory.[190] In the further alternative it is sufficient, in the case of an original literary, dramatic, musical or artistic work, that it is made by an officer or employee of, or published by, an international organization specified by Order in Council.[191]

Publication

Under the 1956 Act 'publication' was relevant to the existence of connecting-factors and to the duration of copyright, and unauthorized publication was a type of primary infringement.[192] But now publication is largely irrelevant to duration,[193] and the relevant type of infringement is specified in terms of issuing copies to the public, in the sense of first putting them into circulation.[194] 'Publication' nonetheless remains central to the existence of connecting factors, so its meaning (as defined by s. 175 of the new Act)[195] may conveniently be considered at this point.

The basic rules, applicable to all types of work, are that 'publication' refers to the issue of copies of the work to the public,[196] but that unauthorized acts are disregarded,[197] as is a publication which is merely colourable in the sense that it is not intended to satisfy the reasonable requirements of the public.[198] Nonetheless the requirement is not onerous: it is sufficient to expose a few copies of the work for sale on a shop counter for two or three weeks, without advertising it, if the anticipated immediate demand is insignificant and the intention is to satisfy whatever public demand may arise.[199] Moreover publication takes place where copies are put on offer to the public, and not where they are received by importers.[200] On the other hand in *Bodley Head v. Flegon*,[201] which involved Solzhenitzyn's novel, *August 1914*,

Brightman J. held that 'samizdat' circulation in Russia, i.e. underground circulation of typed or duplicated copies of uncensored works, could not be regarded as an effort to satisfy the reasonable requirements of the Russian public, but was a clandestine circulation which intentionally disregarded such requirements, since they could not lawfully be voiced by potential readers or satisfied by the author – hence the first publication took place in the West, and British copyright existed.

Although the new Act is not pellucid on these points, it seems that the copies must be of the whole, and not merely a substantial part, of the work; and must be of the work itself, and not merely an adaptation.[202] Thus the issue of copies of a film may publish a dramatic work used as the screenplay, but not a novel on which the screenplay is based.

More specifically, however, in the case of a literary, dramatic or musical work, 'publication' includes making the work available to the public by means of an electronic retrieval system,[203] but does not include performance, broadcasting or cable transmission of the work.[204] An artistic work is not published by its exhibition, broadcast or cable transmisson, nor by the issue to the public of copies of a film including it; nor, in the case of a work of architecture in the form of a building or a model for a building, a sculpture or a work of artistic craftsmanship, by the issue to the public of copies of a graphic work representing it or of photographs of it.[205] Thus a painting *is* published if it is photographed and copies of the photograph are issued, but this is *not* so in the case of a sculpture. But a building, or an artistic work incorporated in a building, is published by the construction of the building.[206] A sound recording or film is not published by its being played or shown in public, broadcast or transmitted by cable.[207]

DURATION

The duration of a copyright varies according to the type of the work in question, and is further affected by the existence of connecting factors. It should be borne in mind that the expiry of a copyright always occurs at the end of a calendar year.

Literary, dramatic, musical and artistic works
Section 12(1) of the new Act lays down the general rule that copyright in a literary, dramatic, musical or artistic work expires fifty years after the end of the calendar year in which the author dies.[208] This is the same period as formerly applied to *published* works, copyright in unpublished works being in principle perpetual. In accordance with the proposals contained in the 1986 White Paper,[209] the new Act abolishes this distinction and applies the same restriction on duration to unpublished works as continues to apply to published works. Moreover the former perpetual copyrights, conferred on universities and colleges by the Copyright Act 1775, are now made to expire at the end of the fiftieth calendar year after that in which the new Act comes into force.[210]

There is an exception for computer-generated works, where copyright expires fifty years after the end of the calendar year in which the work was made.[211] Otherwise, however, there is no longer any distinction between the various types of original work. In particular, the former extension for works published after the author's death, which applied to literary, dramatic and musical works and engravings, but not to other artistic works, whereby copyright would continue for fifty years after the year of publication,[212] has been abolished, though not so as to affect works which were created before the commencement date and in relation to which the fifty year period had begun to run before that date.[213] Similarly the former rule for photographs, whereby copyright expired fifty years after the end of the year of publication, has not been retained, except in relation to photographs published before the commencement date.[214] In the case of literary, dramatic and musical works whose author had died, but which had not been made available to the public, before the commencement of the new Act, copyright expires at the end of the fiftieth calendar year after that of the commencement, and the same applies to unpublished engravings whose author had died, and to unpublished photographs taken after the commencement of the 1956 Act.[215]

In the case of a work of joint authorship,[216] the fifty years commences at the end of the year in which the survivor dies.[217] If the identity of one or more of the joint authors is known, but that of one or more others is not, the period is determined by reference to the life or lives of those whose identity is known.[218]

If a work is of unknown authorship,[219] copyright expires fifty years after the end of the calendar year in which the work is first made available to the public,[220] even if the identity of the author (or any of the joint authors) becomes known after the end of this period.[221] But an act done or arranged at a time when it was not possible by reasonable inquiry to ascertain the identity of the author (or any of the joint authors), and it was reasonable to assume that copyright had expired or that the author (or all the joint authors) had died at least fifty calendar years earlier, does not infringe the copyright.[222]

British copyright in a computer program, like any other literary work, lasts until the end of the fiftieth calendar year after the year in which the author died, and in the case of joint authorship by persons whose contributions are not distinct from each other's, the longest life is used. In France, however, an act of 3 July 1985 limits the duration of copyright in a computer program to twenty-five years from its creation, and the EC Commission, in its Green Paper,[223] contemplated a harmonized term applicable in all Member States, running from the creation of the program and disregarding the author's lifetime, but left open whether the appropriate duration would be twenty, twenty-five or fifty years. Subsequently Art. 7 of its proposed Directive[224] has specified a duration of fifty years from the creation of the program.

Sound recordings and films
Under s.13 of the new Act, copyright in a sound recording or film expires fifty years after the end of the calendar year in which the recording or film was made or, if it is released within that period, fifty years after the end of the calendar year in which it is released.[225] A sound recording or film is released when it is first published, broadcast or transmitted by cable; or in the case of a film or a film sound-track, when the film is first shown in public.[226] In determining release unauthorized acts are disregarded.[227] These rules, which differ from those laid down in the 1956 Act,[228] follow the provisions for films of the Paris Act to the Berne Convention, and extend them to sound recordings.[229]

Broadcasts and cable programmes
Copyright in a broadcast or a cable programme expires fifty years after the end of the calendar year in which the broadcast was made or the programme was transmitted.[230] In the case of a repeat broadcast or cable programme, copyright expires at the same time as the copyright in the original broadcast or programme, and accordingly no copyright arises in a repeat which is broadcast or transmitted after copyright in the original has expired.[231]

Typographical arrangements of published editions
Copyright in the typographical arrangement of a published edition expires twenty-five years after the end of the calendar year in which the edition was first published.[232]

Crown and Parliamentary copyrights
There are special rules as to the duration of Crown and Parliamentary copyrights, i.e. copyrights which initially vested in the Crown or a legislative body under ss. 163–67. In the case of a literary, dramatic, musical or artistic work, Crown copyright lasts until 125 years after the end of the calendar year in which the work was made; or, if the work is published commercially within seventy-five years after the end of the calendar year in which it was made, then the copyright lasts until fifty years after the end of the calendar year of its first commercial publication.[233] But Parliamentary copyright in these types of work is limited to fifty years from the end of the calendar year in which the work was made.[234] However, Crown copyright in Acts of Parliament or Measures of the General Synod ceases at the end of the fiftieth calendar year after the year in which the Royal Assent was given, and Parliamentary copyright in Bills ceases when the Bill is enacted or lost.[235] In the case of other types of work, the normal rules as to duration apply to Crown or Parliamentary copyrights.[236]

The duration of Crown copyright in works created before the commencement of the 1988 Act is regulated by para. 41 of Sch. 1 to the new Act, which looks to the state of affairs existing at the commencement of the new Act and uses concepts as defined in the 1956 Act. In such cases, Crown copyright continues to subsist in accordance with the 1956 Act in the case of published literary, dramatic or musical works; artistic works other than engravings or photographs, whether published or not; published engravings; published photographs; unpublished photographs taken before 1 June 1957; published sound recordings; unpublished sound recordings made before 1 June 1957; and published or registered films. In the case of unpublished literary, dramatic or musical works, such a copyright expires in accordance with s. 163(3) of the new Act, or at the end of the fiftieth calendar year after that in which the new Act comes into force, whichever is later. In the case of unpublished engravings, and of unpublished photographs taken before 1 June 1957, the copyright expires at the end of the fiftieth calendar year after that in which the new Act came into force. In the case of films which were neither published nor registered, and of unpublished sound recordings made between the commencements of the 1956 and 1988 Acts, it expires at the end of the fiftieth calendar year after that in which the new Act came into force, unless the work is published before the end of that period, in which case it expires at the end of the fiftieth calendar year after that of the publication.

International organizations
Copyright of which an international organization is first owner under s. 168 subsists until the end of the fiftieth calendar year after that in which the work was made, unless a longer period is specified by Order in Council for the purpose of complying with international obligations.[237] In the case of an unpublished work in which immediately before the commencement of the new Act copyright subsisted by virtue of s. 33 of the 1956 Act, the predecessor of s. 168, the copyright continues until its expiry in accordance with the 1956 Act, or until the end of the fiftieth calendar year after the commencement of the new Act, whichever is earlier.[238]

PRESUMPTIONS

Sections 104–06 of the new Act[239] lay down certain presumptions as to the subsistence of copyright which apply in infringement actions:

(i) In the case of a literary, dramatic, musical or artistic work, a presumption, until the contrary is proved:

(a) where an author was named on copies of the work as published or on the work itself when made, that the person named is the author and that copyright did not initially vest in his employer, the Crown, Parliament or an international organization under ss. 11(2), 163, 165 or 168;[240] or
(b) where no author was so named, but the work was first published in a qualifying country and a publisher was named on copies of the work as first published, that the person named was the owner at the time of publication.[241]

In *Warwick Film Productions v. Eisinger*[242] Plowman J. held that in a case of anonymous publication to which the second presumption applied, a plaintiff other than the named publisher must either trace title from the publisher or must rebut the presumption, and for the latter purpose it is not enough to show that the publisher was not the author, for the presumption is not based on any inherent probability, and it operates to exclude the author's title at the time of publication. Thus it is not enough for the plaintiff to prove that X was the author and that the plaintiff derives title from X, e.g. under an assignment from X's executor. The presumption is not confined to actions brought by the publisher, and it is not legitimate to speculate what facts might have existed which would render the presumption true in fact, such as an assignment by the author to the publisher.

(ii) In the case of a literary, dramatic, musical or artistic work, where the author is dead or his identity cannot be ascertained by reasonable inquiry, a presumption, in the absence of evidence to the contrary, that the work is an original work and that the plaintiff's allegations as to the first publication and the country of first publication are correct.[243]

(iii) In the case of a literary, dramatic, musical or artistic work in which Crown copyright subsists, and of which printed copies contain a statement as to the year of first commercial publication, a presumption, in the absence of evidence to the contrary, that this statement is correct.[244]

(iv) In the case of a sound recording, where copies as issued to the public (even after the infringement) bear a mark naming a person as copyright owner at the date of issue, or specifying the year or country of first publication, a presumption, until the contrary is proved, that these statements are correct.[245]

(v) In the case of a film, where copies as issued to the public (even after the infringement) bear a statement naming a person as author or director, or as copyright owner at the date of issue of the copies, or specifying the year or country of first publication, a presumption, until the contrary is proved, that these statements are correct.[246]

(vi) In the case of a film, where the film as shown in public, broadcast or transmitted by cable (even after the infringement) bears a statement that a named person was the author or director, or that a named person was the copyright owner immediately after the film was made, a presumption, until the contrary is shown, that these statements are correct.[247]

(vii) In the case of a computer program, where copies issued to the public in electronic form (even after the infringement) bear a statement that a named person was the copyright owner at the date of the issue, or that the program was first published in a specified country, or that copies were first issued to the public in electronic form in a specified year, a presumption, until the contrary is proved, that these statements are correct.[248]

In addition s. 169 applies to an unpublished literary, dramatic, musical or artistic work of unknown authorship. If there is evidence that the author (or any of the joint authors) was a qualifying individual by connection with a country other than the United Kingdom, then it is to be presumed, until the contrary is proved, that he was such a qualifying individual and that copyright accordingly subsists in the work. Moreover in such a case a body appointed under the law of the author's country to protect and enforce copyright in such works will, if designated by Order in Council, be recognized in the United Kingdom as having the authority conferred by the law of the foreign country to act in place of the copyright owner, including by bringing proceedings in its own name. But the foreign body will not be able to assign the British copyright, and the section is excluded if the body has received notice of an assignment by the author. Moreover, the section does not invalidate assignments made or licences granted by the author or his successor.

3

Infringement

TYPES OF INFRINGING ACT

Introduction

The copyright in a work comprises a number of exclusive rights, some in relation to the making, publishing, importing, marketing or possessing of physical copies of the work ('the physical rights'), and others in relation to the performing, showing or playing in public, broadcasting or cable-transmitting of the work ('the performing rights'). Thus one classification of infringing acts relates to whether the act infringes the physical or the performing rights. Another (and cross-) classification divides infringing acts into acts of primary or secondary infringement. Primary infringement is dealt with by ss. 16–21 of the new Act,[1] and secondary infringement by ss. 22–27.[2] In general the new Act applies to existing works (i.e. works made before its commencement date) as well as future works (made after that date),[3] but the new provisions on infringement apply only to acts done after the commencement date, and the provisions on infringement of the 1956 Act continue to apply to acts done before that date.[4]

Section 16(1) of the new Act outlines the acts restricted by the copyright in a work, i.e. the acts of primary infringement, and confers on the owner of a copyright the exclusive right to perform these acts in relation to his work in the United Kingdom (and the relevant British dependent territories);[5] and s. 16(2) specifies that copyright in a work is infringed by a person who, without the licence of the copyright owner, performs, or authorizes another person to perform, any of the acts restricted by the copyright.[6] In broad terms, the acts of primary infringement are the making or publishing of copies of the work; the performing, showing or playing in public, broadcasting or cable-transmitting of the work; the making of an adaptation of the work; and the doing of any of these acts in relation to such an adaptation. Secondary infringement relates to the importing, marketing or possessing of infringing copies; the permitting of the use of a place of public entertainment for an infringing performance; and the supplying of apparatus, premises or copies used for an infringing performance.

Section 16(3) retains the established rule[7] that it is infringement to perform a restricted act in relation to any substantial part of the copyright work; and adds that it is immaterial whether the act relates to the work directly or indirectly, and whether any intervening acts themelves infringe copyright.[8] For there to be infringement, there must be substantial objective similarity between the plaintiff's work and the defendant's allegedly infringing article or performance, *and* the latter must have been derived, i.e. actually copied, directly or indirectly, from the former. The alleged copy, adaptation or performance must be both objectively similar to and actually derived from the plaintiff's copyright work. Objective similarity alone is not sufficient; for example, the defendant's article will not infringe if it was created independently, or derived from a common source. But the defendant's article need not copy the whole of the plaintiff's work; it is enough that a substantial part of the work is copied; and the question is whether what was copied constitutes, in a qualitative rather than a quantitative sense, a substantial part of the plaintiff's work, rather than a substantial part of the defendant's article or performance.[9]

In the case of primary infringement, a defendant who commits a restricted act (whether in relation to the physical or the performing rights) is liable for the infringement regardless of any (reasonable or unreasonable) ignorance or mistake on his part as to the existence of the copyright or the fact of its infringement, with the sole exception that he will escape liability for damages (but not any other remedy) if he proves that, at the time of the infringement, he did not know, and had no reason to believe, that copyright subsisted in the work.[10] This is a heavy burden to discharge, especially as it is not enough for the defendant to show that he reasonably supposed that he was not infringing because he had mistakenly obtained a licence from the wrong person.[11] In particular, this defence will hardly ever succeed in the case of a computer program, since programs are always modern creations and are usually connected by authorship or first publication with the United States, which is a party to the Berne Copyright Convention.

On the other hand, to establish secondary infringement by importing or marketing infringing copies, the plaintiff formerly had the burden of proving that, to the defendant's knowledge, the making of the article constituted an act of primary infringement (or, in the case of an imported article, its making would have constituted an act of primary infringement if the article had been made in this country).[12] Now, however, it is enough if the copyright owner shows that the importer or marketer knew *or had reason to believe* that the article was an infringing copy.[13] Somewhat similarly, in the case of secondary infringement of performing rights, a defendant who permits the use of a place of public entertainment, or the use of apparatus on his premises, or who supplies a copy of a sound recording or film, escapes liability if he had no reason to believe in the likelihood of infringement;[14] but a supplier of apparatus is not protected if its normal use involves a public performance, unless he believed on reasonable grounds that it would not be used for an infringing performance.[15]

Infringements of the physical rights

Making a copy of the work

Sections 16(1)(a) and 17(1)[16] of the new Act specify that the copying of a work is an act restricted by the copyright in every type of work. By s. 17(2), in relation to a literary, dramatic, musical or artistic work, copying means reproducing the work in any material form, including storing the work in any medium by electronic means,[17] but s. 17(6) adds that copying (in relation to any description of work) includes the making of copies which are transient or are incidental to some other use of the work. The latter provision seems to achieve a result desired by the software houses, that the mere loading of a pirate copy of a program into the transient memory of a computer should amount to infringement of copyright in the program, a result almost certainly not reached by the previous law, and indeed, one which seems to deprive the reference in s. 17(2) to 'material' form of almost all significance. Section 17(6) also reduces the importance of the proviso to s. 21(4), by which a conversion of a program from one computer language or code into another does not constitute a translation or adaptation when it occurs incidentally in the course of running the program, since the reading into memory, from a 'pirate' copy, of a program in source code will now constitute reproduction of the source code in a material form, even though its electronic conversion by an interpreter into object code will not constitute adaptation. Moreover, unlike the American Copyright Act, which explicitly authorizes the owner of a copy of a computer program to make copies and adaptations which are essential for utilization of the program or by way of archiving (generally known as 'back-up'),[18] the British Act, by s. 56, merely protects a transferee by giving him the same rights as the original purchaser if certain conditions are met.[19]

In relation to an artistic work, copying includes the making of a copy in three dimensions of a two-dimensional work, and the making of a copy in two dimensions of a three-dimensional work.[20] This was formerly qualified by a largely ignored proviso, contained in s. 9(8) of the 1956 Act, that the making of a three-dimensional object did not infringe copyright in a two-dimensional artistic work, if the object would not appear, to persons who were not experts in relation to objects of that description, to be a reproduction of the work. The latter provision is not repeated, but the significance of the main provision whereby three-dimensional copies infringe copyright in two-dimensional artistic works is greatly diminished by s. 51, which effectively eliminates the operation of ordinary copyright in the sphere of industrial designs, by excluding from the scope of copyright in a design document[21] or a model recording or embodying a design[22] which is not itself an artistic work the making of articles, or copies of articles made, to the design. Industrial designs are now protected, not by ordinary copyright, but under the Registered Designs Act 1949 (as amended by Part IV of the 1988 Act) and by the new unregistered design right created by Part III of the 1988 Act.[23]

In relation to a film, television broadcast or cable programme, copying includes making a photograph of the whole or any substantial part of any image forming part of the film, broadcast or programme.[24] But the making for private and domestic use of a recording of a broadcast or cable programme, solely for the purpose of enabling it to be viewed or listened to at a more convenient time, does not infringe any copyright in the broadcast or cable programme or in any work included in it;[25] and the making for private and domestic use of a photograph of an image forming part of a television broadcast or cable programme, or a copy of such a photograph, does not infringe any copyright in the broadcast or cable programme or in any film included in it.[26] These exemptions go beyond s. 14(4) of the 1956 Act, which only protected the home viewer as regards the copyright in the broadcast as such. In relation to the typographical arrangement of a published edition, copying means making a facsimile copy (including one reduced or enlarged in scale) of the arrangement.[27]

Publishing the work
The 1956 Act made it primary infringement of copyright in an original work to publish the work,[28] but this was construed by the House of Lords in *Infabrics Ltd. v. Jaytex Ltd.*[29] as confined to the first publication in the United Kingdom and the relevant dependent territories of a work previously unpublished therein.

The corresponding provisions, ss. 16(1)(b) and 18, of the new Act do not refer to 'publishing', but to 'the issue to the public of copies of the work', and make such issuing primary infringement of copyright in a work of any type.[30] Section 18(2) defines such issue as referring to the act of putting into circulation (in the United Kingdom) copies not previously put into circulation in the United Kingdom or elsewhere, and not to any subsequent distribution, sale, hiring or loan of those copies, nor to any subsequent importation of those copies into the United Kingdom. This seems in some ways wider and in other ways narrower than the interpretation of infringement by publication adopted by the House of Lords in *Infabrics v. Jaytex*:[31] under the new Act the copies in question must not have been previously put into public circulation anywhere, even outside the United Kingdom and the dependent territories to which the Act extends;[32] but it is now immaterial that other copies of the work have been put into public circulation, even by the copyright owner and in the United Kingdom. In substance the new Act seems to adopt a concept of publication, as referring to the normal activities of a book-publishing house or analogous activities in the case of other types of article, rejected by the House of Lords in *Infabrics v. Jaytex*.

In the case of sound recordings, films and computer programs, s. 18(2) of the new Act extends the concept of issuing copies to the public, so as to include, not only the first putting of the copies into public circulation, but also any rental of copies to the public, and s. 178 defines 'rental' as any arrangement under which a copy is made available, either (a) for payment in money or money's worth, or (b) in the course of a business, as part of services or amenities for which payment is made, and (in either case) (c) on terms that it will or may be returned.[33] In effect this creates a separate right to authorize the rental of legitimate copies. The provision no doubt reflects the concern of film producers, record companies and software houses that persons who obtain these products by rental may make and retain illicit copies of them. In the case of computer programs the duration of this rental right is, however, restricted by s. 66(5), so as to expire at the end of the fiftieth calendar year after the year in which copies of the program in electronic form were first issued to the public.[34]

The introduction of a separate rental right in sound recordings, films and computer programs by the 1988 Act accords to a large extent with the policy of the EC Commission. In the light of the increasing market-penetration and durability of compact discs, and of the importance of the rental market in video films, the Commission declared in Chapter 4 of its *Green Paper on Copyright* its intention to submit a proposal for a directive under Art. 100A of the EEC Treaty (as amended by the Single European Act) requiring the introduction in all Member States of a specific right to authorize the commercial rental of sound recordings and videograms, so as to enable the copyright owner to control the hiring out of legitimate copies. Such rights already existed in some Member States, such as Denmark, but not, before the 1988 Act, in the United Kingdom.[35] As regards sound recordings, the Commission envisaged that such rights should be conferred on the author of the work recorded, the performer, and the producer of the recording, but the 1988 Act confers it merely on the producer. As regards videograms, the Commission envisaged that the right should be conferred on the producer of the film, and the 1988 Act so provides. The Commission envisaged that these rights should last for fifty years from the end of the year in which the recording or film was made, but under the 1988 Act the fifty years runs from the release of the recording or film. As the Commission envisaged, free lending, e.g. by public libraries, is not to be covered by these rights.

Section 66, however, enables the Secretary of State, by statutory instrument, in effect to grant a statutory licence whereby, in specified cases, legitimate copies of sound recordings, films or computer programs may be rented to the public, subject only to the payment of a reasonable royalty or other payment agreed on by the parties or, in default of agreement, determined by the Copyright Tribunal on an application by one of the parties under s. 142.[36] Alternatively a film producer, record company, software house, or group of such persons may establish a licensing scheme, and obtain certification of the scheme by the Secretary of State under s. 143, in which case (by s. 66(2)) any statutory licence under s. 66 will not apply.

By s. 66(3), a statutory instrument under s. 66 may limit the statutory licences granted by reference to factors relating to the work, the copies rented, the renter or the circumstances of the rental. No doubt in the case of films and sound recordings a statutory rental licence will not be made available until a suitable period has expired in which the copyright owner has had an effective opportunity to utilize his creation in other ways. As regards computer programs, a statutory licence would seem appropriate in the case of games programs which are marketed in an electronically copy-protected form and which have already been marketed for, say, a year. These bear some analogy with films and sound recordings, as forms of entertainment which customers may desire to utilize for a limited time. But a statutory licence does not seem appropriate in the case of programs designed for use in the course of a business, since in such cases the user needs the program permanently if he needs it at all, and rental could provide a ready means of making and retaining illicit copies. Of course a user might wish to try out several competing business-application programs briefly for the purpose of deciding which to purchase, but such desires seem unlikely to weigh heavily against the risk of subverting the purpose of copyright.

Making, copying or publishing an adaptation of the work
The new Act makes it primary infringement of copyright in a literary, dramatic or musical work to make an adaptation of the work, or to perform a restricted act (such as making a copy, publishing copies, or performing in public) in relation to an adaptation of the work.[37] An adaptation is made when it is

recorded, in writing or otherwise,[38] but it is infringement to perform a restricted act in relation to an adaptation which has not been so recorded.[39]

'Adaptation' is defined as:

(i) a translation of a literary or dramatic work;[40]
(ii) a version of a dramatic work in which it is converted into a non-dramatic work;[41]
(iii) a version of a literary work in which it is converted into a dramatic work;[42]
(iv) a version of a literary or dramatic work in which the story or action is conveyed wholly or mainly by way of pictures in a form suitable for reproduction in a book, or in a newspaper, magazine or similar periodical, e.g. a strip-cartoon;[43]
(v) an arrangement or transcription of a musical work;[44]
(vi) a version of a computer program in which it is converted into or out of a computer language or code or into a different computer language or code, otherwise than incidentally in the course of running the program.[45]

Section 21(5), rephrasing s. 2(6) of the 1956 Act, declares that no inference is to be drawn from the provisions on adaptation as to what does or does not amount to copying. Thus a painting may reproduce a photograph;[46] and a knitted fabric may reproduce a drawing in the form of a point-pattern giving instructions for setting a knitting-machine.[47] It has even been held, probably wrongly, that a stage-revue sketch may reproduce in material form a cartoon, thus circumventing the absence of any performing rights in artistic works.[48]

Dealing with infringing copies
By ss. 22, 23 and 27 of the 1988 Act,[49] it is secondary infringement to deal in various ways with an infringing copy of a work. By s. 27, an article is an infringing copy in relation to a copyright work if: (i) its making constituted an infringement of the copyright, or (ii) in the case of an article which has been or is proposed to be imported into the United Kingdom, its making in the United Kingdom would have constituted either an infringement of the copyright or a breach of an exclusive licensing agreement relating to the work.[50] It is clear from this definition that the concept extends to copies of an adaptation of a literary, dramatic or musical work.

The reference to copies whose making in this country would have infringed an exclusive licensing agreement is new, and overrules the decision in *CBS v. Charmdale*,[51] but there is now an express saving for cases of exhaustion under European Community law.[52] Moreover there is a presumption that the copy was created at a time when copyright subsisted.[53]

By s. 27(6), if copies which were lawfully made pursuant to certain provisions permitting copying for limited purposes are subsequently dealt with for other purposes, they are treated as infringing copies for the purpose of the dealing in question and for all subsequent purposes. This applies to copies which are made for educational purposes in accordance with ss. 32, 35, 36 or 141, or for the purpose of advertising an artistic work for sale in accordance with s. 63, but are subsequently sold, hired out, or offered or exposed for sale or hire.[54] Similarly copies made by librarians in response to false declarations are treated as infringing copies.[55] Again, a copy made incidentally for purposes of broadcasting or cable transmission in accordance with s. 68 becomes an infringing copy as regards any other use, and for all subsequent purposes if it is not destroyed within twenty-eight days of the first broadcast or cable transmission.[56] Similarly a copy legitimately made by a purchaser of a work in electronic form becomes an infringing copy if it is not transferred along with the original purchased copy or with a copy used in place of an original which is no longer usable.[57]

The dealings with an infringing copy which constitute secondary infringement are specified in ss. 22 and 23 of the 1988 Act as: (i) importing into the United Kingdom, otherwise than for the importer's private and domestic use;[58] (ii) selling, hiring out, or offering or exposing for sale or hire;[59] (iii) in the course of a business, exhibiting in public or distributing;[60] (iv) otherwise distributing to such an extent as to affect prejudicially the copyright owner;[61] and (v) possessing in the course of a business.[62] 'Business' is defined by s. 178 as including a trade or profession, but probably does not include education. Nonetheless acting in the course of a business, within the meaning of the new Act, is clearly wider than acting by way or for purposes of trade, within the meaning of the 1956 Act, since 'business' will cover the supply of services as well as goods, and one may possess in the course of a business many things, such as reference books or computer programs, which one intends for use within the business, although one has no intention of supplying them to customers. Although use as such is not an act of infringement unless it involves copying, the imposition of liability for mere possession, if in the course of a business, in effect extends liability to the business user of infringing copies, even where his use does not involve copying and he is not engaged in supplying the copies to others.[63] Even in the light of the extended definition of copying by s. 17(6) as including the making of transient or incidental copies, the imposition of liability for possessing in the course of a business seems of particular significance in relation to computer software.

Formerly there was liability for secondary infringement by dealing with infringing copies only if one dealt 'knowingly', but under the new Act it is sufficient if one 'knows or has reason to believe' that the article is an infringing copy of the work. Under the old law a heavy burden lay on the plaintiff to prove knowledge. To some extent constructive knowledge would suffice, since it was enough that the defendant had notice of facts which would suggest to a reasonable person that a breach of copyright was occurring, and would put him on inquiry, or that he turned a blind eye to an obvious means of knowledge. But where a previously innocent dealer received the plaintiff's complaint of infringement, he was allowed a reasonable opportunity of investigating the matter, e.g. for a fortnight, before he was fixed with knowledge.[64] Probably the right to an opportunity for investigation remains.

It is also, by s. 24(1) of the new Act, secondary infringement of copyright in a work to make, import, sell, hire out, offer or expose for sale or hire, or possess in the course of a business an article specifically designed or adapted for making copies of that particular work, if one knows or has reason to believe that it is to be used to make infringing copies; and by s. 24(2), to transmit a work by means of a telecommunications system (other than by broadcasting or inclusion in a cable programme service), if one knows or has reason to believe that infringing copies will be made by means of the reception of the transmission in the United Kingdom or elsewhere. Presumably the reference to infringing copies made outside the United Kingdom refers to copies made in British dependent territories to which the Act extends,[65] and to copies made elsewhere which are later imported or proposed to be imported into the United Kingdom.[66] In the latter case, presumably the transmitter must have reason to expect such importation.

Circumvention of electronic copy-protection

Special provision is made by s. 296 of the new Act to deal with devices designed to circumvent attempts by copyright owners who issue copies of their works to the public in electronic form to prevent or obstruct by electronic means the copying of such copies.

The section applies where copies of a copyright work have been issued to the public, by or with the licence of the copyright owner, in an electronic form[67] which is copy-protected, i.e. by any device or other means intended to prevent or restrict copying of the work or to impair the quality of copies made.[68] The work will most often be a computer program, but it may alternatively be a database or some other digitized presentation of text or visual images, or even an analogue copy of a sound recording or film. The section confers rights, not on the copyright owner as such, but on the publisher of the copy-protected copies, i.e. the person who first puts them into public circulation.[69] The publisher is given the same rights as a copyright owner has in respect of an infringement of copyright against a person who, knowing or having reason to believe that it will be used to make infringing copies, makes, imports, sells or hires out, or offers, exposes or advertises for sale or hire, any device or means specifically designed or adapted to circumvent the form of copy-protection employed, or who publishes information intended to enable or assist persons to circumvent that form of copy-protection.[70] Evidently 'device or means' includes both a piece of hardware (such as a special ROM chip) and a program in electronic form (such as the well-known program, FUPROLOK, which has been distributed in the public domain in response to the copy-protection device, PROLOK, which was at one time widely used by publishers of leading business software for MS-DOS computers).

In addition the publisher is given the same rights to delivery up, seizure and disposal, in relation to such a device or means which is in the possession of a person who intends that it should be used to make infringing copies of copyright works as a copyright owner has (under ss. 99, 100 and 114 of the Act) in relation to an infringing copy.[71] Moreover the presumptions which are, by ss. 104–06 of the Act, applicable in proceedings for infringement of copyright,[72] and the exception to the privilege against self-incrimination made applicable in proceedings relating to intellectual property by s. 72 of the Supreme Court Act 1981,[73] are extended by s. 296(6) to proceedings under s. 296.

Infringements of the performing rights

Primary and secondary infringements
Under the new Act it is primary infringement of copyright in a literary, dramatic or musical work to perform the work, or an adaptation of the work, in public.[74] 'Performance' is defined specifically as including performances by way of delivery of lectures, addresses, speeches or sermons, and more generally as including any mode of visual or acoustic presentation, including presentation of a sound recording, film, broadcast or cable programme of the work.[75] Similarly it is primary infringement of copyright in a sound recording or film to play or show the work in public.[76]

In the case of a broadcast or cable programme, it is primary infringement to show or play the work in public to a paying audience.[77] For this purpose an audience is a paying audience if they have paid for admission to the place, or to a place including the place, where the broadcast or programme is to be seen or heard, or if goods or services are supplied there at prices which are substantially attributable to the facilities afforded for seeing or hearing the broadcast or programme, or at prices which exceed those usually charged there and are partly attributable to those facilities for seeing or hearing the broadcast or programme. Residents or inmates of the place, and members, whose payment is only for membership, of a club or society to whose main purposes the provision of facilities for seeing or hearing broadcasts or programmes is only incidental, are not regarded as paying for admission.[78] If the audience have not paid for admission there is no infringement of copyright in the broadcast or programme, nor in any sound recording or film contained in it.[79]

In addition it is primary infringement of copyright in a literary, dramatic, musical or artistic work, a sound recording, a film, a broadcast or a cable programme: (i) to broadcast the work (or, in the case of a literary, dramatic or musical work, an adaptation of the work), or (ii) to include the work (or an adaptation of the work) in a cable programme service.[80] Where copyright in a work is infringed by a performance or playing or showing in public by means of apparatus for receiving visual images or sounds conveyed by electronic means, the person by whom the visual images or sounds are sent, and the performers, are not responsible for the infringement.[81] Where a broadcast made from a place in the United Kingdom is, by reception and immediate retransmission, included in a cable programme service for the same area in pursuance of a requirement imposed under s. 13(1) of the Cable and Broadcasting Act 1984, the cable transmission does not infringe copyright in the broadcast or in any work included in the broadcast, but if the inclusion of a work in the broadcast infringed copyright the cable transmission will be taken into account in assessing damages against the broadcaster.[82]

Where the copyright in a literary, dramatic or musical work is infringed by a performance at a place of public entertainment, anyone who gave permission for the place to be used for the performance is liable for secondary infringement, unless when he gave permission he believed on reasonable grounds that the performance would not infringe copyright.[83] 'Place of public entertainment' is defined as including premises occupied mainly for other purposes but from time to time hired out for public entertainment.[84] In view, however, of the wide interpretation sometimes placed on primary infringement by 'authorizing' another's acts,[85] this head of secondary infringement seems of little practical importance.

In addition, s. 26 of the 1988 Act creates new forms of secondary infringement where copyright in a work is infringed by a public performance, playing or showing of the work by means of apparatus for playing sound recordings, showing films, or receiving visual images or sounds conveyed by electronic means.[86] In addition to the primary infringement committed by the person who carried out the performance, there may also be secondary infringement by the supplier of the apparatus used, the occupier of the premises where the performance took place, and the supplier of a copy of a sound recording or film played or shown. The supplier of the apparatus (or any substantial part of the apparatus) used is liable for secondary infringement if, when he supplied it, he knew or had reason to believe that it was likely to be so used as to infringe copyright; or in the case of apparatus whose normal use involves a public performance, playing or showing, if he did not believe on reasonable grounds that it would not be so used as to infringe copyright.[87] The 1986 White Paper indicates that the latter alternative will cover background music systems, jukeboxes, and discotheque equipment.[88] The occupier is liable if he gave permission for the apparatus to be brought onto the premises and he then knew or had reason to believe that it was likely to be so used as to infringe copyright.[89] The supplier of a copy of a sound recording or film used is liable if, when he supplied it, he knew or had reason to believe that the copy supplied, or another copy made directly or indirectly from it, was likely to be so used as to infringe copyright.[90]

'In public'

Performing rights in musical works and associated lyrics, and in sound recordings, are administered principally by collecting societies, viz. the Performing Right Society (PRS) and Phonographic Performance Ltd (PPL). The concept of performance etc. 'in public' has been widely construed in favour of copyright owners, and the collecting societies are almost always successful in their infringement actions. But, as will be seen in chapter 5, the conduct of, and in particular the terms of licences granted by, collecting societies, are subject to control by the Copyright Tribunal (formerly the Performing Right Tribunal) under Chapter VII (ss. 116–44) of Part I of the 1988 Act.

It was once held by the Court of Appeal, in *Duck v. Bates*,[91] that an amateur performance of a play at a hospital before an audience consisting of nurses, attendants, doctors and their families, students of the hospital, and friends of the actors, with no charge for admission, was not a performance in public, since it was a domestic and private performance. But this decision marks the limit of the exemption, and it is clear that an amateur performance without charge for admission is not necessarily or even usually exempt, for the courts constantly emphasize that the material relationship is not that between performers and the audience, but that between the copyright owner and the audience. In other words, although there is an exception for truly domestic performances, e.g. a performance of a play by children of the hosts and guests at a country house, any performance which, if permitted, would significantly affect the value of the copyright will be held to be 'in public'. Thus the following performances have been held to be 'in public': the playing of music at a hotel before resident guests and diners,[92] or at a proprietary social and dancing club before members and their guests,[93] or at a football supporters' club before members and guests;[94] the performance of a play before members of a Women's Institute;[95] the relaying of broadcasts or records to workers in a factory;[96] and the playing of records before potential customers in a record shop.[97]

Section 34 of the new Act[98] exempts a performance of a work by a teacher or pupil in the course of the activities of an educational establishment,[99] if the audience is limited to teachers and pupils at and others directly connected with the activities of the establishment, other than simply as parents or custodians of pupils. Section 67 of the new Act[100] exempts the playing of sound recordings as part of the activities of non-profit-making, charitable or similar, clubs, societies and organizations, so long as the proceeds of any charge made for admission are applied solely for the purposes of the organization.

Fraudulent or unauthorized reception of transmissions
Section 297 of the new Act creates an offence of dishonestly receiving a broadcast or cable transmission with intent to avoid payment of any applicable charge, and makes a corporate officer responsible for such offences committed by his company with his consent or connivance.

Section 298 creates a civil liability for making, importing, selling or hiring out an apparatus or device designed or adapted to enable or assist persons to receive broadcasts, cable transmissions or encrypted transmissions when they are not entitled to do so, or for publishing information calculated to enable or assist such reception. The obligation is owed to a person who makes charges for the reception of broadcasts or cable transmissions, or who sends encrypted transmissions, and entitles him to the same rights and remedies as for infringement of copyright, subject to a defence against liability for damages if the defendant had no reason to believe that his acts infringed these rights; and to delivery up, seizure and disposal of an infringing apparatus or device as if it were an infringing copy. Moreover the privilege against self-incrimination is overridden in relation to proceedings under s. 298 as in the case of proceedings relating to copyright.

Sections 297 and 298 apply in favour of broadcasts and transmissions made from the United Kingdom or from a reciprocating country designated by Order in Council, and ancillary tele-communications services are also covered.[101]

Liability for infringements committed by others

Under general principles, an employer is liable for torts, including copyright infringement, committed by his employees in the course of their employment. In the case of copyright, the legislation extends vicarious liability by providing, in s. 16(2) of the 1988 Act,[102] that a person is guilty of primary infringement of copyright in a work if he *authorizes* another person to commit an act of primary infringement (whether of the physical or the performing rights). In addition, as we have seen,[103] ss. 25 and 26 provide for cases of secondary infringement of performing rights.

'Authorization' has sometimes been construed widely. Thus in *PRS v. Ciryl*,[104] Bankes L.J. explained that authorization may be inferred from acts which fall short of being direct or positive; indifference, exhibited by acts of commission or omission, may reach a degree from which authorization or permission may be inferred. In *Falcon v. Famous Players*,[105] the same judge defined 'authorize' as 'sanction, approve, and countenance', and this dictum was approved by Jacobs J. (for the Australian High Court) in *Moorhouse v. University of New South Wales*.[106] But this wide approach has now been rejected by the House of Lords in *CBS Songs v. Amstrad Consumer Electronics*,[107] which preferred instead the view of Atkin L.J. in *Falcon v. Famous Players*[108] that to authorize means to purport to grant to a third person the right to do the relevant act, whether the intention is that the grantee should do the act on his own account or on account of the grantor, and emphasized that authorization involves that the grantor of the authority should be in a position to control the relevant conduct of the grantee.

The effect of the decisions is as follows:

(i) The supplier of a film of a play to a cinema authorizes its exhibition there, and thus infringes copyright in the play.[109]

(ii) If a club, or the proprietor of a coffee-bar, engages a band, and leaves to the band the selection of the music to be played, it authorizes the performance of music in infringement of copyright.[110]

(iii) In *Moorhouse v. University of New South Wales*,[111] an Australian university was held to have authorized a student to infringe where the student wrongfully photocopied a book, not directly relevant to his studies, belonging to the university library, on a coin-operated photocopying machine belonging to the university and located in the library. By placing the coin-operated photocopying machines in the library, the university was considered to have impliedly invited library-users to make such use of the photocopying facilities as they thought fit, and this *prima facie* implication was not effectively rebutted by a warning in the published library guides that students had a responsibility to obey the Copyright Act, nor by an ill-drafted notice attached to the machines. This decision was distinguished in *CBS Songs v. Amstrad Consumer Electronics*[112] on the ground that the university was in a position to control the use of the photocopiers.

(iv) On the other hand a supplier by way of sale or hire of a machine capable of making copies does not authorize infringements which are committed by the direct or ultimate purchasers or users by means of the machine, even if such unlawful copying is known to be almost inevitable, and even if the supplier's advertisements draw attention to the ability of the machine to make infringing copies, for, it is said, once the supplier has sold or hired out the machine, he has no control over how it is used.[113] Moreover in such a case the supplier is not liable as a joint tortfeasor with a customer who uses the machine so as to infringe, since that would require inducement, incitement or persuasion to infringe directed at an individual infringer in relation to a particular infringement.[114]

SIMILARITY AND DERIVATION

As the Court of Appeal emphasized in *Francis Day & Hunter v. Bron*,[115] for the defendant's article (or performance) to infringe copyright in the plaintiff's work, there must be both: (a) substantial objective similarity between them; and (b) causal connection or derivation, i.e. the defendant's article (or performance) must actually be copied from the plaintiff's work. Even if the works are absolutely identical, there is no infringement unless one was derived from the other, and the burden is on the plaintiff to prove derivation from his work. A high degree of objective similarity, coupled with access by the defendant to the plaintiff's work, is cogent evidence of copying,[116] but even complete identity is not in itself conclusive, for it may be proved that the defendant could not have had access to the plaintiff's work. Similarly in *Corelli v. Gray*[117] Sargant J. explained that copyright does not confer an absolute monopoly on authors, such as is conferred on inventors by patents. If two identical works were in fact produced independently of each other, there would be no infringement of copyright, for copyright is merely a negative right to prevent appropriation of an author's labours by another, and the onus of establishing appropriation rests on the plaintiff. Thus in the case before him the similarities between the plaintiff's novel and the defendant's dramatic sketch could in principle have been due to (i) mere chance; (ii) both sketch and novel being taken from a common source; (iii) the novel being taken from the sketch; or (iv) the sketch being taken from the novel; and only in the fourth case would the plaintiff's action for infringement succeed. Usually dispute centres on derivation rather than objective similarity, but it is by virtue of the latter requirement that one does not infringe copyright in a literary work consisting of instructions for making a product by following the instructions and making the product, for there is no visual similarity between the instructions and the product.[118]

By section 16(3)(a) of the new Act,[119] it is sufficient if the defendant's product or performance copies a substantial part of the plaintiff's work. Unaltered copying, e.g. by way of photocopying, almost always infringes, even if it is of a quantitatively very small proportion of the plaintiff's work. Thus a photocopy of a single normal page of an encyclopedia would infringe.[120] But usually, as Lords Reid and Pearce emphasized in *Ladbroke v. Hill*,[121] the substantiality of the part copied depends much more on its quality than its quantity. Lord Reid explained that it was relevant whether the part copied was novel and striking, or merely a commonplace arrangement of ordinary words or well-known data. Lord Pearce emphasized that the copying of a part which by itself is not original will normally not infringe, for matter which only attracts copyright by reason of its collocation will, when robbed of such collocation, not be a substantial part of the copyright. Lord Pearce's approach was followed in *Warwick Film Productions v. Eisinger*,[122] where Plowman J. held that where the plaintiff acquires copyright through secondary work, e.g. by editing an earlier version of a trial transcript, the defendant does not infringe if he copies only material which is not original to the plaintiff's work.[123]

It is immaterial whether the copying is direct or indirect (i.e. by the copying of a copy), as in *Ex parte Beal*,[124] where the defendant had photographed an engraving by the plaintiff of a picture by the plaintiff, and Blackburn J. explained that it was immaterial whether the defendant had copied the plaintiff's picture directly or through intervening copies.[125] But the chain of derivation must run in the right direction, and not as in *Purefoy v. Sykes Boxall*,[126] where the defendant's catalogue of his products was copied from the plaintiff's products but did not infringe copyright in the plaintiff's catalogue, since the plaintiff's catalogue was derived from his products and not vice versa. Moreover copying may infringe even where it is unconscious – the defendant may have read or heard the plaintiff's work, then forgotten about it, but eventually produced a similar work by the use of his unconscious memory; but it must be proved that the defendant was actually familiar with the plaintiff's work, and unconscious copying is difficult to establish.[127] Where infringement is doubtful, the likelihood of the two works' entering into competition with each other is a relevant factor, but infringement is possible even if there is no likelihood of competition.[128]

In the case of artistic works, s. 64 of the new Act[129] permits an author to make a subsequent work, without infringing copyright in the earlier work, so long as he does not repeat or imitate the main design of the earlier work. There is no similar express provision protecting authors of literary works, but probably they will be given greater leeway to repeat features of works whose copyright they have assigned than will be accorded to third-party copyists.[130]

Despite the oft-cited maxim that copyright does not protect a mere idea, but only its embodiment or expression in some particular form,[131] the Court of Appeal held in *Corelli v. Gray*[132] that it would infringe to take a series of incidents in combination from a novel for use in a dramatic sketch, even though not a single sentence in them was similar in form, for copyright protects, not merely the form of words in a novel, but the situations contained in it; and it was enough that five scenes in a sketch of six scenes were taken from the novel and not found in any other works. Similarly, in *Kelly v. Cinema Houses*[133] Maugham J. held that there is infringement if the plot of a play or novel is taken bodily, with or without minor additions or subtractions, for a play or film. In *Fernald v. Jay Lewis*[134] it was held infringement to include in a film every feature of a single, but important, four-page episode from an episodic novel, the film using startlingly similar dialogue. But parodies are usually held not to infringe.[135]

In the case of a very simple drawing, e.g. of a hand marking a cross on a ballot-paper, only an identical copy, or one with only microscopic variations, will infringe.[136] In the case of a painting of a well-known subject, such as the Houses of Parliament and Westminster Bridge, copyright will subsist in the choice of view-point, the exact balance of foreground, middle-ground and back-ground features, and the figures or other objects introduced, for it is in these respects that the artist makes his original contribution.[137] More generally, it is relevant whether the feeling and artistic character of an artistic work have been copied.[138]

Where the plaintiff has compiled information, e.g. in the case of a street-directory of the residents of a district, the defendant is entitled to use the plaintiff's work for the purpose of discovering sources, and to use sources so discovered. The defendant is also permitted, after creating his own work, to check the plaintiff's work for matters omitted from his own, and then to make consequential additions of information obtained through his own efforts. But he is *not* entitled, in order to save himself the labour of searching common sources, to make use of the plaintiff's labour by copying his material, even after making some check of its accuracy.[139]

In *Kelly v. Morris*, Page Wood V.-C. emphasized that, in the case of a dictionary, map, guide-book or directory, where there are certain common objects of information which must, if described correctly, be described in the same words, a subsequent compiler must set about doing for himself what the first compiler has done. He must count the mile-stones for himself, or go through the whole process of triangulation as if he had never seen any former map. Generally, he is not entitled to take one word of the information previously published without working out the matter for himself, and the only use that he can legitimately make of a previous publication is to verify his own results when obtained. In the instant case the defendant was not entitled to take a single line of the plaintiff's directory for the purpose of saving himself labour and trouble in getting his information. In fact, he had simply copied the plaintiff's book and then sent out canvassers to see if the information so copied was correct. If the canvassers did not find the occupier at home, or could get no answer from him, the information copied was reprinted bodily. Moreover one canvasser performed his work carelessly. The defendant's work had not been compiled by the legitimate application of independent personal labour.

Recently in *Elanco v. Mandops*,[140] which involved instruction leaflets for herbicides, the defendant had first simply copied the plaintiff's leaflet, and then, after complaint, rewritten it in a different format and language. In granting an interlocutory injunction, Buckley L.J. emphasized that the defendant was entitled to use information which was available in the public domain, but not to copy the plaintiff's leaflet, and thus use the plaintiff's skill and judgement and save itself the trouble and cost of assembling its own information from its own researches or from documents in the public domain, making its own selection of material and producing its own leaflet. On the other hand a true summary or digest of a work, made with skill and labour, and expressed in different language, so as to produce an original work, may not infringe.[141]

Computer programs

On the assessment of objective similarity in the case of computer programs there is little English case-law, but it is clear that one must proceed by analogy with an ordinary literary work. Thus the most obvious way of determining similarity, at any rate where the defendant had access to the plaintiff's source code and has expressed his own source code in the same computer language, is by verbal comparison of print-outs of the parties' source code, in much the same way as one may compare 'ordinary' documents, with a view to discovering literal (or verbatim) or near-literal (or almost verbatim) similarities in lines or blocks of code. For this purpose expert evidence from competent programmers will of course be necessary and admissible, since the complex and unfamiliar nature of computer programs would prevent a layman from instinctively recognizing and evaluating similarities.

In fact this is the approach which has been adopted in the two English cases in which the matter has been considered. Comparison of print-outs of source code was envisaged by Megarry V.-C. in *Thrustcode Ltd. v. W.W. Computing Ltd.*,[142] which involved programs for controlling manufacturing processes. Megarry V.-C. also emphasized that it was not enough to establish infringement to show that the parties' programs produced similar results, but this remark must be read subject to the arguments below as to the sufficiency in some cases of non-literal (or structural) similarity.

More recently, in *MS Associates Ltd. v. Power*,[143] which involved programs for translating source code from the BASIC to the 'C' language, Falconer J. considered expert evidence comparing the parties' source code and dealing with similarities in the names used for functions in the libraries of 'C' functions; in particular lines of code; in functions included – obviously a structural rather than literal type of similarity; in the grouping of functions; in the routines used in particular functions; in the names used for variables; and in certain errors. In holding (on an application for an interlocutory injunction pending a full trial) that the plaintiff had shown an arguable case that it had a real prospect of succeeding in the action, he indicated that a single function (in casu, the 'GET' function) should be regarded as a substantial part of the plaintiff's program.

Similarly in *Whelan Associates v. Jaslow Dental Laboratories*[144] an American court admitted expert testimony and excluded any test of lay recognition, not only in relation to the issue of derivation, but also as regards objective similarity as such. In terms of American law, this was a new approach to objective similarity as such, justified by the complex nature of computer programs, with which the layman is unfamiliar and in respect of which he is unable instinctively to recognize similarity. In the case of literary (as distinct from artistic works), English law has never had any requirement of lay recognition, or any difficulty in admitting expert evidence where the subject-matter makes it appropriate to do so.

No doubt it will be equally permissible to demonstrate literal similarity by means of a byte-by-byte comparison of print-outs, probably in hexadecimal notation, of the parties' object code. This is particularly likely to be appropriate if the defendant is alleged to have produced his object code by directly copying the plaintiff's object code, probably electronically; or to have electronically disassembled the plaintiff's object code, manually modified the resulting assembly code in some respects, and then reassembled it electronically.

Literal or near-literal similarity, though sufficient (if coupled with derivation) to establish infringement, cannot be essential for this purpose, since the British legislation specifies that it is infringement of copyright in a program to make or reproduce an adaptation of the program, and that a version of a program in which it is converted into a different computer language or code constitutes a translation and thus an adaptation of the program. If source code is translated into a different source language – whether electronically, by means of a suitable translation program, or by the human intellect of a programmer versed in both languages, who rewrites the program in much the same way as a person might translate an ordinary document from one human language into another – there may be very little literal similarity between the two versions of the source code. Again, if object code is translated, by electronic disassembly, any necessary manual modification, and then reassembly, perhaps in order to enable the program to run on a computer with a different CPU, there may be very little literal similarity between the sequences of bytes in the two versions of object code. Thus some acceptance of non-literal similarity, as a basis for infringement, is unavoidable.

In the United States the recent decision of the Court of Appeals for the Third Circuit in *Whelan Associates v. Jaslow Dental Laboratories*[145] has established that copyright protection of a computer program may extend beyond the progam's literal code to its structure, sequence and organization. The case involved database programs for assisting in the operation of a business supplying dental equipment. Infringement was found in the substantial similarity of structure and sequence in the parties' programs. These were written in different source languages, the plaintiff's in EDL for an IBM Series One computer, and the defendant's in BASIC, so as to enable it to run on other computers. There was no literal similarity, in view of the different languages, but the defendant had had access to the plaintiff's source code. The court reasoned that the purpose or function of a utilitarian work constitutes its unprotectable idea – in the instant case, to aid in the business operations of a dental laboratory. Since the function performed by the plaintiff's program could be implemented through a variety of structures, the structure chosen constituted a protectable expression. In the result, infringement was found on the basis of expert evidence of substantial similarity in respect of data-file structures, screen outputs, and in five particular, but qualitatively important, sub-routines. The plaintiff's data-file structures were said to be sufficiently complex and detailed as to convey information, and were not the only ones capable of fulfilling the program's purpose. Similarities in screen outputs were considered of some indirect probative value, though it was recognized that screen outputs constituted separate audiovisual works under the American Copyright Act and that different programs could produce similar screen output.

Earlier in *SAS Institute v. S&H Computer Systems*,[146] a Federal District Court had found infringement by reference to 'literal, near-literal, and organisational copying', and indicated that copying of the design would be sufficient; and subsequently in *Dynamic Solutions v. Planning & Control*[147] another Federal District Court agreed with the decision in *Whelan* that 'to the extent that structural similarities are not necessary to the purpose or function of the program, they constitute a protectable expression'. On the other hand in *Plains Cotton Co-op Association v. Goodpasture Computer Serv.*[148] the Court of Appeals for the Fifth Circuit took the view that many of the similarities between the programs with which it was concerned were dictated by externalities of the cotton market, and therefore treated the sequence and organization as an unprotectable idea; and, much earlier, in *Synercom Technology v. University Computing Co.*[149] a Federal District Court had held that copying of input-formats did not infringe, since blank forms did not receive protection unless they conveyed information in themselves, and the input-formats in question conveyed information only about the sequencing and ordering of data.

The decision in *Whelan* has been strongly criticized,[150] on the grounds, first, that the 'purpose' test is open to manipulation, by broad or narrow interpretation. The purpose of the plaintiff's program could have been construed as maintaining client lists, client histories, normal dental patterns, available office hours, material costs and accounts receivable, and producing reports on ordering, scheduling, profits and workloads. Secondly, it has been argued that protection of program structure is excessive in relation to the object of granting copyright in programs, to encourage creativity by preventing 'free-riding' and thus enabling recovery of development costs. Copyists of structure still need to rewrite the literal code, which delays them from entering the market, so that meanwhile the original owner can charge monopoly prices and establish a reputation enabling him later to continue charging higher prices. Moreover protection of structure, while encouraging innovation in the development of new structures, will impede development of 'spin-off' or 'refinement' programs; that is, variations of or improvements on the original program. In such cases, programmers will have to re-invent the wheel and re-develop structure logic before introducing the variation or improvement, and this will increase the cost and reduce the availability of such programs. So, it is argued, the *Whelan* ruling should be refined by defining a program's purpose by way of a detailed description, so that a program with a non-trivial variation will be regarded as having a different purpose and thus not infringing the copyright in the original.

Despite such criticism, the *Whelan* decision seems justifiable in terms of normal principles of copyright law, in both the United Kingdom and the United States. There is a close analogy with the acceptance of non-literal copying as a basis of infringement of copyright in 'ordinary' literary works.[151] In the United Kingdom, the facts of the *Whelan* case would seem to involve a simple case of infringement by direct translation of source code from one computer language to another. More difficult questions would arise in a case where the defendant had only had access to the plaintiff's object code, and had not disassembled it electronically, but had merely run it to observe what functions it offered, how it presented them to the user, and how it formatted data received, and had then written his own source code (perhaps in a different language to the plaintiff's) with the object of producing a program which would seem to the user equivalent to the plaintiff's program in functions and interface. Such copying would seem to satisfy the requirement of derivation, and there would probably be sufficient similarity in the 'structure, sequence and organization' of the programs to justify a finding of infringement.

Some limit on the extent of protection for computer programs is, however, contemplated by the EC Commission's Proposal of January 1989[152] for a Directive on harmonization in this area. Departing from the Green Paper of June 1988, Art. 2(3) of the proposed Directive specifies that copyright protection is not to extend to the ideas, principles, logic, algorithms, or programming languages underlying a program, and that this exclusion extends to 'the specification of interfaces' in so far as this constitutes ideas and principles which underlie a program. Some light is thrown on the concept of 'interface' by the Preamble to the proposed Directive, which refers to the principles describing any means of logical or physical interconnection and interaction which is required to permit elements of hardware and software to work with other software and hardware and with users in the ways they are intended to function. Thus it seems that only features of interface which are essential in terms of function will be caught by the exclusion.

EXCEPTIONS

Chapter III (ss. 28–76) of Part I of the 1988 Act collects a variety of exceptions, under which certain acts which would otherwise infringe copyright are permitted so far as copyright infringement is concerned, though not as against any other ground of illegality, such as breach of contract.[153] Unless otherwise specified, an act authorized by Chapter III is permitted as against copyright in all types of work.[154] Section 28(3) emphasizes that no inference is to be drawn from the statutory exceptions as to the scope of *prima facie* infringement, and s. 28(4) adds that the exceptions are to be construed independently of each other. By s. 76, an act which is permitted by Chapter III in respect of a literary, dramatic or musical work is also permitted in relation to another work of which the work in question is an adaptation. There are also two exceptions based on public policy at common law.

In accordance with the proposals in Chapter 11 of the 1986 White Paper, the new Act does not preserve the statutory licence granted by s. 8 of the 1956 Act (at a royalty of $6\frac{1}{4}$ per cent of the ordinary retail selling price) to record and issue 'cover versions' of recorded music (and associated lyrics), subject to a transitional saving in respect of records made within a year of the abolition in pursuance of a notice given earlier.[155] In future recording licences will be subject to the powers of the new Copyright Tribunal to control licensing schemes administered by collecting societies.[156] Also abandoned are the provisions contained in s. 13(7) and (8) of the 1956 Act which enabled a film whose copyright had expired to be shown (and its sound-track played) in public without infringing the copyright in any literary, dramatic or musical work included, and newsreels to be shown fifty years after the end of the calendar year of the events depicted.

Education

There are a number of statutory exceptions connected with education. Some apply in relation to educational establishments, others in connection with education generally. Section 174 of the new Act defines 'educational establishment' as any school, within the meaning of the Education Act 1944, and any other description of educational establishment specified by statutory instrument;[157] and references to teachers and pupils of an educational establishment include anyone giving or receiving instruction at the establishment. Moreover, certain provisions relating to educational establishments have been extended by statutory instrument so as to cover teachers employed by local education authorities to give instruction elsewhere to pupils unable to attend an educational establishment.[158]

Firstly, s. 29(1) of the new Act specifies that fair dealing with a literary, dramatic, musical or artistic work for the purposes of research or private study does not infringe copyright in the work nor in the typographical arrangement of a published edition. For good measure s. 29(2) adds that fair dealing for these purposes with the typographical arrangement of an edition does not infringe the copyright in the edition. But s. 29(3) specifies that copying by a person other than the researcher or student himself is not fair dealing if it is done by or on behalf of a librarian and does not comply with the restrictions on multiple copying by librarians imposed under ss. 38 or 39; or if it is done by some other third person and that person knows or has reason to believe that it will result in copies of substantially the same material being provided to more than one person at substantially the same time and for substantially the same purpose.

The section replaces ss. 6(1) and 9(1) of the 1956 Act, with some of the amendments proposed in the 1986 White Paper.[159] The amendments extend the exception to cover the copyright in the typographical arrangement of a published edition, but the proposal in the White Paper to exclude commercial research was rejected by Parliament. As envisaged in the White Paper, no definition of 'fair dealing' is offered. It is well established, however, that a publisher cannot invoke this exception on the ground that his customers would use his publication for purposes of research or private study,[160] and the new Act makes clear that multiple copying is not within the exception, but otherwise its ambit remains uncertain. Obviously the proportion of the work or edition copied, and whether the work is out-of-print, are relevant factors. The exception is not, however, limited to persons or acts connected with an educational establishment. In addition, by s. 60, a new provision, where an article on a scientific or technical subject is published in a periodical accompanied by an abstract indicating its contents, it is not infringement of copyright in the abstract or the article to copy the abstract or issue copies of it to the public, unless a licensing scheme certified under s. 143 covering the matter is in operation.

Secondly, s. 33 of the new Act[161] permits the inclusion of a short passage from a published literary or dramatic work in a collection which is intended for use in educational establishments and is so described in its title and in the publisher's advertisements, and which consists mainly of non-copyright material. But the work from which the passage is taken must not itself be intended for use in such establishments, and there must be a sufficient acknowledgement identifying the work by its title or other description and also identifying the author (unless it was published anonymously, or is unpublished and his identity is unknown).[162] A further restriction prevents the same publisher from including more than two excerpts from copyright works by the same author in such anthologies published within five years.

Thirdly, s. 32(1) of the new Act permits the copying of literary, dramatic, musical and artistic works in the course of instruction or preparation for instruction, provided that the copying is done by a person giving or receiving instruction and not by means of a reprographic process.[163] Similarly s. 32(2) permits the copying of a sound recording, film, broadcast, or cable programme, without infringement of the copyright therein, by the making of a film or a film sound-track in the course of instruction, or of preparation for instruction, in the making of films or sound-tracks, provided that the copying is done by a person giving or receiving instruction. Curiously these provisions do not refer in terms to any connection with an educational establishment.[164] In addition s. 32(3)[165] authorizes things done for the purposes of an examination, by way of setting the questions, communicating the questions to the candidates, or answering the questions, though (by s. 32(4), a new provision) this does not cover the making of a reprographic copy of a musical work for use by an examination candidate in performing the work.

Fourthly, s. 34 declares that the performance of a literary, dramatic or musical work, before an audience consisting of teachers and pupils at an educational establishment and other persons directly connected with the activities of the establishment (but not including a parent of a pupil as such), by a teacher or pupil in the course of the activities of an educational establishment, or at such an establishment by any person for the purposes of instruction, is not a public performance.[166] Similarly the playing or showing of a sound recording, film, broadcast or cable programme before such an audience at an educational establishment for the purposes of instruction is declared not to be a playing or showing in public.[167]

Fifthly, s. 35 of the new Act enables an educational establishment to make recordings of broadcasts or cable programmes, and copies of such recordings, for its own educational purposes, without infringing copyright in the broadcast or programme or any work contained in it, except insofar as a licensing scheme, certified by the Secretary of State under s. 143, is in operation.[168]

Finally, s. 36 enables an educational establishment to make reprographic copies of passages from published literary, dramatic or musical works for the purposes of instruction, without infringing copyright in the works or the typographical arrangement of published editions, up to a limit of 1 per cent of any particular work in any quarter. This does not apply, however, where licences authorizing the copying in question are available and the copyist is or should be aware of this; but the terms of a licence granted to an educational establishment authorizing the reprographic copying for the purposes of instruction of passages from published literary, dramatic or musical works are invalid insofar as they purport to restrict the proportion of a work which may be copied (whether on payment or free of charge) to less than 1 per cent per quarter. The section reflects the government's expectation that voluntary blanket licensing should provide the framework for multiple copying in the educational context. The 1986 White Paper also envisaged that the Secretary of State should be empowered to require an individual copyright owner to join a blanket licensing scheme, and to order compulsory licensing of a particular class of work,[169] and these recommendations are now implemented in ss. 135–39 of the new Act.[170]

Libraries and archives

Sections 37–43 of the new Act[171] authorize certain librarians and archivists, and persons acting on their behalf, to make copies of certain works, or parts of works, subject to certain conditions. In general these sections operate subject to regulations made by the Secretary of State subject to annulment by either House of Parliament. Under s. 37, such regulations – currently the Copyright (Copying by Librarians and Archivists) Regulations 1989[172] – prescribe the description of library or archive to which, and the conditions under which, these exemptions apply. In general these provisions enable a prescribed librarian to make a copy of an authorized item for supply to, and to supply it to, another person, but only if: (i) the person satisfies the librarian, by means of a signed declaration,[173] that he requires it for purposes of research or private study, and will not use it for any other purpose; (ii) the same person is not supplied with more than one copy of the same item; and (iii) the person supplied pays a sum not less than the cost, including a contribution to the general expenses of the library, attributable to the production of the copy.[174]

Subject to these conditions, s. 38 enables a prescribed librarian[175] to make and supply a copy of an article or item[176] in a periodical, without infringing copyright in the text, any illustrations accompanying the text, or the typographical arrangement. A similar power is conferred by s. 39 to make and supply a copy of a reasonable proportion of a published edition of a literary, dramatic or musical work (other than an article in a periodical). The predecessor of the latter power[177] was largely illusory, since it was restricted to situations where the librarian did not know, and could not by reasonable inquiry have ascertained, the name and address of a person entitled to authorize the making of the copy as regards the original work (as distinct from the typographical arrangement), a situation which would seldom arise in the case of a work published recently in the United Kingdom, since one could inquire of the publisher as to the ownership and management of the copyright in the original work. Fortunately this restriction has been removed by the new Act. But, to prevent the related production of multiple copies of the same material,[178] s. 40 now requires the librarian to be satisfied, before supplying a copy under ss. 38 or 39, that the person's requirement of a copy is not related to any similar requirement of another person, and requirements are regarded as similar and related where they are for copies of substantially the same material at substantially the same time and for substantially the same purpose and are requirements of persons receiving instruction to which the material is relevant at the same time and place.

A further power to make and supply a copy for research or private study is now conferred on a prescribed librarian or archivist by s. 43,[179] which applies to documents containing works which had not been published prior to the deposit of the document in the library or archive. A copy of the whole or part of such a literary, dramatic or musical work may be supplied, unless the librarian is or should be aware that the copyright owner has prohibited copying.

Section 41 enables a prescribed librarian to make a copy of the whole or part of a published literary, dramatic or musical work and supply it to another prescribed library, but not (except in the case of an article in a periodical) if he knows or could ascertain by reasonable inquiry the name and address of a person entitled to authorize the making of the copy. Section 42 enables a prescribed librarian or archivist to make a copy from any item in the permanent collection of his library or archive in order to preserve or replace the item by placing the copy in its permanent collection in addition to or in place of the item, or in order to replace in the permanent collection of another prescribed library or archive an item which has been lost, damaged or destroyed. But this power does not apply where it is reasonably practicable to purchase a copy of the item to fulfil the authorized purpose, and is confined to items held for purposes of reference on the premises of the copying library or of loan to other libraries.[180] All libraries and archives in the United Kingdom are prescribed as permitted to make and supply copies under ss. 41 and 42, but the recipient library or archive must not be conducted for profit.[181]

Section 44[182] enables a copy to be made of an article of cultural or historical importance or interest for deposit in an appropriate library or archive, where such making and deposit is necessary to enable the article lawfully to be exported from the United Kingdom. Section 61 permits the making of a sound recording of a performance of a song, for the purpose of including it in an archive maintained by a non-profit-making body designated by statutory instrument,[183] without infringement of any copyright in the words

71

or the music, if the words are unpublished and of unknown authorship, no other copyright is infringed and the making of the recording is not prohibited by the performer. Single copies of the recording may then be made by the archivist and supplied to persons who satisfy him that they require them for purposes of research or private study and will not use them for other purposes. Section 75 enables the Secretary of State to designate non-profit-making bodies as authorized to make recordings, and copies of recordings, of broadcasts or cable programmes for placing in archives.[184] This overrides copyright not only in the broadcast or cable programme, but also in works included therein.

News reports; criticism or review; and incidental inclusion

Section 30(2) and (3) of the new Act[185] authorizes fair dealing with any type of work, other than a photograph, for the purpose of reporting current events. The report must, however, be accompanied by a sufficient acknowledgement, unless the report is in the form of a sound recording, film, broadcast or cable programme. 'Sufficient acknowledgement' is defined by s. 178 as an acknowledgement identifying the work by its title or other description, and also identifying the author unless either the work has been published anonymously, or it has not been published and his identity cannot be discovered by reasonable inquiry.

In addition, s. 58, a new provision, enables a written or other record of spoken words which embody a literary work, and which has been made without infringing a prohibition by the speaker, and, where copyright already subsisted in the work, without infringing the copyright, for the purpose of reporting current events or of broadcasting or cable transmission, to be used and copied for that purpose, without infringing copyright in the literary work, provided that: (a) the record was made directly from the spoken words (rather than taken from a previous record or a broadcast or cable transmission); (b) the use made of the record is not of a kind prohibited by the speaker or copyright owner before the record was made; and (c) the use is effected or authorized by a person who is lawfully in possession of the record.

Section 30(1) of the new Act[186] authorizes fair dealing with any type of work for the purpose of criticism or review of the work itself, or of another work, or of a performance of a work. The critique or review must, however, be accompanied by a sufficient acknowledgement, as defined by s. 178 above. This exception was considered by the Court of Appeal in *Hubbard v. Vosper*,[187] where it was emphasized that criticism is not confined to criticism of the literary style, but extends to criticism of the ideas, thoughts, doctrine, philosophy and subject-matter of the work. The question of fair dealing is one of degree or impression, and involves consideration of the number and length of the quotations, the use made of them, and their proportion to the comments. It may be fair dealing to quote the entirety of a short work, e.g. a tombstone epitaph.

In *Hubbard v. Vosper* Lord Denning also explained that the exception is not confined to works which have been published to the world at large, but extends to ones which have otherwise been circulated widely, such as a circular sent by a company to its shareholders. But in *Beloff v. Pressdram*,[188] which involved an unpublished memorandum by a journalist concerning her conversation with a leading politician, which had been leaked to *Private Eye*, probably by a colleague, and then published therein, Ungoed-Thomas J. regarded the fact that the memorandum was unpublished and never intended for publication as an important factor against the defence of fair dealing; and ultimately concluded that the leak vitiated the defence.

Section 31 permits the incidental inclusion of any type of work in an artistic work, a sound recording, a film, a broadcast or a cable programme.[189] Moreover, copies of anything made under this section may be issued to the public, and such things may be played or shown in public, broadcast or included in a cable programme.[190] But a musical work, an accompanying lyric, or a sound recording, broadcast, or cable programme of or insofar as it includes a musical work or lyric, must not be included deliberately.[191]

Public administration
Sections 45 and 46 of the new Act[192] deal with parliamentary and judicial proceedings,[193] Royal Commissions and statutory inquiries. They authorize things done for the purposes of such proceedings, or of reporting such proceedings if held in public, other than the copying of a published report. They also authorize the issue to the public of copies of a report of a Royal Commission or statutory inquiry, as against the owner of copyright in a work contained therein.

Section 47 permits certain acts in relation to material which is open to public inspection pursuant to a statutory requirement or is on a register maintained in pursuance of a statutory requirement, if done by or with the authority of the person required to make the material open to public inspection or the person maintaining the register. By s. 47(1), any copyright in such material as a literary work is not infringed by the copying of so much of the material as contains factual information, for a purpose not involving the issue of copies to the public. By s. 47(2), material open to public inspection may be copied, and copies of it issued to the public, for the purpose of enabling it to be inspected at a more convenient time or place or otherwise facilitating the exercise of the rights of inspection.[194] By s. 47(3), material which is open to inspection or is on a register and which contains information about matters of general scientific, technical, commercial or economic interest, may be copied, and copies of it issued to the public, for the purpose of disseminating the information. These exceptions may be extended by statutory instrument to material made open to public inspection by international organizations or under international agreements, and to registers maintained by international organizations.[195] In addition s. 49 authorizes the copying, and the supply of copies to anyone, of public records which are open to public inspection under the Public Records Act, by or with the authority of officers appointed under that Act.

Section 48 enables the Crown to copy, and issue to the public copies of, previously unpublished literary, dramatic, musical or artistic works which have been communicated to the Crown by or with the licence of the copyright owner, and which are recorded or embodied in a document or other fixation which is owned by or in the custody or control of the Crown. The power is exercisable only for the purpose for which the work was communicated, or related purposes, and is subject to a contrary agreement between the Crown and the copyright owner.

By s. 50, without prejudice to any defence of statutory authority otherwise available, acts specifically authorized by past or future statutes, such as the publication of patent specifications by the Comptroller-General of Patents, do not infringe copyright, unless the Act in question contains a saving for copyright.[196]

Broadcasts and cable transmissions

Since the copyright in a work may be divided, e.g. so that the right to make physical copies is in different hands from the performing rights, special provision is necessary to ensure that a person entitled to broadcast a work or transmit it by cable is able to make copies necessary for the purpose. Accordingly s. 68 of the new Act[197] authorizes a person who is entitled by virtue of a licence or assignment to broadcast or include in a cable programme a literary, dramatic, musical or artistic work, an adaptation of such a work, a sound recording or a film to perform certain acts for the purposes of the broadcast or programme. He is permitted to make a sound recording or film of the literary, dramatic or musical work, or adaptation, in question; or to take a photograph or make a film of the artistic work in question; or to make a copy of the sound recording or film in question. But a copy made under this exception must not be used for any other purpose, and is treated for the purpose of an unauthorized use as an infringing copy. Moreover the copy must be destroyed within twenty-eight days of being first used for a broadcast or in a cable programme; otherwise it is treated as an infringing copy for all subsequent purposes.

Section 69 authorizes acts necessary in the context of the supervisory functions of the British Broadcasting Corporation, the Independent Broadcasting Authority or the Cable Authority. By s. 73, copyright in a broadcast made from the United Kingdom, and in any work included in the broadcast, is not infringed by its immediate re-transmission by cable, insofar as (a) this is done in pursuance of s. 13(1) of the Cable and Broadcasting Act 1984, or (b) the cable transmission is to the same area as that at which the broadcast was aimed, and the broadcast is not a satellite transmission nor an encrypted transmission. If the broadcast itself infringed copyright in a work included, damages awarded against the broadcaster will take account also of the cable transmission.

Section 74 of the new Act enables the Secretary of State by statutory instrument to designate non-profit-making bodies as authorized to make and issue to the public copies of television broadcasts or cable programmes, for the purpose of providing sub-titled or otherwise suitably modified copies for persons who are deaf or hard of hearing or otherwise physically or mentally handicapped, unless a licensing scheme certified under s. 143 is in operation. This overrides copyright not only in the broadcast or programme, but also in works included therein. The National Sub-titling Library for Deaf People has been designated under s. 74.[198]

Solo readings or recitations

By s. 59 of the new Act,[199] the reading or recitation in public of a reasonable extract from a published literary or dramatic work does not infringe copyright in the work, provided that it is accompanied by a sufficient acknowledgement. Moreover it is permissible to include such a reading or recitation in a sound recording, broad-cast or cable transmission, so long as the recording, broadcast or transmission consists mainly of other material.

Artistic works

Section 62 of the new Act[200] permits certain acts in relation to buildings, sculptures, models for buildings, and works of artistic craftsmanship, subject to the proviso (except in the case of buildings) that the work be permanently situated in a public place or in premises open to the public. It is permissible to make a graphic work of, to photograph or film, or to broadcast or include in a cable transmission a visual image of, the work in question. Moreover, copies of a graphic work, photograph or film made under this exception may be issued to the public, and such derivative works may be broadcast or included in cable trans-missions without infringing copyright in the building or other principal work in question.[201]

By s. 65,[202] anything done for the purposes of reconstructing a building does not infringe any copyright in the building or in any drawings or plans in accordance with which the building was (with the copyright owner's licence) constructed. In relation to buildings constructed before the commencement of the new Act, the relevant copyright owner in relation to the drawing or plans is the person who owned the copyright in the drawings or plans at the time of the construction of the building under the law then in force.[203] Section 63 permits the copying of an artistic work, and the issue of copies to the public, for the purpose of advertising the sale of the work.

Typefaces

The design of an original typeface (including an ornamental motif used in printing)[204] is protected, apparently as a graphic work, but the protection is severely limited by ss. 54 and 55 of the 1988 Act. In the first place, if articles specifically designed or adapted for producing material in the typeface are marketed, in the United Kingdom or elsewhere, by or with the licence of the copyright owner, protection expires at the end of the twenty-fifth calendar year after that of the first such marketing.[205] Secondly, it is not infringement of copyright in the design of a typeface to use the typeface in the ordinary course of typing, composing text, type-setting or printing, nor to possess or import an article for the purpose of such use, nor to do anything in relation to material produced by such use; even if an infringing copy of the work is used.[206] Rather the remedies available are against those who make, import or market articles specifically designed or adapted for producing material in the typeface, for such articles are treated as articles for making infringing copies for the purposes of s. 24 (on secondary infringement), ss. 99 and 100 (on delivery up, seizure and forfeiture), and ss. 107(2) and 108 (on offences and forfeiture in criminal proceedings).[207]

Use of computer programs
American law specifically provides for a right of the owner of a legitimate copy of a computer program to make back-up copies. Section 117 of the American Copyright Act provides that it is not infringement for the owner of a copy of a program to make or authorize the making of another copy or an adaptation of the program, provided that either: (i) the new copy or adaptation is created as an essential step in the utilization of the program in conjunction with a machine and it is used in no other manner, or (ii) the new copy or adaptation is for archival purposes only and all archival copies are destroyed if continued possession of the program ceases to be rightful. The section adds that an exact copy prepared in accordance therewith may be leased, sold or otherwise transferred along with the copy from which it was prepared as part of the lease, sale or other transfer of all rights in the program, and not otherwise; but that an adaptation so prepared may be transferred only with the authorization of the copyright owner.

The British legislation contains no equivalent provision. Section 56 of the 1988 Act merely provides in effect that where:

(i) a copy of a work (including a program) in electronic form has been purchased (after the commencement of the new Act)[208] on terms which, expressly or impliedly or under any rule of law (e.g. against derogation from grant), allow the purchaser to copy the work, or to adapt it or make copies of an adaptation, in connection with his use of it; and

(ii) there are no express terms to the contrary (i.e. ones which prohibit transfer of the copy by the purchaser, impose obligations which continue after a transfer, prohibit the assignment of any licence or terminate any licence on a transfer); then

(iii) a transferee may do anything which the transferor was licensed to do: but

(iv) any copy, adaptation or copy of an adaptation which is not also transferred becomes an infringing copy.

These provisions also apply where the original purchased copy has become unusable and a further copy is transferred instead; and to a further transfer.[209] In addition s. 21(4) excludes from the definition of 'translation' and 'adaptation' a version created incidentally in the course of running the program.

Hence in the United Kingdom the right of the first user of a legitimate copy to make back-up copies or other copies for his own use depends on an express or implied licence from the copyright owner, or on the doctrine of non-derogation from grant, which was, rather surprisingly, applied to copyright by the House of Lords in *British Leyland Motor Corp. v. Armstrong Patents Co. Ltd.*,[210] so as to prevent a manufacturer of a complex mechanical product from invoking his copyright in design drawings to prevent another undertaking from producing or marketing spare parts for the product.

As regards programs, any express terms purporting to regulate the buyer's right to use the program which arrive with the software are almost certainly communicated too late to bind him, unless he then communicates his agreement to them, perhaps by returning a card to the publisher with a view to registering for support. There may be an exception if the user has previously purchased other copies of the same program and thus become familiar with the terms of the express licence which the publisher seeks to grant and impose in respect of the program. But even then, unless the purchase is directly from the publisher, the terms are probably not contractually binding unless the purchaser communicates his assent to the publisher. Moreover, any argument that, even if not contractually binding, the terms are effective as part of the copyright would no doubt be answered by invoking the rule against derogation from grant.

Hence, unless the purchaser has signed a licensing agreement with the copyright owner, his right to make back-up copies or other copies for his own use will be governed by the implied licence which is customary in the relevant context. In the case of software to run on a micro-computer, probably the terms usually to be implied are that the user may make as many copies as he likes for back-up purposes or for the purpose of using the program on a single computer at any given moment, but that he must not use the copy received or any copies made from it on more than one computer at the same moment.

Moreover, unless otherwise agreed, it seems probable that it is an implied term of a contract to supply software, other than perhaps a game program, that the copy supplied shall not be electronically copy-protected, so as to prevent or hinder the making of copies which will run without the original being present in the machine; and thus that one who receives an electronically protected version, without having agreed to this, may reject it under s. 14 of the Sale of Goods Act 1979 on the grounds that it is unmerchantable or not reasonably fit for its purpose, and refuse to pay or claim back the price, as well as claiming damages.

In Chapter 5 of its Green Paper,[211] the EC Commission favoured a broad use-right in respect of computer programs, covering reproduction, rental, adaptation and translation, as necessary to enable the copyright owner to charge according to the actual use made of his program. Accordingly Art. 4 of its Proposal of January 1989[212] would make it primary infringement of copyright in a program: (a) to reproduce it by any means, in any form, and whether in whole or in part, and this would include reproduction by way of loading, viewing, running, transmitting or storing the program; (b) to adapt the program; and (c) to distribute the program, by way of sale, licensing, leasing, renting out, or importing for such purposes. In addition Art. 6 provides for secondary infringement by importing, possessing, or dealing with an infringing copy of a program, knowing or having reason to believe it to be such; and by making, importing, possessing, or dealing with articles specifically designed to facilitate the removal or circumvention of a copy-protection device which has been applied to the program.

On the other hand, in its Green Paper the Commission took the view that a licence to use should cover all acts (including adaptations) inherent in the authorized use, though suppliers would be permitted to require notification of any adaptations made. It also favoured both the elimination of any exception allowing copying for private purposes, and the explicit creation of a right to make back-up copies, which would have to be destroyed when the right to use the program expired. In the result, however, Art. 5(1) of the Proposal merely ensures that where a program has been sold or made available to the public otherwise than by a written licence agreement signed by both parties, the user shall be entitled to carry out any acts of reproduction or adaptation which are necessary for the use of the program. In addition Art. 5(2) permits copies so marketed to be rented to the public by non-profit-making public libraries.

Public policy at common law

It is well established that public policy at common law prevents the enforcement of copyright in a work which is grossly immoral,[213] or of a work which has been fraudulently published as that of a well-known author.[214] Similarly it would be contrary to public policy to enforce at the behest of the author or publisher copyright in a work which was created and published in breach of a binding obligation to respect confidence, and indeed in such a situation the copyright may be held on a constructive trust for the person to whom the confidence obligation was owed.[215] More doubtfully, in *Beloff v. Pressdram*[216] Ungoed-Thomas J. held that the defence of public interest in disclosure applies to copyright infringement as well as to breach of confidence, though he confined the defence to the disclosure of serious illegalities and other matters dangerous to the public, clearly recognizable as such.[217] Section 171(3) of the new Act explicitly saves the operation of any rule of law preventing or restricting the enforcement of copyright, on grounds of public interest or otherwise.

EXHAUSTION

The question of exhaustion concerns the effect on intellectual-property rights of the marketing, by the owner of the rights or with his consent, of articles which fall within the scope of these rights. Are the rights exhausted by such marketing, so that the owner cannot invoke them so as to prevent further marketing or use of the articles in question? The marketing carried out or authorized by the owner may take place in the same country as the further marketing or use which he is seeking, by invoking his intellectual-property rights, to prevent, in which case one is concerned with internal exhaustion; or they may take place in different countries, in which case one is concerned with international exhaustion.

As will be seen, traditional English law does not systematically adopt the principle of exhaustion, either internally or internationally, but European Community law imposes a doctrine of international exhaustion in respect of trade between Member States. This prevents the owner of an intellectual-property right from using his right to prevent the importation into or marketing or use within one Member State of goods which have been marketed by him or with his consent in another Member State.

English law
Under English law the problem of exhaustion is dealt with differently for the various types of intellectual-property right.

Patents and registered designs
Under s. 60(1)(a) and (c) of the Patents Act 1977,[218] it is infringement of a patent to dispose of, offer to dispose of, use, import, or keep for purposes of disposal or use, the patented product or a product obtained directly by means of the patented process.

British law (apart from European Community law) has neither a doctrine of internal nor of international exhaustion of patent rights. If goods within the scope of a British patent are sold, whether in the United Kingdom or elsewhere, by the owner of the patent or with his permission, their subsequent sale or use in, or importation into, the United Kingdom, will nonetheless infringe the patent unless it is expressly or impliedly licensed by the patent owner. A sale by the patentee himself will impliedly license all further dealings with the goods, except insofar as a clear and express prohibition on certain of them is imposed by the terms of the sale. But if such a prohibition is so imposed, it will be effective against third parties, at any rate if they acquire the goods with notice of it. Thus sale abroad by the British patentee impliedly licenses importation into and sale and use in this country, unless a clear and express prohibition is imposed thereon.[219] But a condition imposed by the patentee on a sale in the United Kingdom to a wholesaler, prohibiting retail-sale below a specified price, has been held binding on a retailer who bought with knowledge of the condition.[220] Moreover if the owner of both a British and a foreign patent for the same invention assigns the foreign patent, or grants a licence to manufacture and sell in the foreign country, there will be no implied licence to import into this country and sell or use here, and such importation, sale and use will infringe.[221]

As regards registered designs, s. 7 of the Registered Designs Act 1949 (as amended by the Copyright, Designs and Patents Act 1988) gives the registered proprietor the exclusive right in the United Kingdom to import for sale or hire or for use for the purposes of a trade or business, and to sell, hire out, or offer or expose for sale or hire, an article in respect of which the design is registered and to which the design, or one not substantially different, has been applied. Thus it is infringement, without the licence of the registered proprietor, to import into this country for sale, or to sell here after importation, an article falling within the scope of the monopoly which has been made abroad. On the analogy with patents, presumably a sale abroad by the registered proprietor himself would imply a licence to import and sell here unless the terms of the sale provided otherwise, but a sale abroad by a person licensed to make and sell in that country would imply no such licence, and one who imported such goods into this country or sold them here would infringe.

Trade marks

In the case of registered trade marks, however, it seems that British law *does* provide for exhaustion. Section 4(3)(a) of the Trade Marks Act 1938 authorizes the use of a registered mark by any person in relation to goods which are connected in the course of trade with the registered proprietor (or a registered user) of the mark, and to which the proprietor (or a registered user) has applied and has not subsequently removed or obliterated the mark, or in respect of which he has at any time expressly or impliedly consented to the use of the mark. In *Revlon Inc. v. Cripps & Lee Ltd.*[222] the Court of Appeal held that for this purpose, in the case of a mark owned in various countries by different members of a group of companies and used to denote connection with the group as a whole, s. 4(3)(a) prevents a member of the group which is the registered proprietor or a registered user of the mark in the United Kingdom from invoking the registered mark against goods which have been marked and marketed elsewhere by any member of the group, since, even if the application of the mark by one member of the group cannot be treated as an application by another member, as was suggested by Templeman L.J. but rejected by Buckley and Bridge L.JJ., at any rate each member must be regarded as consenting to any use of the mark by other members. Such reasoning implies that marketing abroad by an independently-owned foreign licensee of the registered proprietor of a British mark would exhaust his rights, and render parallel importers immune from infringement of the British mark.

In the *Revlon* case, the only difference in quality between the goods marketed in the United Kingdom by the mark-owner and the parallel imports was obvious from the original labelling of the latter, with which the parallel importer had not interfered. If, however, there is a difference in quality which is not obvious from the labelling and is not otherwise disclosed by the parallel importer in such a way as to eliminate the likelihood of deception or confusion, he will be liable at common law for passing off, though probably not for infringement of the registered mark.[223]

Copyright and unregistered design right

As has been seen,[224] ss. 22 and 23 of the Copyright, Designs and Patents Act 1988[225] make it secondary infringement of copyright in a work for a person, without the licence of the copyright owner, to import[226] into or market[227] within the United Kingdom an article which is, and which he knows or has reason to believe is, an infringing copy of the work. 'Infringing copy' is defined by s. 27[228] as an article the making of which constituted infringement of the copyright in the work in question, or (in the case of an article which has been or is proposed to be imported into the United Kingdom) an article the making of which in the United Kingdom would have been constituted either an infringement of such copyright or a breach of an exclusive licence agreement relating to the work. The reference to breach of an exclusive licence is new, and is designed to overrule the decision in *CBS v. Charmdale*[229] on this point. But articles whose free importation into the United Kingdom is required by European Community law are explicitly excluded from being infringing copies.[230]

Thus, apart from European Community law, the question whether importation into this country, or subsequent sale here, infringes copyright turns primarily on whether the making of the articles would have constituted primary infringement if they had been made in the United Kingdom. Hence copies which were made abroad by the owner of the British copyright can lawfully be imported into this country and sold here by third parties,[231] unless the owner has granted an exclusive licence for this country.[232]

But if the articles were made abroad by someone who was not entitled to make such copies here, their commercial importation into and sale in this country (otherwise than under a reasonable mistake) will infringe the copyright. This will be so even where the same person owns the copyright in this country and in the country where the copies are made, and the maker abroad has a licence from the owner to make and market copies in the foreign country, and even if the owner, the maker abroad, and an exclusive licensee for this country are all members of the same group of companies. For a licence to make and market copies abroad does not imply a licence to make copies here or to import into this country copies made abroad or to sell such imported copies here; and if the holder of such a licence were to make copies here, such making would infringe; and the corporate veil is respected in this context.[233]

Similar rules apply as regards the new unregistered design right created by Part III of the 1988 Act. Section 227 provides for secondary infringement by importing or marketing an infringing article in similar terms to ss. 22 and 23,[234] and s. 228 defines 'infringing article' in similar terms to s. 27.

European Community law
The domestic British rules on exhaustion give way to European Community law where the goods have been marketed in another EEC Member State. Articles 30–36 of the EEC Treaty prohibit the Member States from imposing or maintaining restrictions on

imports or exports of goods between Member States, subject to a few exceptions, including one relating to restrictions which are justified for the protection of industrial or commercial property and which do not constitute a means of arbitrary discrimination or a disguised restriction on trade between Member States. On the basis of these provisions, the European Court has since 1970[235] deduced a doctrine of Community-wide exhaustion of intellectual-property rights, which applies to all types of such right, including patents,[236] trade marks,[237] copyright,[238] or any similar right.[239]

The doctrine prevents the holder of an intellectual-property right in one Member State from invoking his right in that State so as to prevent the importation into or sale or use within that State of goods falling within the scope of the right which have been marketed by him or with his consent in another Member State. It is immaterial whether the right-owner holds parallel rights in both countries[240] or has no parallel right in the country of the marketing, for example because his invention is of a type which cannot be patented there.[241] But the marketing must have taken place within the Community and not, for example, in a State with which the Community has a trade agreement.[242] The marketing may have been effected by the owner of the intellectual-property right itself, or by another company which forms part of the same group as the owner, or by an independently-controlled undertaking which holds a licence granted by the owner.

Marketing by a compulsory licensee does not exhaust the rights of the owner against whom the licence is imposed.[243] Nonetheless, where the law of a Member State provides for licences under a patent or other intellectual-property right to be available as of right, it must not discriminate, in relation to such licences, against imports from other Member States, as compared with its treatment of local production. In *Allen & Hanburys Ltd v. Generics (UK) Ltd*,[244] a British patent had been granted under the Patents Act 1949, and its duration had been extended from sixteen to twenty years by the Patents Act 1977. During the additional four years, however, the 1977 Act made licences available as of right, on terms to be agreed by the parties or, in default of agreement, fixed by the Comptroller-General of Patents, Designs and Trade Marks. The European Court ruled, first, that Articles 30 and 36 of the Treaty prevent the courts of a Member State from granting an injunction, prohibiting the importation from another Member

State of a product covered by a patent in respect of which licences are available as of right, against an importer who has undertaken to accept such a licence, if a similar injunction could not be granted in similar circumstances against a local manufacturer of the product; secondly, that Articles 30 and 36 of the Treaty prevent the competent administrative authorities from imposing on the grantee of a licence of right terms preventing importation of the patented product from other Member States, if the authorities could not refuse to grant a licence to an undertaking which would manufacture and market the product in the State in question; and, thirdly, that it made no difference that the patent was for a pharmaceutical product and that the imports would come from a Member State where such products could not be patented.

This ruling will no doubt also apply to the licences of right which will be available, especially during the second five years of the term, under the new unregistered design right, created in the United Kingdom by Part III of the Copyright, Designs and Patents Act 1988.[245] Moreover, the Court's ruling is a good indication of the attitude it will take to the Comptroller-General's powers to order the grant of compulsory licences, a matter on which the wording of the (British) Patents Act 1977 evinces a hostility to imports which is obviously incompatible with Community law.

Moreover, subject to certain conditions Community law enables a parallel importer of goods in respect of which intellectual-property rights have been exhausted to repackage them and to substitute one trade mark belonging to the holder whose rights have been exhausted for another mark belonging to him. In *Hoffmann-La Roche v. Centrafarm*[246] the European Court ruled the prohibition by Art. 36(2) of the Treaty on disguised restrictions on trade between Member States prevents the owner of a trade mark in two Member States from invoking his mark in one of the Member States against goods to which the mark has lawfully been applied in the other Member State and which have subsequently been repackaged and re-marked with the mark by a third party, if the following conditions are satisfied: (i) it is established that such use of the mark by the owner will, in view of his marketing scheme, contribute to the artificial partitioning of the national markets; (ii) it is shown that the repackaging cannot adversely affect the original condition of the product (as where it was double-packaged and the repackaging only affects the external packaging, or where the repackaging is inspected for the purpose by a public authority); (iii) the mark owner receives prior notice of the marketing of the repackaged product; and (iv) the new packaging contains a statement identifying the repackager.

This ruling was followed and elaborated in *Pfizer v. Eurim-Pharm*,[247] to the effect that Community law overrides trade-mark rights so as to enable an importer of a pharmaceutical product which has been manufactured in a Member State by a subsidiary of the mark owner, and marked with the owner's consent, to repackage the product and market it in another Member State, if the repackaging is confined to replacing the external wrapping, without interfering with the internal packaging, and making the trade mark affixed by the manufacturer to the internal packaging visible through the new external wrapping, and the new external wrapping also indicates clearly that the product was manufactured by the mark-owner's subsidiary and repackaged by the importer.

Shortly after its decision in *Hoffmann-La Roche v. Centrafarm*,[248] the Court ruled in *Centrafarm v. American Home Products Corp.*[249] that the prohibition on disguised restrictions also prevents the owner of different marks in two Member States from invoking one of the marks in the Member State where it is protected against products which have been lawfully marketed in the other Member State bearing the mark owned there by the same proprietor, if it is established that the owner of the different marks has followed the practice of using them for the purpose of artificially partitioning the markets.

Recently, however, in *Warner Bros. v. Christiansen*,[250] which involved video-cassettes of films, the European Court has qualified the doctrine of exhaustion, at any rate in relation to copyright, by ruling that Community law does not prevent the law of a Member State from making the hiring out of legitimate copies without the consent of the copyright owner an act of infringement, nor from applying such a rule to copies which had been marketed with the copyright owner's consent in another Member State whose law does not contain such a rule.

Moreover, the Community-law doctrine of exhaustion does not apply to performing rights, and so does not protect a person who receives in one Member State a broadcast made in another Member State, and immediately retransmits it by cable to subscribers in the first-mentioned State, from infringing copyright in a film which is the subject of the broadcast.[251] Nor, normally, do assignments or licences of performing rights which divide markets along national lines infringe the EEC competition rules.[252] And even where goods, such as copies of a sound recording or film, are imported and marketed in accordance with the doctrine of exhaustion, Community law does not enable them to be used for a public performance in the State of importation.[253]

The European Court has also, on the basis of Articles 30–36 of the Treaty, created a doctrine of common origin, which, however, appears to be confined to trade marks.[254] This applies where similar trade marks in two Member States were once in the same hands but have subsequently come into separate hands, whether as a result of a consensual transaction or an expropriation by a public authority of enemy property, and whether the separation occurred before or after the establishment of the common market. In such a case Community law prevents the owner of the mark in one of the Member States from using his mark to interfere with the importation into, and disposal and use within, that State, of goods from the other Member State which have been lawfully marked there by or with the consent of the owner of the mark in that country.

Except to the extent that the doctrines of exhaustion or common origin interfere with the exercise of intellectual-property rights, such rights may be utilized in a Member State against goods from other Member States without infringing the Treaty provisions on free movement.[255] In particular, Community law does not at present interfere with the enforcement in a Member State of intellectual-property rights whose existence is due to the adoption in that State of an unusual but non-discriminatory rule, such as that contained in s. 50(1) of the (British) Patents Act 1949,[256] whereby in determining the novelty of an invention, specifications more than fifty years old were disregarded.[257] Nor does Community law prevent the owner of, for example, a copyright which is subsisting in a Member State fom using it to prevent the importation into and sale in that State of goods which have been marketed without his consent in another Member State in which his copyright has expired.[258]

Moreover, Community law does not prevent a Member State from granting intellectual-property protection, e.g. by way of registered designs, for spare parts for products such as motor vehicles; and even if the owner of an intellectual-property right, such as a registered design for the front wings of, or other spare parts for, a car of his manufacture, has a dominant position in a relevant market, he does not commit an abuse prohibited by Art. 86 of the EEC Treaty by merely refusing to grant licences to manufacture or import and sell the protected goods to third parties who are willing to pay a reasonable royalty, though he may be guilty of abuse if he arbitrarily refuses to supply such spare parts to independent repairers, or charges excessive prices for such supplies, or ceases production of such parts while numerous cars of the type in question are still in use.[259]

4
Remedies

THE NEW BRITISH LAW

Introduction

Remedies for infringement of copyright are now regulated by Chapter VI (ss. 96–115) of Part I of the 1988 Act, which replaces Part III of the 1956 Act. Section 96 of the new Act[1] provides that, subject to the following provisions of Chapter VI, an infringement of copyright is actionable by the copyright owner, and in an action for infringement of copyright all such relief, by way of damages, injunctions, accounts or otherwise, is available to the plaintiff as is available in respect of the infringement of any other proprietary right. This does not, however, empower the courts to create additional substantive obligations for the benefit of copyright owners, so as to remedy alleged deficiencies in the scheme of statutory liabilities – such as a common-law duty of care on the part of a manufacturer of equipment capable of being used for unlawful copying, requiring him to discourage his customers from using the equipment so as to infringe.[2]

By s. 101, an exclusive licensee[3] has, except against the copyright owner, the same rights and remedies in respect of matters occurring after the grant of the licence as if the licence had been an assignment, and the licensee's rights are concurrent with those of the copyright owner, but defences available against the owner are also available against the licensee. Where there are concurrent rights of action, then in an infringement action: (i) the other person entitled must, unless the court otherwise orders, be joined as a plaintiff or added as a defendant before the action proceeds beyond an application for interlocutory relief;[4] (ii) damages will be assessed in the light of the terms of the licence and the concurrent pecuniary remedies obtained or available; (iii) an award of damages or profits in favour of one of the parties entitled precludes an account of profits in favour of the other; and (iv) profits will be apportioned between the parties entitled in accordance with any agreement between them or, if there is no such agreement, as the court considers just.[5] Moreover s. 27(3) extends the definition of 'infringing copy', so as to overrule *CBS v. Charmdale*[6] and include an article whose making in the United Kingdom would have constituted a breach of an exclusive licence under the relevant copyright, as well as one whose making here would have infringed the copyright itself. The same transitional provisions apply to the remedies of an exclusive licensee as to those of a copyright owner, except that an exclusive licence granted before the commencement of the 1956 Act is ignored.[7]

Injunctions

A successful plaintiff in an action for infringement of copyright will normally seek and obtain, apart fom any other remedies, a final injunction restraining the defendant from committing further infringements after the judgment is given. Despite the equitable origin and, therefore, in principle discretionary character of injunctions, the grant of a final injunction to a successful copyright plaintiff is almost automatic, since its refusal would amount to judicial connivance at the compulsory purchase by the defendant, without statutory authority, of the plaintiff's proprietary rights. Hence a final injunction will be refused only for special reasons, such as that the copyright has expired before the trial or that the plaintiff has been guilty of unreasonable delay in asserting his rights.

Copyright plaintiffs often seek also an interlocutory injunction prohibiting the defendant from committing allegedly infringing acts until the case is decided. The grant of interlocutory injunction in copyright, as in other cases, is governed by the principles laid down by Lord Diplock in *American Cyanamid v. Ethicon*.[8] The plaintiff must show a serious case to be tried, but it is not for the court to reach even a provisional conclusion as to contested facts on the basis of affidavit evidence. If a serious case is shown, an injunction will be granted or refused in accordance with the balance of convenience, taking into particular account the relative difficulty of assessing damages for infringement (if the plaintiff succeeds) and damages for the defendant's lost liberty to compete (payable under the plaintiff's cross-undertaking if the defendant succeeds) and the relative abilities of the parties to pay such damages.

Another important form of interlocutory relief is the *Anton Piller* order.[9] Such an order is obtained *ex parte*, often before the issue of the writ in the main action, and requires the defendant to permit the plaintiff, with his solicitor, to enter named premises and search them for and remove evidence of infringement, and/or to disclose the names of his suppliers of and customers for infringing articles. By s. 72 of the Supreme Court Act 1981, overruling *Rank Film Distributors v. Video Information Centre*,[10] the privilege against self-incrimination cannot be invoked in intellectual-property cases, but self-incriminating answers cannot be used in other proceedings. In principle an *Anton Piller* order should only be granted where there is very strong evidence both of infringement and that the evidence will otherwise disappear, and the applicant should make a full and frank disclosure of all material circumstances. In practice there is ground for suspicion that these requirements are not always complied with.

Damages
Under the 1956 Act there was a distinction between infringement damages under s. 17, and conversion damages under s. 18. As Lord Wright M.R. explained in *Sutherland v. Caxton*,[11] under s. 17 the measure of damages was the depreciation caused by the infringement to the value of the copyright as a chose in action; while under s. 18 the measure was the value of the infringing copies, which by force of the section were deemed to be the plaintiff's property, from the mere fact of being brought into existence. Now however conversion damages have been abolished by the new Act, so that the former law thereon is obsolete, but for the most part the former law on infringement damages remains operative.

By s. 96(1) of the new Act,[12] it is a defence to a claim for damages, but not any other remedy, for primary infringement of copyright for the defendant to prove that at the time of the infringement he did not know, and had no reason to believe, that copyright subsisted in the work in question. The subsection does not, however, protect one who, knowing or having reason to believe that copyright exists, makes a mistake as to its ownership and obtains permission from the wrong person.[13] Moreover, as a matter of common sense, the defence will seldom be available where the work is clearly modern, in view of the wide territorial application of the Act and the length of time for which copyright endures.[14] On the other hand, to establish secondary infringement the plaintiff must usually prove that the defendant knew of or had reason to believe in the illicit character of the copies dealt with or the likelihood of an illicit performance.[15]

In general, damages for infringement may be awarded on the same basis as in the case of patent infringement; i.e. where appropriate, by reference to the plaintiff's competitive losses as a publisher in respect of lost sales and forced price-reductions, and otherwise on a royalty basis.[16] Damages may also be awarded for depreciation in the value of the copyright due to the issue of a cheap and inferior infringement which vulgarizes the work.[17]

In addition to the damages normally available, s. 96(2) of the new Act specifies that, in an action for infringement of copyright, the court may, having regard to all the circumstances, and in particular to (a) the flagrancy of the infringement, and (b) any benefit accruing to the defendant by reason of the infringement, award such additional damages as the justice of the case may require. This replaces s. 17(3) of the 1956 Act, which required the court to be satisfied also that effective relief would not otherwise be available to the plaintiff. In omitting the reference to effective relief, the new Act implements a proposal of the Whitford Report,[18] the 1981 Green Paper[19] and the 1986 White Paper,[20] but strangely the Act does not adopt their further proposal to widen the court's discretion by omitting reference to benefit to the defendant. In *Ravenscroft v. Herbert*,[21] Brightman J. explained that flagrancy implies scandalous conduct, deceit and such like, but includes deliberate infringement of copyright; and the reference to 'benefit' implies that the defendant has reaped a pecuniary advantage in excess of the damages which he would otherwise have to pay.

It seems obvious that s. 17(3) of the Act was intended to permit the award of exemplary damages, i.e. damages going beyond compensation for the plaintiff's losses and designed to punish and deter. Indeed in *Williams v. Settle*[22] the Court of Appeal upheld an award of £1000 as exemplary damages against a professional photographer who had sold to newspapers a photograph taken at the plaintiff's wedding, which included his father-in-law, who had since been murdered. But in *Rookes v. Barnard*[23] Lord Devlin left open whether s. 17(3) authorized the award of exemplary (as distinct from aggravated) damages, and commented that the award in *Williams v. Settle* could be justified more easily as aggravated damages; and in *Broome v. Cassell*,[24] Lord Kilbrandon opined that s. 17(3) did not authorize the award of exemplary damages. Subsequently in *Beloff v. Pressdram*,[25] Ungoed-Thomas J. took the view that s. 17(3) allowed only for aggravated compensatory damages, largely for the plaintiff's suffering from injured feelings, distress and strain, and prevented the award of exemplary, or even aggravated, damages for infringement of copyright otherwise than under the sub-section. On the other hand the Whitford Report considered that exemplary damages were and should be available in cases of flagrant infringement.[26] Unfortunately, however, the new Act does not refer in terms to *exemplary* damages.

Under s. 18 of the 1956 Act, a copyright owner was entitled to additional remedies against an infringer of the copyright by way of damages or other relief in respect of the conversion of infringing copies, on the basis of a statutory fiction that such copies belonged to the copyright owner. Moreover an award of conversion damages was based on the full value of the infringing copies, without any deduction for the cost or value of the materials used or the work done in making them.[27] Eventually the fiction proved unpopular, especially in the context of industrial designs,[28] and, in accordance with the recommendations of the Whitford Report[29] and the proposals in the 1986 White Paper,[30] the new Act abolishes the fiction of ownership and the conversion remedies, except in relation to proceedings begun before its commencement.[31]

Delivery up and disposal

To replace the conversion remedy, the new Act, as well as strengthening the provision for additional damages, provides for orders for the delivery up and disposal of infringing copies or articles. Section 99 enables a copyright owner[32] to apply to the court[33] for an order, against a person who has an infringing copy of the work[34] in his possession, custody or control in the course of a business, that the infringing copy be delivered up to the copyright

owner or some other person directed by the court.[35] The procedure
also applies to an article which is specifically designed or adapted
for making copies of a particular copyright work, if the person
having it in his possession, custody or control knows or has reason
to believe that it has been or is to be used to make infringing
copies, even if he is not acting in the course of a business;[36] and
also applies, in favour of a publisher of copies of a work lawfully
issued to the public in a copy-protected electronic form, to a
device which is specifically designed or adapted to circumvent that
form of copy-protection and is in the possession of a person who
intends it to be used to make infringing copies of copyright
works.[37] But an application under s. 99 must be made within six
years of the making of the infringing copy or article, unless the
copyright owner was under a disability or the relevant facts were
concealed;[38] and the court will not make an order for delivery up
unless it also makes, or considers that there are grounds for
making, a further order for the disposal of the copy or article
under s. 114.[39]

After obtaining an order for delivery up under s. 99, the
copyright owner may apply to the court for an order for disposal of
the copy or article delivered up under s. 114, and the person
against whom the order for delivery up was made may apply for a
decision refusing an order for disposal. Meanwhile the copy or
article must be retained by the person to whom it was so
delivered.[40] Under s. 114 the court may order that the copy or
article delivered up be forfeited to the copyright owner, or
destroyed, or otherwise dealt with as the court thinks fit. But the
remedy is discretionary, and the court must consider whether
other remedies for infringement would be adequate to compensate
and protect the copyright owner.[41] Persons interested in the copies
or articles must be notified and are entitled to appear and appeal;
and if the court refuses to make an order for disposal, the copy or
article must be returned to the prior possessor.[42]

Section 100 gives a copyright owner (or his agent) a right in
certain circumstances to seize and detain an infringing copy,
without first obtaining an order for delivery up under s. 99, with a
view to obtaining an order for its disposal under s. 114, but the
power is hedged about with so many restrictions as to be almost
illusory. The copy must be found exposed or otherwise immediately
available for sale or hire, and notice of the time and place of the

proposed seizure must be given in advance to a local police station. The person making the seizure may enter premises to which the public has access, but may not seize anything in the possession, custody or control of a person at a permanent or regular place of business of his, and may not use any force. Moreover a notice in the form prescribed by statutory instrument[43] must be left at the time and place of the seizure, giving particulars of the person by whom or on whose authority and the grounds on which the seizure was made. Evidently copyright owners will be inclined to proceed under s. 99, or by means of a classical *Anton Piller* order, rather than under s. 100. After a seizure under s. 100, the copyright owner may apply for an order for disposal under s. 114, and the victim of the seizure may apply for a decision refusing such disposal.

An order for delivery up to the copyright owner or other person of an infringing copy or article (in the same sense as in s. 99) may also be made under s. 108 by a court which is seised of a prosecution for an offence under s. 107.[44] The copy or article must have been in the possession, custody or control of the person prosecuted at the time of his arrest, charge or summons, and in the case of an infringing copy (as distinct from an article specially designed or adapted for making copies of a particular work) must have been held by him in the course of a business, but the order may be made even if the person is acquitted. The order may be made on the application of the prosecutor or of the court's own motion, but cannot be made more than six years after the copy or article was made,[45] and should not be made if it appears unlikely that an order for disposal will be made under s. 114. An order made under s. 108 by a magistrates' court is appealable to the Crown Court. If an order for delivery up is made under s. 108, the person receiving the copy or article must retain it pending a decision to make or refuse an order for disposal under s. 114, which applies in the same way as after the making of an order for delivery up under s. 99.

Offences

Section 107 of the new Act[46] creates a number of criminal offences involving infringement of copyright. Broadly, any infringement committed in the course of a business constitutes an offence as well as a civil wrong. There are two levels of offence: the more serious

offences are punishable summarily by up to six months' imprisonment and/or a fine not exceeding the statutory maximum, or on
indictment by up to two years' imprisonment and/or an unlimited
fine; while the less serious are only punishable summarily by up to
six months' imprisonment and/or a fine not exceeding level 5 on
the standard scale.[47] In the case of a more serious offence, a
constable may obtain a search warrant from a magistrate.[48]

The more serious offences are the following acts, done without
the licence of the copyright owner in respect of an article which is,
and which the actor knows or has reason to believe is, an infringing
copy:

(i) making for sale or hire;
(ii) importing into the United Kingdom otherwise than for one's
own private and domestic use; or
(iii) distributing either in the course of a business, or otherwise
but to such an extent as prejudicially to affect the copyright
owner.[49]

The less serious offences are constituted by the following acts:

(i) without the licence of the copyright owner, in the course of a
business, selling, hiring out, offering or exposing for sale or hire,
or possessing with a view to committing an infringing act, an
article which is, and which the actor knows or has reason to
believe is, an infringing copy;[50]
(ii) making or having in one's possession an article specifically
designed or adapted for making copies of a particular copyright
work, knowing or having reason to believe that it is to be used to
make infringing copies for sale or hire or for use in the course of a
business;[51]
(iii) causing a literary, dramatic or musical work to be performed, or a sound recording or film to be played, in public
(otherwise than by reception of a broadcast or cable transmission) so as to infringe copyright, and with knowledge or
reason to believe that copyright would be infringed.[52]

The presumptions contained in ss. 104–06 do not apply in
criminal prosecutions, except for the purposes of forfeiture orders,[53]
but where an offence is committed by a corporation any director,
manager or similar officer who consented to or connived at its
commission is also guilty of the offence.[54]

Stoppage by Customs

By ss. 111 and 112 of the new Act,[55] the owner of copyright in a published literary, dramatic or musical work may give notice in writing to the Commissioners of Customs and Excise requesting them for a specified period to treat as prohibited goods printed copies of the work which are infringing copies. A similar notice may be given by the owner of copyright in a sound recording or film in relation to copies of the infringing work expected to arrive at a specified time and place. Such a notice makes prohibited the importation of the goods in question, other than for the importer's private and domestic use, and thus enables them to be forfeited. Regulations made by the Commissioners may require evidence from and impose other conditions on the person giving the notice, including conditions as to the payment of fees and the giving of security for and indemnity against liabilities and expenses.

EUROPEAN HARMONIZATION

Commercial piracy

In Chapter 2 of its Green Paper,[56] the EC Commission examined at length the economic and legal situation in the Member States in relation to commercial piracy – i.e. the making of illicit copies of copyright works (including 'bootleg' copies of 'live' performances) for the purpose of commercial distribution, and the commercial distribution of such copies. An attempt was made to assess the economic scale of piracy taking place in relation to different types of work and to different countries, and much greater abuse was found to exist in relation to sound recordings, films and computer programs than in relation to books. For example, it was found that in 1984 pirate audio tapes represented 64 per cent of the Greek market in terms of volume and 28 per cent of that market in terms of value; and that in 1986 pirate video tapes represented 40–45 per cent of the Dutch, and 70–75 per cent of the Portuguese, markets.

The Commission proceeded to analyse the substantive rules applicable, and the procedures and remedies available, in the Member States. The position in the United Kingdom emerged as reasonably satisfactory, even though the Commission overlooked the decision of the English Court of Appeal in *Rickless v. United Artists Corp.*,[57] which established that (even before the 1988 Act)

performers *did* have a civil remedy against 'bootlegging' of their
'live' performances.[58] But various legal deficiencies were discovered
– for example, in the Netherlands there is no copyright in sound
recordings as such; there are important limitations on the availability of search and seizure procedures in the Benelux countries;
injunctive relief is not available in France and Portugal; and
imprisonment is not possible for copyright offences in Belgium.

From the survey the Commission concludes that the repression
of piracy of sound and video recordings in the Community requires
the existence of clear substantive legal provisions in favour of
authors, producers, performers and broadcasting organizations in
respect of their right to authorize the reproduction for commercial
purposes of their recordings and broadcasts, and that there is need
also for appropriate procedures facilitating legal action against and
proof of acts of piracy, and in particular provisions on search and
seizure. Moreover, it recognizes the need for efficient remedies to
be available to copyright owners in infringement cases, and for
deterrent criminal sanctions to be available to deal with organized
professional piracy. Further, an appropriate organizational framework is needed to enable co-operation between copyright owners
and law-enforcement authorities. Finally it concludes that specific
controls, e.g. on commercial tape-duplication equipment, are
desirable in appropriate areas.

Hence the Commission contemplates proposing to the Council
in the near future a binding Community measure requiring
Member States to confer on film producers and makers of sound
recordings exclusive rights over the reproduction of their works for
commercial purposes and their commercial distribution. The contemplated measure would also confer similar rights on performing
artistes in relation to their fixed performances, and on broadcasters and cable transmitters in respect of their broadcasts or
transmissions. It would also subject to licensing by a public
authority the possession of equipment suitable for the commercial
duplication of digital audio tape recordings, and provide for the
registration of such licensed equipment. Only as regards such
equipment do these proposals appear to involve a change in
British law.

Less urgently, the Commission contemplates proposing a regulation extending Council Regulation 3842/86,[59] which lays down
measures to prohibit the release for free circulation of counterfeit

goods (i.e. goods which infringe trade marks), so as to cover also 'pirate' goods (i.e. goods which infringe copyright). It also intends to propose the extension of the regime of mutual assistance between the administrative authorities of the Member States and the Commission in customs and agricultural matters provided for by Regulation 1468/81,[60] so as to cover co-operation in respect of trade mark and copyright infringements.

The Commission also envisages making non-binding recommendations to the Member States on the enabling of copyright owners to request public prosecution of pirates; and on the introduction of minimum standards in respect of search-and-seizure procedures, criminal sanctions and civil remedies in relation to piracy. It seems likely that in these respects no further action will be needed in the United Kingdom. The Commission also favours the creation of registers at Community or international level of the ownership of copyrights in sound recordings and films, and the conclusion of an international agreement on seizure of counterfeit and pirate goods, covering importation and exportation as well as internal controls.

Home copying

In Chapter 3 of its Green Paper, the Commission takes the view that home copying of sound recordings and films causes undesirable losses to copyright owners insofar as home copying substitutes for purchases of pre-recorded material, and that substantial, but unquantifiable, losses are occurring in the case of sound recordings. In the cases of films, it considers that at present such losses are small. It recognizes, however, increased dangers to copyright owners from the imminent availability to consumers of digital audio tapes and recorders, and eventually of similar technology for videos, since digital technology permits almost endless copying of copies without loss of quality.

Accordingly it contemplates the adoption of measures at Community level requiring digital audio tape recorders for home use to conform to technical specifications designed to limit their ability to make copies. This will involve prohibiting the manufacture, sale or importation of non-conforming machines, and also the manufacture, sale or importation of devices designed to circumvent the copy-restricting technology. Possession of non-conforming machines for professional or specialist use will require a licence from a public authority, and such licences will be registered. The Commission does not consider it necessary at present to introduce a similar system in relation to video recorders, since the release of digital video technology for home use is not yet imminent.

As regards non-digital (ordinary, analogue) copying of sound recordings and films, it notes that some Member States (such as Germany and France) have imposed a levy on recording equipment and blank tapes, or on blank tapes only, and accordingly have authorized home copying; while others (such as the United Kingdom and Ireland) maintain the illegality of home taping and do not impose a levy. As a result of a disagreement between the Commissioners, the Green Paper rejects the idea of harmonization at Community level as regards the existence or rate of such levies. The Commission contemplates that Member States should remain free to retain existing levies, or to introduce such levies where they do not yet exist, and should also remain free to maintain their refusal to introduce them. It notes that existing levies do not involve systematic controls at borders, and takes the view that the small divergencies which they cause between price-levels in different Member States (levies on blank tape amounting to about 8–10 per cent of the retail price) do not necessitate action at Community level. Thus the British government will presumably continue to reject the requests of producers of sound and video recordings for the introduction of levies on blank tape.

In the United Kingdom s. 69 of the 1988 Act now permits the making for private and domestic use of a recording of a broadcast or cable programme, provided that this is done solely for the purpose of enabling it to be viewed or listened to at a more convenient time. The permission is effective as against the copyrights in the broadcast or programme and in any work included in it. In addition s. 70 permits the making for private and domestic use of a photograph of an image forming part of a television broadcast or cable programme, or a copy of such a photograph, as against the copyrights in the broadcast or programme and in any film included in it. These exemptions go beyond s. 14(4) of the 1956 Act, which only protected the home copyist of a broadcast as regards the copyright in the broadcast as such. Otherwise, however, home taping (e.g. from records or tapes) amounts in law to infringement of copyright, though it is entirely impracticable to enforce copyright to any useful extent against home copyists – a situation which, as Lord Templeman emphasized in *CBS Songs v. Amstrad Consumer Electronics*,[61] brings the law into disrepute. It seems a pity that Parliament, whether or not it was willing to impose levies on blank tapes or recording equipment, did not insist on authorizing home taping (i.e. other than for business use) in all cases.

5
Licences

GENERAL RULES

Dealings with copyright are regulated by ss. 90–93 of the new Act, replacing ss. 36–38 of the 1956 Act.[1] By s. 90, copyright is transmissible by assignment *inter vivos*, by testamentary disposition, or by operation of law (e.g. on bankruptcy or intestacy), as personal or moveable property.[2] An assignment may be total or partial, i.e. limited to some of the acts comprised in, or part of the period of, the copyright,[3] and where different persons are for any reason entitled to different aspects of the copyright in a work, the copyright owner for any purpose of the Act is the person who is entitled to the aspect of copyright relevant for that purpose.[4] An assignment must, however, be expressed in writing and signed by or on behalf of the assignor.[5] By s. 91(1) and (2),[6] it is also possible by signed agreement for the prospective owner of a future copyright, i.e. a copyright which will or may come into existence in respect of a work or works to be created in the future or on the occurrence of some other future event (such as publication in a qualifying country of an existing work of a non-qualifying author),[7] to assign it, so that the copyright will vest in the assignee upon its coming into existence.

A licence granted by a copyright owner (or prospective owner) need not be in writing, and binds all his successors in title except a purchaser in good faith for value without actual or constructive notice of the licence or a successor in title of such a purchaser.[8] However, the Act confers special advantages on an exclusive licensee (i.e. under a licence exclusive of all other persons, including the licensor), but only if it is expressed in writing and signed by the licensor.[9] It then confers on the licensee the same rights against a successor in title of the licensor who is bound by the licence as he has against the licensor himself,[10] as well as conferring on the licensee rights of action against third parties who infringe the copyright, and rendering a copy made abroad without the consent of the licensee an infringing copy if imported into this country.[11] Where copyright is owned jointly, the joint owners together constitute the copyright owner for the purposes of the Act, so that a valid licence requires the consent of them all.[12]

LICENSING SCHEMES

Especially in the sphere of performing rights, it has long been the practice for copyright owners to join together as members of collecting societies, so as to enable their copyrights to be managed collectively (and thus conveniently and effectively). Thus performing and broadcasting rights in musical works (and associated lyrics) have long been administered by the Performing Right Society (or PRS), and similar rights in sound recordings by Phonographic Performance Ltd. (or PPL). More recently the Copyright Licensing Agency has become active in the sphere of reprographic copying, especially in the educational sector.

The arrangements between a collecting society and its members may involve the members assigning their copyrights to the society, or they may merely empower it to grant licences on their behalf. In any event the functions of collecting societies are to establish and operate licensing schemes, so that a user obtains, for a single payment to the society, a licence covering all the works under the society's control, and to distribute the proceeds of the licences among the members. Such societies also enforce the copyrights against infringers. Obviously the members benefit from savings on managerial costs, and in many cases such schemes are the only practicable way in which the owners can reap any real benefit from their rights. Users also benefit from the availability from a single source for a single payment of a licence covering a large number of works.

On the other hand there have long been fears that the collecting societies might abuse what amounts to a monopoly position, and Part IV of the 1956 Act established a Performing Right Tribunal, with power to review and alter the terms of licensing schemes in respect of performing and similar rights operated by collecting societies. Current policy encourages the establishment and operation of collecting societies to administer rights over physical copying, as well as performances, but recognizes the need for controls over their activities.[13] Accordingly, Chapter VIII (ss. 145–52) of Part I of the new Act reconstitutes and renames the Performing Right Tribunal as the Copyright Tribunal, and Chapter VII (ss. 116–44) extends and restates its jurisdiction over licensing schemes and certain other licences. The expanded jurisdiction of the Tribunal also replaces the statutory licence to make and issue 'cover versions' of recorded music, formerly granted by s. 8 of the 1956 Act.

The Copyright Tribunal

Chapter VIII of the new Act renames and reconstitutes the Performing Right Tribunal, established under s. 23 of the 1956 Act, as the Copyright Tribunal.[14] It now consists of a chairman and two deputy chairmen, who must be legally qualified and are appointed by the Lord Chancellor, and between two and eight ordinary members appointed by the Secretary of State.[15] But for an individual case the Tribunal consists of the chairman or a deputy chairman (who acts as chairman) and two or more ordinary members.[16] It decides by majority, the acting chairman having a casting vote.[17] As indicated by s. 149, its jurisdiction is now conferred by ss. 118–27, 139, 142,[18] 144 and 190[19] and Sch. 6[20] of the new Act. Its procedure is regulated by rules made by the Lord Chancellor in the form of a statutory instrument.[21] Its powers extend to awarding and assessing costs between the parties.[22] An appeal on a point of law lies from a decision of the Tribunal to the High Court (or in the case of proceedings of the Tribunal in Scotland, to the Court of Session).[23]

Controls over licensing schemes

Sections 117–23 of the new Act empower the Copyright Tribunal to make orders in respect of licensing schemes[24] operated by licensing bodies[25] which:

(a) relate to copyright in literary, dramatic, musical or artistic works, or films (and their sound-tracks);

(b) cover the works of more than one author;[26] and

(c) relate to licences for copying the work, performing, playing or showing it in public, or broadcasting it or transmitting it by cable.[27]

These sections also apply to all licensing schemes (whether or not operated by licensing bodies and whether or not the works of several authors are involved) which relate:

(i) to copyright in sound recordings (other than film sound-tracks when accompanying films), broadcasts or cable programmes, or typographical arrangements of published editions; or

(ii) to the rental right in sound recordings, films or computer programs.[28]

By s. 119, while a licensing scheme is in operation, a person who claims that he requires a licence in a case of a description to which the scheme applies, or an organization which claims to be representative of such persons, and who or which is in dispute with the operator of the scheme, may refer the scheme, insofar as it relates to cases of that description, to the Copyright Tribunal.[29] The scheme then remains in operation until the proceedings on the reference have been concluded.[30] On the reference the Tribunal considers the matter in dispute and makes such order, either confirming or varying the scheme so far as it relates to cases of the relevant description, as it determines to be reasonable in the circumstances.[31] The order may be of indefinite duration or for such period as the Tribunal determines.[32] In addition, s. 118 permits a reference to the Tribunal in respect of a *prospective* licensing scheme by an organization claiming to be representative of persons claiming to require licences in cases of a description to which the scheme would apply. Unless the Tribunal declines to entertain the reference on the ground that it is premature, it makes an order confirming or varying the proposed scheme, either generally or as regards cases of the relevant description, as it determines to be reasonable in the circumstances; and the order remains in force indefinitely or for a period determined by the Tribunal.

By s. 123, a scheme confirmed or varied by an order of the Tribunal under ss. 118 or 119 operates (as regards the relevant description of case) so long as the order is in force.[33] While the order is in force a person who pays to the operator any charges payable in respect of a licence to which the order applies (or if the amount cannot be ascertained, gives an undertaking to the operator to pay them when ascertained), and complies with the other terms applicable to such a licence under the scheme, is treated, as regards infringement, as if he had been granted a licence in accordance with the scheme.[34]

By s. 120, while an order made under ss. 118 or 119 is in force, a further reference to the Tribunal in respect of the same description of case may be made by the operator, or a prospective licensee, or an organization representing prospective licensees. Such a reference may not, however, without the special leave of the Tribunal, be made within twelve months of the previous order (or if the order was to last for fifteen months or less, until the last three months before its expiry).[35] During the further reference the scheme remains in operation, and on the further reference the Tribunal proceeds to make an order in the same way as on the original reference, and with the same effects.[36] Yet further references may be made, subject to the same delay after the previous order.[37]

By s. 121, a person who claims, in a case covered by a licensing scheme, that the operator has refused, or failed within a reasonable time after being asked, to grant to or procure for him a licence in accordance with the scheme, may apply to the Tribunal.[38] If the Tribunal is satisfied that the claim is well-founded, it will make an order declaring that the applicant is entitled to a licence on terms which it considers applicable in accordance with the scheme.[39] The order will remain in force indefinitely or for a period determined by the Tribunal.[40] While the order is in force, if the person in whose favour it was made complies with the terms of the order (including terms as to charges payable to the operator), he is treated for purposes of infringement as the holder of a licence from the copyright owner on the terms specified in the order.[41] Such an order may be reviewed by the Tribunal from time to time on application by the operator or the original applicant, subject to the usual time-limits.[42]

Section 121 also applies where the case is excluded from a licensing scheme, in the sense that the terms of the scheme except certain matters (including those in question in the case) from the licences for which it provides, or that the case is so similar to ones in which licences are granted under the scheme that it is unreasonable that the case should not be dealt with in the same way.[43] In such a case, a person who claims that the operator has unreasonably refused, or failed within a reasonable time after being asked, to grant to or procure for him a licence, or proposes unreasonable terms, may apply to the Tribunal.[44] If the Tribunal is satisfied that the claim is well-founded, it will make an order declaring that the applicant is entitled to a licence in respect of specified matters on terms which it considers reasonable in the circumstances.[45] Such an order has similar operation, as regards duration, effect and variation, as an order under s. 121 declaring entitlement to a licence in accordance with a scheme.[46]

Controls over other licences granted by licensing bodies

Sections 124–28 apply to certain proposed or expiring licences, granted by a licensing body otherwise than in pursuance of a licensing scheme. By s. 124, such licences are subject to these controls if:

(a) the licence relates to copyright in literary, dramatic, musical or artistic works, or films (and their sound-tracks), whether it permits 'physical' copying or performance (including broadcasting or cable transmission) of the work or both, provided that it covers works of more than one author; or

(b) the licence relates to copyright in a sound recording (other than a sound-track accompanying a film), a broadcast or a cable programme, or the typographical arrangement of a published edition; or

(c) the licence relates to the rental right in sound recordings, films, or computer programs.

By s. 125, the terms of a proposed licence may be referred to the Tribunal by the prospective licensee. In such a case, unless the Tribunal declines to entertain the reference on the ground that it is premature, it will make an order, confirming or varying the terms, as it considers reasonable in the circumstances. The order will remain in force indefinitely or for a period fixed by the Tribunal, though it may be reviewed by the Tribunal on an application under s. 127.

By s. 126, where a licence is due to expire within the next three months, whether by effluxion of time or as a result of notice given by the licensing body, the licensee may apply to the Tribunal on the ground that it is unreasonable in the circumstances that the licence should cease to operate. The licence then remains in operation until the proceedings are concluded. If the Tribunal finds the application well-founded, it makes an order for the continuance of the licence on terms which it considers reasonable, and the order operates indefinitely or for a period fixed by the Tribunal, though it may be reviewed by the Tribunal under s. 127.

By s. 127, an order under ss. 125 or 126 may be reviewed from time to time by the Tribunal on application by the licensing body or the person entitled to the benefit of the order, subject to the usual time-limits. On review the Tribunal confirms or varies its order as it considers reasonable in the circumstances. By s. 128, while an order under s. 125 or s. 126 is in force, if the person entitled to the benefit of the order complies with the terms (including as to charges payable to the licensing body) specified in the order, he is treated for purposes of infringement as holding a licence granted by the copyright owner on the terms specified in the order.[47] Moreover the benefit of an order can be assigned, unless assignment is prohibited, in the case of an order under s. 125, by the terms of the order, or in the case of an order under s. 126, by the terms of the original licence.[48]

If under s. 125, s. 126 or s. 127 the Tribunal makes or reviews an order so as to vary the amount of charges payable, it may direct that the variation shall have effect from a date earlier than the order making the variation, but not earlier than the date of the relevant reference or application, nor earlier than the date of the grant of the licence (in the case of proceedings founded on s. 125) or the expiry date of the original licence (in the case of proceedings founded on s. 126).[49]

Relevant factors

As has been seen, the various provisions empowering the Copyright Tribunal to review a licensing scheme or other licence require it to confirm or vary the terms 'as it may determine to be reasonable in the circumstances'. This is slightly amplified by s. 129, which instructs the Tribunal, in determining what is reasonable in relation to a licensing scheme, to have regard to the availability of other schemes, or the granting of licences, to other persons in similar circumstances, and to the terms of such schemes or licences, and to exercise its powers so as to secure that there is no unreasonable discrimination between licensees (or prospective licensees) under the scheme or licence to which the current reference or application relates and licensees under other schemes operated by, or other licences granted by, the same person. But, by s. 135, this and the other more detailed guidelines for the Tribunal specified in ss. 130–34 do not affect the Tribunal's general obligation in any case to have regard to all relevant considerations.

Section 130 deals specifically with the licensing of reprographic copying[50] of published literary, dramatic, musical or artistic works, or of the typographical arrangement of published editions. It requires the Tribunal to have regard to the extent to which published editions of the works in question are otherwise available, the proportion of the work to be copied, and the nature of the use to which the copies are likely to be put.

Section 131 deals with licences for the recording by or on behalf of educational establishments[51] of broadcasts or cable programmes which include copyright works, or the making of copies of such recordings, for educational purposes. It requires the Tribunal, in considering what charges (if any) should be paid, to have regard to the extent to which the owners of copyright in the works included have already received, or are entitled to receive, payment in respect of their inclusion.

Sections 132 and 133(2) deal with licences relating to certain sound recordings, films, broadcasts or cable transmissions. Where such a work includes an entertainment or other event, the Tribunal is to have regard to any conditions imposed by the promoters of the entertainment or other event, other than conditions regulating charges to be imposed on licensees or conditions as to payments to the promoters for the grant of facilities for making the work; and refusal to grant a licence cannot be regarded as unreasonable if it could not be granted consistently with such conditions.[52] Moreover where such a work includes a performance, the Tribunal is to take into account, in considering what charges should be paid for a licence, any reasonable payments which the copyright owner is liable to make pursuant to a licence in respect of the performance.[53] Similarly, by s. 133(1), in fixing charges for a licence for the rental to the public of copies of sound recordings, films or computer programs, the Tribunal is to take into account any reasonable payments which the owner of the copyright in the sound recording, film or program is liable to make in consequence of the granting of the licence, or of the acts authorized by the licence, to owners of copyright in works included therein.

Section 134 deals with licences to include literary, dramatic, musical or artistic works, or sound recordings or films, in a broadcast or cable transmission, where one broadcast or cable transmission is, by reception and immediate re-transmission, to be further broadcast or transmitted by cable. Insofar as both transmissions are to the same area, the Tribunal, in considering what charges (if any) should be paid for licences for either transmission, is to have regard to the extent to which the copyright owner has already received, or is entitled to receive, payment for the other transmission which adequately remunerates him in respect of transmissions to that area. Insofar as the further transmission is to another area, the Tribunal is to ignore the further transmission in considering charges for licences for the first transmission, except where the extension of area by the further transmission results from requirements imposed under s. 13(1) of the Cable and Broadcasting Act 1984, in which case the Tribunal is to secure that the charges payable for licences for the first transmission adequately reflect the extension of area by the further transmission.

Reprographic copying
'Reprographic copying' is defined by s. 178 as copying by means of a process for making facsimile copies, or of a process involving the use of an appliance for making multiple copies, and as including any copying by electronic means of a work held in electronic form, but as not including the making of a film or sound recording.

Indemnities under general schemes or licences
Section 136[54] applies to schemes for licensing reprographic copying of published literary, dramatic, musical or artistic works, or the typographical arrangement of published editions, and to licences granted by licensing bodies for such copying, where the scheme or licence does not specify the works to which it applies with such particularity as to enable licensees to determine whether a work falls within the scheme or licence by inspection of the scheme or licence and the work.[55] The section causes to be implied in such a scheme or licence an undertaking by the operator or licensing body to indemnify a licensee against any liability incurred by him

by reason of his having infringed copyright by making (or authorizing the making) of reprographic copies of a work in circumstances within the apparent scope of his licence – that is, in circumstances where it is not apparent from inspection of the licence and the work that it does not fall within the description of works to which the licence applies, and the licence does not expressly provide that it does not extend to copyright of the description infringed.[56] The indemnity extends to liability to pay costs, and to costs reasonably incurred by a licensee in connection with actual or contemplated proceedings against him for infringement of copyright, as well as to sums payable in respect of infringement.[57] A scheme or licence may, however, contain reasonable provision as to the manner in and time within which claims under the implied undertaking are to be made, and reasonable provision for enabling the operator or licensing body to take over the defence of infringement proceedings.[58]

Educational copying

As we have seen,[59] ss. 32–36 of the new Act authorize in a number of cases the doing for educational purposes of acts which would otherwise infringe copyright. In particular, s. 36[60] permits the making by or on behalf of an educational establishment for the purposes of instruction of reprographic copies of passages from published literary, dramatic or musical works, up to a limit in the case of any establishment of one per cent of any work in any quarter, unless licences authorizing the relevant copying are available and the copyist is or should be aware of their availability. Such licences may not, however, restrict the proportion of a work which may be copied by an educational establishment (with or without payment) to less than the statutory one per cent per quarter.

For reprographic copying by educational establishments on a larger scale current policy envisages the use of licensing schemes.[61] Accordingly, where there is in existence a licensing scheme or licence which is subject to the jurisdiction of the Copyright Tribunal under ss. 118–23 or 125–28, and which covers *inter alia* the making by or on behalf of educational establishments for the purposes of instruction of reprographic copies of published literary, dramatic, musical or artistic works, or of the typographical arrangement of published editions, s. 137 enables the Secretary of

State, after notifying and hearing representations from copyright owners, the licensing body, and representatives of educational establishments, to make an order extending the scheme or licence to cover works of a similar description which have been unreasonably excluded from the scheme, provided that this will not conflict with the normal exploitation of the works in question or unreasonably prejudice the legitimate interests of their owners. The owner of a work thus included may appeal against the order to the Copyright Tribunal,[62] or (normally only after two years from the order) apply to the Secretary of State for the order to be reconsidered,[63] and an order of the Secretary of State on reconsideration, confirming, discharging or varying his original order, is open to appeal to the Copyright Tribunal by the copyright owner or a representative of educational establishments.[64]

Where it appears that there is no relevant licensing scheme or general licence[65] in existence covering, or suitable for extension so as to cover, the making by or on behalf of educational establishments for the purposes of instruction of reprographic copies of a description of published literary, dramatic, musical or artistic works, or of the typographical arrangement of published editions, s. 140 enables the Secretary of State to appoint a person to hold an inquiry as to whether a new licensing scheme or general licence is required for the purpose. If the inquirer is satisfied that it would be of advantage to educational establishments to be authorized to make reprographic copies of the works in question, and that making the works subject to a licensing scheme or general licence would not conflict with the normal exploitation of the works or unreasonably prejudice the legitimate interests of the copyright owners, he may recommend a new licensing scheme or general licence, and will then also specify any conditions and qualifications to which the licences should be subject.

Section 141 enables the Secretary of State, within a year after the making of such a recommendation, to make an order, in the form of a statutory instrument entering into force at least six months after its making, that, to the extent that such provision has not been made in accordance with the recommendation, the making by or on behalf of an educational establishment, for the purposes of instruction, of reprographic copies of the works to which the recommendation relates is to be treated as licensed by the copyright owners.[66] For this purpose provision in accordance with the recommendation may be made either: (i) by means of a certified licensing scheme (under s. 143) under which a licence is available to the educational establishment in question, or (ii) by means of a general licence from a licensing body covering all works of the description to which it applies, which has been granted to or for the benefit of the relevant establishment, referred by or on behalf of the establishment to the Copyright Tribunal under s. 125, or offered to or for the benefit of the establishment but refused without such a reference.[67]

An order under s. 141 will also terminate the operation of any existing licence for such copying, other than a licence granted under a certified licensing scheme or a general licence, insofar as it is more restrictive or onerous than the licence provided for by the order.[68] The licence under the order will be free of royalties, but subject to other terms specified in the recommendation or the order, and the order may provide that copies made in accordance with the licence should become infringing copies if they are subsequently sold, hired out, or exposed for sale or hire, or exhibited in public.[69] The order may be varied from time to time, but not so as to include works not covered by, or to remove terms specified in, the recommendation on which it is based.[70]

Certification of licensing schemes

Section 143 authorizes the Secretary of State (and not the Copyright Tribunal) to certify licensing schemes for the purposes of: s. 35 (on the educational recording of broadcasts or cable programmes); s. 60 (on scientific abstracts); s. 66 (on the rental of sound recordings, films and computer programs); s. 74 (on subtitled copies of broadcasts or cable programmes for the deaf or otherwise handicapped); and s. 141 (on reprographic copying of published works by educational establishments).

Application is made to the Secretary of State by the operator or proposed operator of the licensing scheme, and if the Secretary of State is satisfied that the scheme enables the works to which it relates to be identified with sufficient certainty by persons likely to require licences, and sets out clearly any charges payable and the other terms on which licences will be granted, he will make an order (in the form of a statutory instrument) certifying and scheduling the scheme.[71] The order will specify a date, at least eight weeks after its making, on which the certification will come into operation, but its operation will be delayed if a reference to the Copyright Tribunal under s. 118 is pending.[72]

A certified scheme cannot be effectively varied unless a corresponding amendment is made to the certification order, but the Secretary of State must amend the order in the case of a variation ordered by the Copyright Tribunal on a reference under ss. 118–20, and has a discretion in the case of other amendments.[73] A certification order must be revoked if the scheme ceases to be operated, and may be revoked if it is no longer being operated according to its terms.[74]

Monopolies Commission reports

By s. 144 of the 1988 Act, where a report of the Monopolies and Mergers Commission specifies restrictive conditions in licences under a copyright, or the refusal of a copyright owner to grant licences on reasonable terms, as matters operating, having operated, or likely to operate against the public interest, the powers conferred on the Secretary of State by Part I of Schedule 8 to the Fair Trading Act 1973, for the purpose of remedying such adverse effects, include power to order by statutory instrument the cancellation or modification of such restrictive conditions, and/or to provide that licences in respect of the copyright are to be available as of right. These powers must not, however, be exercised so as to contravene any convention on copyright to which the United Kingdom is a party.[75] In default of agreement, the terms of such a licence of right will be settled by the Copyright Tribunal on an application by the intending licensee, and will enable him to perform all the acts in respect of which a licence is available of right. The licence will operate from the date of the application to the Tribunal.

By s. 98, where licences are available of right under s. 144 and the defendant in an infringement action undertakes to accept such a licence, no injunction can be granted against him, nor can an order for delivery up of infringing copies or articles be made under s. 99, and damages or profits awarded against him in respect of infringements committed after licences became available of right cannot exceed double the amount which would have been payable in respect of the acts in question under such a licence. Moreover a defendant may give the undertaking at any time before final order in the infringement action, and need not admit liability.

COMMUNITY COMPETITION LAW

Individual agreements

Since (in practice) the early 1970s individual agreements for the licensing of intellectual property, especially patents, have been subjected to control under the rules on competition laid down by Art. 85 of the EEC Treaty. Article 85(1) prohibits agreements between undertakings which may affect trade between Member States and which have as their object or effect the prevention, restriction or distortion of competition within the common market. The prohibition is sanctioned by the power of the EC Commission to impose fines and periodic penalty payments on the undertakings involved under Arts. 15 and 16 of Regulation 17/62, and by the automatic invalidation of the agreement by Art. 85(2) of the Treaty.

Article 85(3), however, provides for the exemption from the prohibition of agreements which contribute to improving the production or distribution of goods or to promoting technical or economic progress, while allowing consumers a fair share of the resulting benefit, provided that they do not impose on the undertakings concerned restrictions which are not indispensable to the attainment of the approved objectives, and that they do not afford them the possibility of eliminating competition in respect of a substantial part of the products in question. Such exemption may be granted by the EC Commission, either by an individual decision under Arts. 6–9 of Regulation 17/62, taken after examination of the agreement in question, or in certain cases by a general regulation describing the agreements which are to fall within its scope.

As regards agreements for the licensing of intellectual property, the Commission has long been authorized by Council Regulation 19/65 to exempt by regulation agreements between two undertakings only relating to the acquisition or use of patents or other industrial know-how. Accordingly the Commission eventually adopted Regulation 2349/84 on the Application of Art. 85(3) of the EEC Treaty to Certain Categories of Patent Licensing Agreements (hereafter 'the Patent Regulation'),[76] and later supplemented it by Regulation 556/89 on the Application of Art. 85(3) of the Treaty to Certain Categories of Know-how Licensing Agreements (hereafter 'the Know-how Regulation').[77]

The Patent Regulation crystallizes the Commission's experience gained from the examination of individual patent licences, tempered by the more sympathetic attitude to patents which has been evinced by the Member States and to some extent shared by the European Court.[78] As required by Regulation 19/65, the Patent and Know-how Regulations are limited to agreements to which only two undertakings are party,[79] but this is merely a formal requirement, in the sense that the Regulation is applicable to an agreement signed by two parties, even if it forms part of a network of similar licences of the technology in question between the same licensor and various licensees. Moreover it is to be expected that, in dealing with applications for the individual exemption of a patent or know-how licence to which there are more than two formal parties, the Commission will be strongly influenced by the provisions of the Regulations. It also seems likely that the experience gained with patent and know-how licences will be drawn on if cases arise involving licences under copyright or related rights where the subject-matter has an industrial character. In relation to the United Kingdom, licences to use industrially a registered design, or a design in which unregistered design right exists under Part III of the 1988 Act, or in which copyright still has relevant existence under transitional provisions, would fall into this category.[80]

The Patent Regulation applies both to 'pure' patent licensing agreements, and to agreements combining the licensing of patents and the communication of unpatented technical know-how, but not to agreements for the provision of know-how alone.[81] The Commission's decision in *Boissois/Interpane*[82] indicates, however, that the Patent Regulation does not apply, even though relevant patents exist in some Member States, if unpatented know-how is the dominant element in the package licensed. The Know-how Regulation applies both to 'pure' know-how licensing agreements and to 'mixed' know-how and patent licensing agreements which are not exempted by the Patent Regulation.[83]

'Know-how' is defined by the Art. 1(7)(1) of the Know-how Regulation as a body of technical information which is secret, substantial and identified in an appropriate form. As regards secrecy, the know-how package as a body, or in its precise configuration and assembly of components, must not be generally known or easily accessible, so that part of its value consists in the lead-time gained by the licensee; but there is no requirement that each individual component of the package should be totally unknown or unobtainable elsewhere.[84] As regards substantiality, the know-how must include information which is of importance (and not trivial) for a manufacturing process, or a product or service, or the development of a manufacturing process or a product or service, and must be useful in the sense that it can reasonably be expected to be capable of improving the licensee's competitive position.[85] As regards identification, the know-how must be described or recorded in a manner making it possible to verify that it is secret and substantial and to ensure that the licensee is not unduly restricted in exploiting his own technology. The record may be contained in the licence agreement, or in a separate document, or in some other appropriate form, but must be in existence when the technology is transferred or created shortly afterwards, and must be available when needed.[86] Moreover, any subsequent improvements communicated between the parties in pursuance of the agreement must also be appropriately identified.[87]

Patent or know-how pools, and reciprocal licences between competitors containing territorial restrictions, are excluded from the scope of the Regulations, and are likely to be viewed with particular suspicion.[88]

Exclusivity
Perhaps the most important issue in the context of the control of patent or know-how licences by competition law is the acceptability of exclusivity clauses and related prohibitions on exports – i.e. of provisions in a patent or know-how licence designed to grant to the licensee exclusive rights of manufacturing and perhaps selling the licensed product in his allotted territory, and to reserve similar exclusive rights to the licensor or his other licensees in other territories.

In its decisions on patent licences in the 1970s[89] the Commission took the view that exclusivity and related clauses normally infringed Art. 85(1) of the Treaty, even if the exclusive rights agreed on were limited to manufacturing, so that the parties were free to sell throughout the common market; and *a fortiori* if the exclusive rights extended to marketing and thus impeded exports. Exclusivity would only escape Art. 85(1) if the agreement had no appreciable effect in the common market, for example because the licence was for a territory outside the common market from which imports were for other reasons unlikely or because of the parties' small market shares. In this respect the Commission's approach was largely confirmed by the European Court in *Nungesser and Eisele v. Commission*,[90] though the Court created an obscure, theoretical exception for so-called 'open' exclusive licences, which would escape Art. 85(1) if they related to products unknown to customers in the licensed territory at the time of the agreement. An 'open' exclusive licence would, apparently, grant to the licensee exclusive rights to manufacture, and could prohibit direct sales by the licensor himself in the licensee's territory, but would permit direct sales by one licensee in a sister-licensee's territory, as well as not impeding parallel imports by other traders.

On exemption under Art. 85(3), however, the Patent Regulation represents a very considerable relaxation as compared with the Commission's earlier approach. The earlier decisions[91] showed willingness to exempt licences which were exclusive as to manufacturing only, and thus left the parties free to sell throughout the common market, even if the invention was important and the parties had large market shares, provided that the licensee was seeking to penetrate a new territorial or product market. But if the exclusivity extended to marketing, the Commission required some additional justification for granting exemption, such as that the restriction on marketing was confined to the first sale and was of limited duration, or that passive sales were permitted, or that the restriction was needed to protect a small or medium-sized undertaking attempting to penetrate a new market or promote a new product. Moreover, as the Court confirmed (at last as regards important products) in *Nungesser*,[92] any provision designed to impede parallel imports by third parties would eliminate the possibility of exemption.

In contrast to the restrictive attitude formerly adopted by the Commission, Art. 1 of the Patent Regulation grants a wide measure of exemption to exclusivity clauses and related prohibitions, as regards both manufacturing and marketing. It permits an exclusive licence to be granted for either the whole or a part of the common market,[93] and permits the licensor to undertake that he will himself neither manufacture nor actively market (for example, by advertising or establishing a branch or distribution depot) the

119

licensed product in the territory within the common market allotted to the licensee, and will not license other persons to do so, while any of the licensed patents covering the product remains in force. Conversely, the licensee is permitted to undertake not to manufacture nor actively to market the licensed product in other territories within the common market in which there are parallel patents covering the product, while a parallel patent remains in force in the territory in question. The Know-how Regulation grants similar exemptions for a period of ten years – running, as regards acts by the licensor, and acts by the licensee in territories reserved for the licensor, from the signature of the first licence granted by the licensor in respect of the technology for the licensed territory; or, as regards acts by the licensee in the territories of sister licensees, from the signature of the first licence granted by the licensor in respect of the technology within the EEC.[94] Where, however, the licensed technology is protected in a Member State by 'necessary patents', the Know-how Regulation permits exclusivity in that State for the duration of such patents.[95] In any event the exemption of exclusivity under the Know-how Regulation ceases if the know-how becomes public or insubstantial.[96]

But as regards passive selling (in response to unsolicited requests), the position under the Regulations is more complicated. Under the Patent Regulation the licensor may undertake that he will not himself make passive sales of the licensed product in the licensee's territory while one of the licensed patents remains in force; and the licensee may undertake not to make passive sales of the licensed product in a territory within the common market reserved by the licensor for his own exploitation while a parallel patent remains in force there. But a licensee may undertake not to sell the licensed product passively in a territory within the common market which is licensed to a sister-licensee in a network only for five years from the first marketing of the product within the common market by a member of the network, or for the duration of a parallel patent in the relevant territory, whichever is shorter. Similarly the Know-how Regulation exempts prohibitions of passive selling by the licensor in the licensee's territory, and by the licensee in territories reserved for the licensor, for ten years from the first licence for the licensed territory;[97] but exempts prohibitions on passive selling by the licensee in territories of sister licensees only for five years from the first licence within the EEC.[98]

The Patent Regulation follows the previous decisions in setting its face against obstacles to parallel imports between Member States carried out by third parties.[99] It is permissible for the licensor or the licensee to refuse himself to supply the licensed product to intending parallel importers if there are objectively justified reasons, but other forms of obstruction (such as by instituting or threatening patent-infringement actions against the parallel importer or his suppliers or customers) are unacceptable in all circumstances. Where an improper obstruction is required by the licensing agreement or is carried by way of a concerted practice between the licensor and the licensee, the benefit of the exemption is automatically lost. Otherwise such an obstruction enables the Commission to take an individual decision withdrawing the benefit of the exemption. The Know-how Regulation contains similar provisions.[100]

Other clauses

The Patent Regulation also exempts clauses requiring the licensee to mark the licensed product with an indication of the patentee's name, the licensed patent or the licensing agreement; and clauses requiring him to use only the licensor's trade marks or get-up to distinguish the licensed product, so long as the licensee is permitted to identify himself as the manufacturer.[101] But it is not acceptable to require the licensee under a patent licence so to mark an unpatented product; or even, where only a component is patented, another component of the total product.[102]

Article 2 of the Patent Regulation, and Art. 2 of the Know-how Regulation, list a number of obligations which are declared not normally to be restrictive of competition, but which are exempted in case they should in exceptional circumstances fall within the scope of Art. 85(1). Article 3 of each of the Regulations, on the other hand, lists obligations which are regarded as so undesirable that their inclusion in a licensing agreement disqualifies the agreement from receiving the benefit of the exemption offered by the Regulation in question. Where a licence contains restrictive clauses which are not otherwise mentioned in the relevant Regulation, Art. 4 of each Regulation offers a simplified procedure for gaining an individual exemption, under which an agreement notified to the Commission receives an implied exemption if the Commission fails to object within six months. The Know-how

Regulation specifies that Art. 4 applies in particular to a licence under which the licensee is merely permitted to supply a limited quantity of the licensed product to a particular customer, at whose request the licence was granted, in order to provide him with a second source of supply in the licensed territory, and to similar licences enabling a customer to make the product himself or through a sub-contractor.[103]

Among the clauses 'white-listed' by Art. 2 of both Regulations are ones requiring the licensee to observe specifications concerning the minimum quality of the licensed product which are necessary for a technically satisfactory working of the licensed technology (or, under the Know-how Regulation, one conforming to quality standards respected by the licensor and other licensees), to allow the licensor to carry out related checks, and to procure goods or services from the licensor or his appointee insofar as these are necessary for such working.[104] But other 'tie-ins' are black-listed by Art. 3(9) of the Patent Regulation[105] and Art. 3(3) of the Know-how Regulation. It is also noteworthy that in *Windsurfing International v. Commission*[106] the European Court ruled, in the context of a patent licence, that quality controls only escape from Art. 85(1) where they relate to a product covered by a licensed patent, and not merely to another product which is to be incorporated with the patented product into a larger product which is to be marketed by the licensee,[107] and only where the criteria are agreed on in advance and are objectively verifiable.

Both Regulations 'white-list' minimum royalty or minimum working obligations,[108] but 'black-list' maximum working restrictions.[109] Restrictions on the licensee as to the technical fields in which he may apply the licensed technology are acceptable,[110] but other restrictions as to customers or forms of distribution are proscribed.[111] The Know-how Regulation, however, permits restrictions limiting the licensee's production of the licensed product (being a component designed for inclusion in a larger product) to the quantities which he requires in manufacturing his own (larger) products, and preventing him from selling the licensed product except as an integral part of or replacement part for or otherwise in connection with his own (larger) products, so long as he is left free to determine such requirements.[112] Moreover, it is permissible to prohibit the licensee from granting sub-licences or assigning the licence, and to guarantee to him any more favourable terms which may later be granted to another licensee.[113]

The two Regulations differ somewhat as to the permissible duration of licensing agreements (apart from exclusivity clauses, considered above). Under the Patent Regulation it is permissible to prohibit the licensee from working the patent after the termination of the licensing agreement, if the patent is still in force,[114] but it is not acceptable for a licensing agreement to provide for its automatic continuance beyond the expiry of the licensed patents existing at the conclusion of the agreement, by including patents subsequently obtained by the licensor, unless at that stage each party is given at least an annual right of termination.[115] Royalties may, however, be made payable after expiry of the licensed patents if the licensee continues to use know-how communicated by the licensor which has not entered the public domain.[116] On the other hand it is not acceptable to charge royalties on wholly unpatented products, nor for the use of know-how which has entered the public domain otherwise than by the fault of the licensee.[117] It is however permissible to postpone the actual payment of royalties properly charged in respect of working while the patents are in force or the know-how is secret until a time when this is no longer so.[118] Probably a clause fixing royalties by reference to the selling price of a larger product containing a patented component will not normally infringe Art. 85(1).[119]

Under the Know-how Regulation it is permissible to prohibit the licensee from divulging the know-how, even after the expiry of the licensing agreement, and to prohibit him from exploiting the licensed know-how after termination of the agreement, insofar as it is still secret.[120] Moreover the agreement may make royalties continue to be payable throughout its duration, despite the know-how becoming publicly known, provided that the publication is not by the licensor; and the licensee may be made liable also for damages if he publishes it.[121] On the other hand, the licensee must not be prevented from continuing to use the know-how after termination of the agreement, if it has become publicly known other than by his action in breach of the agreement.[122] Nor is it acceptable to charge royalties on goods or services which are not produced, at least partly, by means of the licensed technology, nor for the use of know-how which has become published by the licensor.[123] Nor may the initial duration of the agreement be automatically prolonged by the inclusion of subsequent improvements, unless the licensee is entitled to refuse them or each party is entitled to terminate at the end of the initial term and at least every three years subsequently.[124]

Under the Patent Regulation it is acceptable for a licence to impose reciprocal obligations for the communication of experience gained in working the licensed invention, and for the grant of licences in respect of improvements and new applications; but not to require the licensee to assign these to the licensor.[125] More stringently, the Know-how Regulation endeavours to insist in addition that the licensee should not be prevented from using, and licensing to third parties, any severable improvements which he makes.[126]

It is acceptable under both Regulations to require the licensee to co-operate with the licensor in suppressing infringements by third parties,[127] but he must be left free to challenge the validity or secrecy of the licensed patents or know-how.[128] The licensor may, however, reserve the right to terminate the licence in the event of such a challenge.[129]

The operation of Art. 85(1) of the Treaty in relation to no-challenge clauses was recently clarified by the European Court in *Bayer AG and Henneche GmbH v. Süllhöfer*,[130] which involved cross-licences between German companies in respect of patents granted or applied for in Germany and other Member States in connection with polyurethane. The cross-licensing agreement was reached in 1968 as a compromise of litigation which was pending in Germany between the parties, but the agreement was not embodied in a court order. On a reference from the German court of final appeal, the European Court ruled that a no-challenge clause contained in a licensing agreement may, in appropriate legal and economic circumstances, amount to a restriction on competition falling within Art. 85(1), and that Art. 85(1) applies even if the agreement is designed to settle pending litigation, though it left open the possible effect of such an agreement being embodied in a court order. The Court explained, however, that there is no restrictive effect in the case of a royalty-free licence, since such a licence does not prejudice the licensee's competitive position. Equally there would be no anti-competitive effect if the licence, although subject to royalties, related to a technology which had already become obsolete, and thus would not be further utilized by the licensee. Moreover, even in the case of a licence subject to royalties, the market position of the parties might be so weak as to deprive the restriction on the licensee's freedom of action of any appreciable effect on the competitive situation. On the other hand, where there is an appreciable restriction of competition, a reciprocal licence in respect of patents granted in several Member States will sufficiently affect trade between Member States to fall within Art. 85(1), even if the agreement is between undertakings established in the same Member State.

It is noteworthy that the court focused only on the effect of such clauses on the licensee's position, and thus effectively rejected an argument often adopted by the Commission, that such clauses, by preventing a knowledgeable person, the licensee, from challenging the patent, reduce the likelihood that the patent will be revoked and third parties thereby freed from its restrictions. Moreover the circumstances in which the dispute arose made it unnecessary for the Court to consider exemption under Art. 85(3).

Under both the Patent and the Know-how Regulations the parties must be left free to fix their own prices for the licensed products,[131] and (save as otherwise provided) to compete with each other and third parties in respect of research and development, manufacture, use and sales, though the licensee may be required to use his best endeavours to exploit the licensed invention.[132] It seems that arbitration clauses are now considered as in themselves acceptable, the safeguard being the Commission's power to intervene and take an individual decision withdrawing the benefit of the 'block' exemption where an award causes the licence to have effects inconsistent with the requirements for exemption;[133] though in granting an individual exemption the Commission may require the parties to notify it promptly of any award.[134]

Collecting societies

In addition to the controls imposed at national level, e.g. in the United Kingdom by the powers over licensing conferred on the Copyright Tribunal by Chapter VII of the 1988 Act,[135] the constitution and activities of a copyright collecting society which is established within the European Community are subject to review for compliance with Art. 86 of the EEC Treaty. Article 86 prohibits the abuse by an undertaking of a dominant position in a substantial part of the common market, in so far as it may affect trade between Member States, and declares that an abuse may arise from the imposition of unfair prices or other unfair trading conditions, or the application of dissimilar conditions to equivalent transactions with other parties. The application of Art. 86, as well as Art. 85 on anti-competitive agreements, is entrusted by Reg. 17/62 to the EC Commission, which is empowered to investigate possible infringements, of its own motion or upon a complaint by an interested party; and to take decisions establishing the existence of infringements, requiring their termination, and if necessary imposing fines or periodical penalty payments on infringers. In addition infringement of Art. 86 may be invoked in ordinary national courts by way of defence to a claim which amounts to or is based on an abuse, and possibly as a cause of action in tort.

The application of Art. 86 to the constitution and activities of a copyright collecting society established within the Community was first established by the Commission's decisions in *Re GEMA*,[136] which involved the German collecting society for both physical and performing rights in musical works,[137] and confirmed by the decision of the European Court in *Belgische Radio en Televisie v. SABAM (No. 2)*.[138] There will usually be no difficulty in establishing that a collecting society has a dominant position, since the whole object of a collecting society is to manage all copyrights of the relevant type within its territory, and in practice a successful collecting society will have largely achieved this object, and any of the larger Member States (at least) will constitute a substantial part of the common market.[139] The question of importance is what will constitute an abuse.

On this the Commission's decisions in *Re GEMA*[140] provide detailed guidance, while the Court's decision in *Belgische Radio en Televisie v. SABAM (No. 2)*[141] confirms generally that account must be taken of the function of a collecting society, to protect its members, especially against major users of their works, such as broadcasters and record manufacturers; and that abuse depends on whether the relevant practices go beyond what is necessary to enable the society effectively to fulfil its function. It is clear from these decisions that an abuse may arise from the terms of the constitution of a collecting society, or from its internal decisions, or from its transactions with members or outsiders; and that a practice may be abusive because of its unfairness either to members or potential members or to users of the works.[142]

Discrimination as regards membership or members' rights
The Commission decision in *Re GEMA (No. 1)* establishes that it
is an abuse for a collecting society to discriminate, in relation to
admission to and rights arising from membership of the society,
against individuals who are nationals of, or undertakings which are
established in, other Member States; or against undertakings
which belong to the same State as the society, but are associated
with similar undertakings which are established in other Member
States. Similarly the Commission ruled in *Interpar v. GVL*[143] that
it is an abuse for a collecting society administering performers'
rights in a Member State to refuse to conclude management
agreements with artistes who are neither nationals of nor resident
in the State in which the collecting society is established, but are
nationals of or resident in other Member States.

The Commission also ruled in *Re GEMA (No. 1)* that, insofar as
membership depends on income received from the society, credit
must be given for similar income from similar societies established
in other Member States; that a society must not confer economic
benefits on some members at the expense of others without
reasonable justification; that a member must qualify for full
benefits from the society after no more than five years; and that it
is an abuse for a collecting society to attempt to exclude the
jurisdiction of the courts to review the society's decisions at the
request of its members.

Excessive requirements relating to assignments
The *GEMA* decisions [144] also establish that a collecting society
must not insist on receiving an assignment from its members of
rights for countries in which the society does not carry out direct
administration of its rights, but authorizes a foreign society to act
as its agent. As regards rights for countries where the society does
carry out direct administration, the *GEMA* decisions insist that a
society must permit a member, without loss of status or economic
advantages, to choose whether to assign to the society all the
categories of right which the society is willing to administer, or
only to assign one or more categories of such rights – e.g. to assign
the general performing right, but not broadcasting or recording
rights. On the other hand, it is acceptable for a society to insist, as
regards the categories of right assigned, that all existing and future
works of the author be included in the assignment. The *GEMA*

decisions also insist that a member must also be permitted to withdraw any category of rights from the society on three years' notice, expiring at the end of a calendar year, so as thereby to regain the relevant rights in full, subject to the society's right to perform existing licences.

Similarly the Court's decision in *Belgische Radio en Televisie v. SABAM (No. 2)*[145] recognizes that a compulsory assignment of all copyrights, both present and future, without distinction between the various forms of exploitation, may amount to an abuse, especially if the assignment continues to operate for an extended period after the member's withdrawal; and that the combined, as well as the individual, effect of the various clauses in the assignment must be considered.

Abuses as regards users

As regards users, the *GEMA* decision establishes that it is an abuse for a collecting society to charge higher royalties on recordings or equipment imported from other Member States than on those manufactured in its own country, and that credit must be given for royalties already paid in other Member States. Moreover the subsequent decision of the European Court in *Musik-Vertrieb v. GEMA*[146] establishes that, under the doctrine of exhaustion arising from Arts. 30–36 of the Treaty, no royalties at all may be charged by a collecting society in respect of imported recordings which have been marketed in another Member State with the consent of the society in question.

The *GEMA* decisions also establish that it is an abuse for a collecting society to charge royalties in respect of works of which it does not hold the copyright, whether because the copyright has expired or because it has not been assigned to the society.

Conflicting interests

In view of the conflicting interests of creators and users of copyright works, in *Re GEMA (No. 1)* the Commission ruled that persons associated with users of a collecting society's copyrights could not be excluded from membership of the society, but their voting rights could be restricted. Subsequently, in *Re the GEMA Statutes*,[147] the Commission permitted GEMA to amend its constitution so as to require that the assignments made to it by its members should prohibit the member from agreeing to share his royalties with a user (such as a broadcaster) who had concluded collective agreements with the society, for the purpose of inducing the user to favour the member's works. It recognized that such individual royalty-sharing arrangements would undermine the collective scheme.

Recent developments

In *Ministère Public v. Tournier*,[148] which involved SACEM, the French collecting society for musical works, the European Court gave an important ruling as follows:

(i) Non-exclusive reciprocal representation agreements between collecting societies established in different Member States do not infringe Art. 85 of the EEC Treaty, but parallel behaviour between the parties to such an agreement, in refusing to deal directly with users in each other's country, may support the inference of an illegal concerted practice unless it is otherwise explicable, for example by reference to the burden which a collecting society would have in organizing its own system of licensing in another Member State.

(ii) Contracts between a collecting society and users of its works do not infringe Art. 85 of the Treaty unless they contain restrictions going beyond what is necessary for the legitimate purpose of protecting the interests of the copyright owners. However, a refusal to grant performance licences to discotheque proprietors in respect of foreign works alone would not be justified if such grants could be made without prejudicing the interests of authors, composers or publishers, and without increasing the society's managerial costs.

(iii) As regards abuse of dominant position, contrary to Art. 86 of the Treaty, by the charging of excessive royalties, it is relevant to compare rates charged in different Member States, provided that the comparison is made on a uniform basis. If a society in one Member State charges royalties appreciably higher than are charged in all the other Member States, the society in question will have to justify the difference by establishing objective disparities between the circumstances in its country and elsewhere in the Community.

6
Moral Rights

INTRODUCTION

English law has traditionally viewed copyright in economic terms, and largely ignored such considerations as the author's honour. But now, as envisaged in the 1986 White Paper,[1] Chapter IV (ss. 77–89) of Part I of the new Act, attempts, *inter alia*, to implement Art. 6-bis of the Paris revision of the Berne Copyright Convention[2] by creating 'moral rights':

(i) to be identified as the author of a copyright literary, dramatic, musical or artistic work, or as the director of a copyright film;
(ii) not to have a copyright work or film of which one is author or director subjected to derogatory treatment;
(iii) not to suffer false attribution of authorship of a literary, dramatic, musical or artistic work, or directorship of a film; and
(iv) not to have a photograph or film which one has commissioned for private and domestic purposes made public.

The 'moral' rights are independent of ownership of the copyright in the work or film, and are of most importance where the copyright does not belong to the author. Infringement of these rights is actionable as a breach of statutory duty owed to the person entitled.[3] No act done before the commencement of the new Act can infringe the moral rights established by Chapter IV, but s. 43 of the 1956 Act (on false attribution of authorship) continues to apply to acts done before such commencement.[4] However, the rights apply to existing as well as new works, and even in the case of existing works authorship is determined for this purpose in accordance with the new Act (and not with the rules applicable at the time of creation of the work).[5]

These rights are not assignable,[6] but they may be waived by the person entitled. It is enough if he consents informally or by contract,[7] or if he signs a written instrument waiving his rights.[8] A waiver may relate either to a specific work, or to works of a specified description, or to works generally; it may relate to future works; it may be conditional or revocable; and if made in favour of the copyright owner, it will be presumed to extend to his licensees and successors in title unless a contrary intention is expressed.[9]

The provisions on consent and waiver, taken with those requiring an author to 'assert' his moral rights, and with the wide scope of the exceptions to these rights specified in Chapter IV, may be thought to depart substantially from the policy underlying the Berne Convention, and to indicate a lack of real enthusiasm on the part of the United Kingdom for the protection of the honour of authors and directors. The Act seems to display a preference, wherever there is a serious conflict of moral and commercial interests, for commercially convenient, rather than honour-protective, solutions. Clearly the practical effect of Chapter IV will depend on the extent that users of copyright works are desirous of and successful in insisting on contracting out of the moral rights created by the Chapter.

IDENTIFICATION AS AUTHOR OR DIRECTOR

Sections 77–79 confer on the author of a copyright literary, dramatic, musical or artistic work (other than a computer program, the design of a typeface, or a computer-generated work),[10] and on the director of a copyright film, the right, if properly asserted, to be identified as the author or director of the work when certain acts are performed in relation to the whole or any substantial part of it.[11] The right continues so long as copyright subsists in the work.[12] On the death of the author or director it may be specifically bequeathed; otherwise, if the copyright in the work forms part of his estate, the 'moral' right passes with the copyright; and failing these conditions it becomes exercisable by his personal representatives.[13] The right is enforceable by an action for breach of statutory duty, brought by the author or director (or, after his death, his successor in title to the right) against the infringer.[14]

The right does not apply to a literary, dramatic, musical or artistic work if the author died before commencement of Part I of the 1988 Act, nor to a film made before such commencement.[15] In the case of literary, dramatic, musical or artistic works created before commencement by an author still living at commencement and in whom the copyright initially vested, the right does not apply to anything which may, by virtue of an assignment or licence granted before commencement, be done without infringing copyright; and where the copyright first vested in someone other than the author, the right does not apply to anything done or licensed by the copyright owner.[16]

Moreover, the right of identification does not apply to things done or authorized by the copyright owner if copyright in the work initially vested in the employer of the author or director under ss. 9(2)(a) or 11(2);[17] nor to works in which Crown or Parliamentary copyright subsists, or in which copyright originally vested in an international organization under s. 168, unless the author or director has previously been identified as such in or on published copies of the work.[18] Also excluded from the right of identification are works made for the purpose of reporting current events;[19] and the publication in a newspaper, magazine or similar periodical,[20] or in an encyclopedia, dictionary, yearbook or other collective work of reference, of a work which was made for the purposes of such publication or has been made available with the author's consent for the purposes of such publication.[21] In addition, certain exceptions to the infringement of copyright also apply to the right of identification.[22]

Apart from the various exclusions, the right to be identified only operates in respect of acts done after it has been properly asserted by the author or director, and only against persons who are bound by the assertion.[23] An assertion may be general, or limited to a specified act or description of acts.[24] An assertion may be effected by means of a statement included in an instrument effecting an assignment of the copyright in the work, in which case it binds the assignee and anyone claiming through him, regardless of notice.[25] An assertion may also be expressed in any other written instrument signed by the author or director, in which case it binds anyone to whose notice it is brought.[26] Delay in asserting the right must be taken account when the court is considering remedies in an action for infringement.[27]

The acts in respect of which the author or director is entitled to be identified are:

(a) In the case of a literary or dramatic work (other than a lyric) – the commercial publication, performance in public, broadcasting or cable transmission of the work or an adaptation of it, or the issue to the public of copies of a film or sound recording including the work or an adaptation.[28]

(b) In the case of a musical work or a lyric – the commercial publication of the work or an adaptation of it, or the issue to the public of copies of a sound recording of the work or an adaptation of it, or the showing in public or issue to the public of copies of a film whose sound-track includes the work or an adaptation of it.[29]

(c) In the case of any artistic work – the commercial publication or exhibition in public of the work, or the broadcast or cable transmission of a visual image of the work, or the showing in public of, or issue to the public of copies of, a film including a visual image of the work.[30]

(d) In the case of a building, a model for a building, a sculpture or a work of artistic craftsmanship – also the issue to the public of copies of a graphic work representing or a photograph of the work.[31]

(e) In the case of a building – also the construction of the (or if there are several, the first) building constructed to the design.[32]

(f) In the case of a film – the showing of the film in public, the broadcast or cable transmission of the film, or the issue of copies of the film to the public.[33]

As regards the manner of identification, s. 77(7) and (8) requires that:

(1) In the case of commercial publication, or the issue of copies of a film or sound recording, the author or director must be identified in or on each copy; or if that is not appropriate, in some other manner likely to bring his identity to the notice of a person acquiring a copy.

(2) In the case of identification on a building, the identification must be by appropriate means visible to persons entering or approaching the building.

(3) In other cases, it must be in a manner likely to bring his identity to the attention of a person seeing or hearing the performance, exhibition, showing, broadcast or transmission.

(4) In all cases, the identification must be clear and reasonably prominent.

(5) In all cases, if the author or director in asserting the right specifies a pseudonym, initials or some other particular form of identification, that form must be used. Otherwise any reasonable form of identification may be used.

DEROGATORY TREATMENT

Sections 80–83 of the new Act confer on the author of a copyright literary, dramatic, musical or artistic work, and the director of a copyright film, the right in certain circumstances not to have his work subjected to derogatory treatment. The right applies to the whole or any part of the work,[34] and 'treatment' means any addition to, deletion from or alteration or adaptation of the work, other than a translation of a literary or dramatic work or an arrangement or transcription of a musical work involving no more than a change of key or register.[35] The treatment of a work is derogatory if it amounts to distortion or mutilation of the work or is otherwise prejudicial to the honour or reputation of the author or director.[36] The right to object to derogatory treatment continues to subsist so long as copyright subsists in the work.[37] On the author's death it devolves and becomes exercisable in the same way as the right to identifcation.[38] The right is enforceable by means of an action for breach of statutory duty brought by the author or director (or his successor on death) against the infringer, and in such an action the court may, if it thinks this an adequate remedy in the circumstances, grant an injunction prohibiting the doing of an act unless a disclaimer is made, in such terms and manner as may be approved by the court, dissociating the author or director from the treatment of the work.[39] The same transitional provisions apply as in the case of the right of identification.[40]

The right to object to derogatory treatment may be waived in the same way as the right to identification.[41] Similarly it does not apply to computer programs, computer-generated works, or works made for the purpose of reporting current events,[42] nor to acts permitted in relation to copyright because of authorized assumptions that copyright has expired.[43] Again, it does not apply in relation to the publication in a newspaper, magazine or similar periodical, or in a collective work of reference, of a work made for the purposes of such publication or made available with the author's consent for the purposes of such publication, but in the case of derogatory treatment this exclusion extends further to a subsequent exploitation elsewhere without any modification of the published version.[44] In the case of derogatory treatment, there is a further exclusion for things done for the purpose of avoiding the commission of an offence or complying with a statutory duty (or, in the case of the BBC, avoiding the inclusion in programmes of things offensive to good taste or decency or likely to encourage or incite crime or lead to disorder or offend public feeling), provided (where the author or director is identified at the time of the derogatory act or has previously been identified in or on published copies of the work) that there is a sufficient disclaimer – i.e. a clear and reasonably prominent indication, given at the time of the derogatory act, along with the identification if then made, that the work has been subjected to treatment to which the author or director has not consented.[45]

In the case of works in which the copyright originally vested in the employer of the author or director under ss. 9(2)(a) or 11(2), or in an international organization under s. 168, or in which Crown or Parliamentary copyright subsists, the right to object to derogatory treatment does not apply to things done or authorized by the copyright owner unless the author or director is identified at the time of the derogatory act or has previously been identified in or on published copies of the work. Moreover, even if he is or has been so identified, there is no infringement of the right if there is a sufficient disclaimer (in the same sense as in the case of things done to avoid the commission of an offence).[46]

The acts which constitute (in effect, primary) infringement of the right to object to derogatory treatment are:

(a) In the case of a literary, dramatic or musical work – the commercial publication, public performance, broadcasting or cable transmission of a derogatory treatment of the work, or the issue to the public of copies of a film or sound recording of or including a derogatory treatment of the work.[47]

(b) In the case of an artistic work (other than a building) – the commercial publication or exhibition in public of a derogatory treatment of the work, or the broadcasting or cable transmission of a visual image of a derogatory treatment of the work, or the

135

showing in public of, or issue to the public of copies of, a film including a visual image of a derogatory treatment of the work.[48]

(c) In the case of a model for a building, a sculpture or a work of artistic craftsmanship – also the issue to the public of copies of a graphic work representing or a photograph of a derogatory treatment of the work.[49]

(d) In the case of a building – if the architect is identified on a building and it is the subject of derogatory treatment, he is entitled to require the identification to be removed.[50]

(e) In the case of a film – the showing in public, broadcasting or cable transmission of a derogatory treatment of the film, or the issue of copies of a derogatory treatment of the film to the public.[51]

(f) In the case of a film – also, along with the film, the playing in public, broadcasting, cable transmission, or issue to the public of copies of a derogatory treatment of the sound-track.[52]

By s. 83, it is also (in effect, secondary) infringement of the author's right to object to derogatory treatment to possess in the course of business, sell, hire out, offer or expose for sale or hire, in the course of a business exhibit in public or distribute, or otherwise distribute so as to affect prejudicially the honour or reputation of the author or director, an article which is, and which one knows or has reason to believe to be, a work or a copy of a work which (i) has been subjected to derogatory treatment and (ii) has been or is likely to be the subject of an act of primary infringement of the right to object to derogative treatment.

FALSE ATTRIBUTION

Section 84 confers on a person the right not to have a literary, dramatic, musical or artistic work falsely attributed to him as author, or a film falsely attributed to him as director.[53] The attribution may be express or implied,[54] and may be of the whole or any part of a work or film.[55] Moreover a false representation that a literary, dramatic or musical work is an adaptation of a person's work, or that a copy of an artistic work was made by the author of the original, counts as a false attribution,[56] as does a false attribution of joint authorship to a work of sole authorship.[57] The right is subject to waiver in the same way as the other moral rights.[58] The right continues until twenty years after the person's death.[59] It is not assignable,[60] but an infringement after the person's death is actionable by his personal representatives and any damages recovered become part of his estate.[61]

The following acts infringe the right:

(a) In the case of a literary, dramatic or musical work or a film – issuing to the public copies of the work in or on which there is a false attribution.[62] In this case the defendant infringes regardless of whether he knows or has reason to believe that the attribution is false.

(b) In the case of an artistic work – exhibiting in public the work, or a copy of it, in or on which there is a false attribution.[63] Again there is no requirement that defendant should know of or have reason to believe in the falsity of the attribution.

(c) In the case of a literary, dramatic or musical work – performing the work in public, broadcasting it or transmitting it by cable as the work of the person, knowing or having reason to believe that the attribution is false.[64]

(d) In the case of a film – showing it in public, broadcasting it or transmitting it by cable as being directed by the person, knowing or having reason to believe that the attribution is false.[65]

(e) Issuing to the public or publicly displaying material containing a false attribution in connection with any of the foregoing acts.[66]

(f) In the case of a literary, dramatic, musical or artistic work or a film – in the course of a business, possessing, selling, hiring out, offering or exposing for sale or hire, exhibiting in public, or distributing a copy of the work in or on which there is a false attribution, knowing or having reason to believe that there is such an attribution and that it is false.[67]

(g) In the case of an artistic work – in the course of a business, possessing, selling, hiring out, offering or exposing for sale or hire, exhibiting in public, or distributing the work itself, when there is a false attribution in or on it, knowing or having reason to believe that there is such an attribution and that it is false.[68]

(h) In the case of an artistic work – in the course of a business, selling, hiring out, offering or exposing for sale or hire, exhibiting in public, or distributing: (i) a work which has been altered after the author parted with possession of it as being his unaltered work, or (ii) a copy of such an altered work as being a copy of his unaltered work, knowing of or having reason to believe in such an alteration.[69]

PRIVATE PHOTOGRAPHS AND FILMS

By s. 85 of the new Act, a person who for private and domestic purposes commissions the taking of a photograph or the making of a film in which copyright subsists has the right not to have copies of the work issued to the public, and not to have the work exhibited or shown in public, broadcast or transmitted by cable. There are exceptions as regards incidental inclusion in an artistic work, film, broadcast or cable programme; parliamentary or judicial proceedings; Royal Commissions and statutory inquiries; acts done under statutory authority; and acts permitted against copyright because of assumptions that copyright has expired.[70] The right does not apply to photographs taken or films made before the commencement of the new Act.[71] It replaces the former rule under s. 4(3) of the 1956 Act that a person who commissioned the taking of a photograph for money or money's worth was entitled to the resulting copyright, under which in *Williams v. Settle*[72] the Court of Appeal upheld an award of exemplary damages against a professional photographer who had sold to newspapers a photograph taken at the plaintiff's wedding and including his father-in-law, who had since been murdered.[73]

The right applies to the whole or any substantial part of the photograph or film,[74] and continues to subsist so long as copyright subsists in the photograph or film.[75] It is subject to waiver by the person entitled;[76] but in the case of a joint commission, each of the commissioners has the right, and the right of each is satisfied if he consents to the act in question, but a waiver by one does not affect the rights of the others.[77] Infringement is actionable as a breach of statutory duty owed to the person entitled.[78]

7

Performers' Rights

INTRODUCTION

Infringement of copyright is often referred to as 'piracy'. In contrast 'bootlegging' refers to conduct in relation to a 'live' performance by a singer, musician, actor or other artiste, which may not infringe any copyright, but (prior to the 1988 Act) had long amounted to a criminal offence against the Performers' Protection Acts 1958–72 (or their predecessors).

As we have seen,[1] for copyright to exist (otherwise than in a broadcast or cable transmission), there must be a fixation recording or embodying the work; there is no copyright in a performance as such. A bootlegger who surreptitiously tapes or films a performance may infringe copyright in the work which is being performed, if that work has previously been reduced to a fixation, but this copyright will often belong to someone other than the performer. If by chance a legitimate sound recording or film of the performance is also being made at the same time, the bootlegger will not infringe copyright in that record or film, since his record or film will be derived, not from the legitimate record or film, but directly from the performance itself, which will amount to a common source of the lawful and unlawful fixations. While the 'bootleg' record or film may itself receive copyright protection, this copyright will apparently belong to the bootlegger and not the performer.

Despite the denial of copyright to performers, prior to the 1988 Act they received some protection against bootlegging by virtue of the Performers' Protection Acts 1958–72. These created, *inter alia*, the following criminal offences in relation to a performance by one or more actors, singers, musicians, dancers or other artistes of a literary, dramatic, musical or artistic work:

(a) knowingly making a record or film directly or indirectly from or by means of such a performance, without the performers' written consent, and otherwise than for the maker's private and domestic use; or

(b) knowingly selling, hiring out, distributing for the purposes of trade, or by way of trade exposing or offering for sale or hire, a record or film made in contravention of these Acts; or

(c) knowingly using such a record or film for the purposes of a public performance or exhibition; or

(d) knowingly making a live broadcast of such a performance without the performer's written consent.

There were defences in respect of things done for the purpose of reporting current events, or of inclusion by way of background or otherwise incidentally.

Owing, however, to lack of police interest and to low penalties imposed after conviction, the criminal sanction was of little value to performers and legitimate record and film companies, and attempts were made to establish a civil remedy for bootlegging. Such a civil remedy was at first denied in *MPPA v. British International Pictures*[2] and *Apple Corps v. Lingasong*.[3] Then came *Ex parte Island Records*,[4] where the Court of Appeal held that, although the Performers' Protection Acts did not give rise to a civil action for breach of statuory duty, bootlegging was nonetheless a civil wrong by way of an innominate tort of interference with a lawful business or with contractual relations by unlawful means, and this innominate tort was actionable both by the performer and by the record company with which he had an exclusive recording contract.

Then in *Lonrho v. Shell*,[5] a case involving not bootlegging but infringement of orders imposing sanctions against Rhodesia, the House of Lords, per Lord Diplock, declared that the innominate tort recognized in *Island Records* did not exist, but added that a performer clearly had a civil remedy against a bootlegger for breach of statutory duty, and left open whether a record company which had an exclusive recording contract with the performer was also entitled to sue for breach of statutory duty in its own name and without joining the performer as a party. The Court of Appeal subsequently ruled in *RCA v. Pollard*[6] that a record company had no right to bring an action for breach of statutory duty against a bootlegger, even if it had an exclusive recording contract with the relevant performer, but later in *Rickless v. United Artists Corp.*[7] it affirmed the availability of such an action to the performer himself and, after his death, his personal representative. *Rickless* also established that, after the performer's death, his personal representative had power to give the written consent required by the Performers' Protection Acts.

The 1986 White Paper, in its Chapter 14, proposed the extension of the protection of the Performers' Protection Acts to performances by variety artistes, such as jugglers and acrobats, who do not normally perform literary, dramatic, musical or artistic works. At the criminal level, it also proposed that the offences, penalties and procedures under the Performers' Protection Acts should be made consistent with those in the copyright field. In particular the *mens rea* for bootlegging offences (as well as copyright offences) should be relaxed so as to include persons who had reasonable cause to believe that they were dealing in offending copies; and criminal courts should be empowered to order the destruction of 'bootleg' records and films, and equipment specifically adapted for the purpose of producing them, even where there was no conviction owing to absence of proof of *mens rea*. It also proposed that legislation should explicitly make civil remedies, such as injunctions and damages, available in respect of trading in 'bootleg' records or films, both to performers and to persons, such as record or film companies, to whom the performer had granted an exclusive contract.

THE NEW LAW

The proposals contained in the 1986 White Paper are now implemented by Part II (ss. 180–212) of the 1988 Act, which replaces the Performers' Protection Acts[8] and explicitly creates civil (as well as criminal) remedies against bootlegging, by way of a civil action for breach of statutory duty,[9] which is made available not only to performers but also to those with whom they have concluded exclusive recording contracts. Like Part I, Part II of the Act applies to the whole of the United Kingdom, including its territorial waters and also including structures and vessels present on its continental shelf for purposes of exploring the sea bed or subsoil or exploiting their natural resources, and extends to things done on ships, hovercraft or aircraft registered in the United Kingdom.[10]

Performances and recordings
Part II defines 'performance' more widely than under the former law. It now covers, not only a dramatic performance (including dance or mime), a musical performance, and a reading or recitation of a literary work,[11] but also a performance of a variety act or a similar presentation, being (in all these cases) a live performance given by one or more individuals.[12] It defines 'recording', in relation to a performance, as a film or sound recording which is made either: (a) directly from the live performance; or (b) from a broadcast or cable transmission of the performance; or (c) directly or indirectly from another recording of the performance.[13] Part II confers rights in relation to performances which took place before its entry into force, but not as against infringing acts done, or done in pursuance of arrangements made, before such entry.[14] The rights conferred by Part II are independent of any other rights, such as any copyright in, or moral rights relating to, any work performed or any film, sound recording, broadcast or cable transmission of the performance.[15]

Persons entitled, duration and dealings
Sections 181–84 confer rights on performers themselves, and sections 185–88 on persons (referred to as 'persons having recording rights') who have exclusive rights, under contracts with performers, to make recordings of their performances with a view to commercial exploitation, i.e with a view to sale, hiring out, or showing or playing in public. The contractual rights must be exclusive even of the performer himself.[16] They may relate to 'one or more' of his performances, but must include the performance in question,[17] and an assignee of an exclusive recording contract is included.[18]

For a performer to have rights under Part II, he must be a qualifying individual (i.e. a citizen or subject of, or an individual resident in, a qualifying country), or the performance must take place in a qualifying country (i.e. the United Kingdom, another EEC Member State, or a reciprocating country designated by Order in Council).[19] For a person to have recording rights under Part II, he must be a qualifying person, i.e. a citizen or subject of, or an individual resident in, or a corporation formed under the law of, or having a place of business at which substantial business activity (other than in respect of goods elsewhere) is carried on in, a qualifying country.[20] If, however, the holder of an exclusive recording contract is not a qualifying person, the relevant Part II rights will vest in the qualifying person (if any) who is (directly or by assignment) licensed by the holder to make the recordings with a view to their commercial exploitation.[21]

Part II rights expire fifty years after the end of the calendar year in which the performance took place.[22] Performers' rights are not assignable *inter vivos*, but may be specifically bequeathed by the performer, and otherwise become exercisable by his personal representatives for the benefit of his estate.[23] The rights of a person having recording rights are not separately assignable, but pass automatically on an assignment of the benefit of the exclusive recording contract.[24] A person having recording rights is bound by a consent given by a predecessor in title.[25]

Infringement
Subject to certain exceptions specified in Sch. 2 and analogous to some of the exceptions to copyright infringement, it is infringement of *the performer's rights* to commit any of the following acts without his consent:[26]

(a) to make, otherwise than for one's private and domestic use, a recording of the whole or any substantial part of a performance;[27]
(b) to broadcast live or transmit live by cable the whole or any substantial part of a performance;[28]
(c) to show or play in public, or broadcast, or transmit by cable, the whole or any substantial part of a performance, by means of a recording which was, and which one knew or had reason to believe was, made without the performer's consent;[29]
(d) to import into the United Kingdom, otherwise than for one's private and domestic use, or in the course of a business to sell, hire out, offer or expose for sale or hire, distribute or possess, a recording of the whole or a substantial part of a performance

143

which was, and which one knows or has reason to believe was, made otherwise than for private purposes and without the performer's consent.[30]

The same acts, other than live broadcasting or cable transmission,[31] infringe *the rights of the person having recording rights*, except that, to infringe the rights of the person having recording rights:

(i) in the case of making a recording, the act must be done without the consent of the performer *and* without the consent of the person having recording rights;[32]

(ii) in the case of acts done in relation to an existing recording:
(a) the act must be done without the consent of the person having recording rights *and also*, in the case of a qualifying performance,[33] without the consent of the performer; *and further*
(b) the recording must have been made, and the defendant must know or have reason to believe that it was made, without the consent of the performer *and* without the consent of the person having recording rights.[34]

By s. 189 and Sch. 2, certain acts, which correspond broadly to certain acts which are excluded from infringing copyright by Chapter III of Part I of the Act, are excluded from infringing rights in performances under Part II. These exclusions relate to: (i) fair dealing for purposes of criticism or review, or of reporting current events; (ii) incidental inclusion in sound recordings, films, broadcasts or cable transmissions; (iii) instruction in making films or sound-tracks, or examinations; (iv) playing or showing at an educational establishment before an audience directly concerned with its activities; (v) recordings of broadcasts or cable transmissions for the purposes of an educational establishment; (vi) copying required for the purpose of exporting the original; (vii) things done for the purpose of, or of reporting, parliamentary or judicial poceedings or those of a Royal Commission or statutory inquiry; (viii) public records open to public inspection; (ix) acts specifically authorized by statute; (x) copying by transferees of recordings of performances in electronic form; (xi) use of recordings of spoken words made for the purpose of reporting current events or broadcasting or cable transmission; (xii) recordings of folksongs for archives; (xiii) playing of sound recordings by non-profit-making clubs or societies; (xiv) recordings made for the purpose of a legitimate broadcast or cable transmission; (xv) recordings made for purposes of supervision or control by the BBC, the IBA or the Cable Authority; (xvi) showing or playing in public of broadcasts or cable transmissions to a non-paying audience; (xvii) immediate re-transmission by cable of a broadcast; (xviii) provision of sub-titled copies of broadcasts or cable programmes for the deaf or otherwise handicapped; (xix) recording of broadcasts or cable programmes for archiving.

In addition, s. 190 enables the Copyright Tribunal, on application, to give consent on behalf of a performer for the making of a recording from a previous recording of a performance, where the identity or whereabouts of the performer cannot be ascertained by reasonable inquiry or the performer unreasonably withholds his consent. As regards the latter condition, the Tribunal must be satisfied that the performer's reasons for withholding consent are not based on any legitimate interest of his, but it is for him to show his reasons, and if he does not the Tribunal may draw appropriate inferences. In any event the Tribunal must take into account whether the original recording was made with the performer's consent and is lawfully in the possession of the applicant, and whether the making of the further recording is consistent with the arrangements under and the purposes for which the original recording was made. If the Tribunal gives consent, it may order payment to the performer in consideration thereof.

Remedies

By s. 194, an infringement of the rights in performances created by Part II is actionable by the person entitled to the right as a breach of statutory duty. Provision is also made by ss. 195, 196 and 203–05, analogous to that made by ss. 99, 100 and 113–15 in relation to copyright, for the delivery up, seizure and disposal of illicit recordings of performances. 'Illicit recording' is defined by s. 197 as a recording of the whole or a substantial part of a performance made otherwise than for private purposes and without the consent of the performer (for the purposes of performers' rights), or without the consent of the performer and also without the consent of the person having the recording rights (for the purposes of such rights). Moreover recordings lawfully made under certain provisions of Sch. 2 for educational purposes or broadcasting become illicit recordings when dealt with for other purposes, but otherwise recordings made in accordance with Sch. 2 are not illicit.[35]

Sections 198 and 202 create offences in respect of unlawful acts done in the course of a business in relation to a performance similar to those created by ss. 107 and 110 in relation to copyright works. Sections 199 and 200 provide (similarly to ss. 108 and 109, on infringing copies of copyright works) for the delivery up in criminal proceedings of illicit recordings, and for the issue of search warrants enabling the police to search premises for illicit recordings. Section 201 creates an offence of representing falsely and without reasonable grounds that one is authorized by another to give consent under Part II in relation to a performance.

8

Industrial Designs

Prior to the 1988 Act, industrial designs (i.e. designs of mass-produced goods) could be protected both under the Registered Designs Act 1949 (hereafter 'the 1949 Act') and under the Copyright Act 1956, as amended by the Design Copyright Act 1968. After various proposals for reform in this highly controversial area were made in the Whitford Report on *Copyright and Designs Law*,[1] the Green Paper on *Reform of the Law relating to Copyright, Designs and Performers' Protection*,[2] and the Green Paper on *Intellectual Property Rights and Innovation*,[3] eventually the government stated its legislative intentions in the 1986 White Paper on *Intellectual Property and Innovation*,[4] and the proposals of the 1986 White Paper have now been implemented by the 1988 Act. Part IV (ss. 265–73) of the new Act amends the 1949 Act and sets out the amended text in Schedule 4. More importantly, the new Act excludes industrial designs from protection by ordinary copyright,[5] and Part III (ss. 213–64) creates instead a new form of protection by way of an unregistered design right.

REGISTERED DESIGNS

Certain industrial designs may be registered under the Registered Designs Act 1949 as amended. Registration creates a full monopoly, i.e against independent creation as well as copying, for a period (assuming all permissible renewals) of twenty-five years.[6]

Definition of 'design'
Section 1(2) of the 1949 Act (as amended) provides that a design which is new may, on application by a person claiming to be the

147

proprietor, be registered in respect of a specified article or set of articles. Section 1(1) and (3), as amended, defines 'design' as follows:

(a) A design comprises features of shape, configuration, pattern or ornament, which are applied to an article by an industrial process.[7]

(b) These features, in the finished article, must appeal to and be judged solely by the eye.[8] Moreover, the appearance of the article must be material, in the sense that aesthetic considerations are normally taken into account to a material extent by persons acquiring or using articles of that description, or would be if the design were applied to the article.[9]

(c) A method or principle of construction is excluded.[10]

(d) Also excluded are features of shape or configuration which either: (i) are dictated solely by the function which the article has to perform;[11] or (ii) are dependent upon the appearance of a thing of which the article is to form part.[12]

It is in excluding features dependent on the appearance of a thing to which the article is to be fitted that the new Act has most substantially altered the definition of a registrable design. The intention is clearly to prevent design registration from creating a functional monopoly in the sphere of components or spare parts for complex machinery.[13]

Little difficulty has arisen in relation to features of pattern or ornament, but the position relating to features of shape or configuration is complex. The leading case is *Amp v. Utilux*,[14] where the House of Lords held that an electric terminal for use inside washing machines was not registrable, since the shape of the terminal lacked eye-appeal and was dictated solely by function, even though the function could have been fulfilled by a differently shaped terminal. As regards eye-appeal, the relevant eye is that of the customer, and to be registrable the design must appeal to some customers, so that it might attract them to buy the article by reason of its appearance. In addition, the reference to dictation by function excludes features of shape which, as in this case, were adopted for purely functional reasons; the exclusion is not limited to cases where only one possible shape is capable of fulfilling the function.

More recently the requirements of eye-appeal and absence of

pure functionality have been clarified by the Privy Council, on appeal from Hong Kong, in *Interlego AG v. Tyco Industries Inc.*[15] In holding that the design for the well-known 'Lego' interlocking toy-bricks was registrable under the 1949 Act, Lord Oliver explained that for this purpose the emphasis is on the visual image conveyed by the manufactured article, and that the design and the article have to be taken as a whole. For a design to be registrable, the shape of the article as a whole (rather than the novel features of the design) has to have eye-appeal, and on the existence of eye-appeal the designer's purpose is relevant, though not conclusive. While the mere coincidence of eye-appeal with functional efficiency would not suffice if in fact every feature of the design were dictated by the function which the article was to perform, on the other hand a shape which as a whole had eye-appeal would be registrable as a design even if some (but not all) of its features were dictated solely by functional considerations. Moreover, eye-appeal does not constitute a function for present purposes – 'functional' refers to the mechanical working of the article. In the instant case, in view of the nature of the article and the purpose of the designer, eye-appeal was established. Although the interlocking knobs and tubes served the function of holding the bricks together, their actual shape and dimensions were designed at least partly with a view to the appearance of the article as a whole. The approach adopted in this decision appears to remain applicable under the amended 1949 Act.

By s. 1(5) of the 1949 Act (as amended) and r. 26 of the Registered Designs Rules 1989,[16] designs to be applied to the following articles are not registrable:

(a) works of sculpture, other than casts or models used or intended to be used as models or patterns to be multiplied by an industrial process;
(b) wall plaques, medals and medallions;
(c) printed matter primarily of a literary or artistic character – including book jackets, calendars, certificates, coupons, dress-making patterns, greeting cards, labels, leaflets, maps, plans, playing cards, postcards, stamps, trade advertisements, trade forms and cards, transfers and similar articles.

Novelty

By s. 1(2) and (4) of the 1949 Act (as amended), a design, to be registrable, must be new. In particular it must not be the same as a design which has been registered in respect of the same or any other article in pursuance of a prior application or has been published in the United Kingdom, in respect of the same or any other article, before the date of the application, nor must it differ from such a design only in immaterial details or in features which are variants commonly used in the trade.[17] A design may be anticipated by a document, such as a patent specification, but only if it contains clear and unmistakable directions such as to give a reader who is grappling with the problem what he wants.[18]

The requirement of novelty is relaxed by s. 6(4)–(6) of the 1949 Act (as amended), which derive from provisions originally added by s. 44 of the Copyright Act 1956, and which now provide that where an application is made by or with the consent of the owner of copyright in an artistic work for the registration of a corresponding design, the design is not to be treated as anticipated by a previous use of the work, unless the use included the marketing (in the United Kingdom)[19] of articles to which the design (or one differing only immaterially) had been applied industrially and took place with the consent of the copyright owner. Section 6 also specifies a number of other exceptions to the requirement of novelty, such as disclosure in confidence or in breach of confidence;[20] first and confidential orders for textiles;[21] display at certain exhibitions;[22] and communication to government departments.[23] Under Art. 4 of the Paris Convention[24] and ss. 13 and 14 of the 1949 Act, an applicant can claim the priority of an earlier application made in a Convention country within the previous six months.

Under s. 4, a registered proprietor may apply for registration in respect of additional articles, or of a slightly modified design, despite previous registration or publication of the original design, but so as to expire with the earlier registration.

Registration and term

Application is made in respect of a specified article or set of articles.[25] 'Set of articles' means a number of articles of the same general character which are ordinarily on sale or intended to be used together, and to each of which the same design, perhaps with minor variations, is applied – e.g. cups and saucers.[26] Apart from such sets, a separate application must be made in respect of each type of article for which registration is desired.[27]

The application must be made by the proprietor.[28] By s. 2 of the 1949 Act as amended by s. 267 of the 1988 Act, in the case of an application made after the commencement of Part IV of the 1988 Act, the original proprietor is either: (a) the author (i.e. the actual creator of the design; or where it was generated by computer without human authorship, the person by whom the arrangements necessary for its creation were made); or (b) where the design was created in pursuance of a commission for money or money's worth, the commissioner; or (c) where the design was created in the course of the author's employment, his employer. But ownership of a design may be assigned or devolve by operation of law, so as to enable the successor in title to apply for registration.[29] If unregistered design right subsists in the design under Part III of the 1988 Act,[30] an application for registration can be entertained only if it is made by the design right owner.[31]

The Registry searches through previous registrations to discover anticipations,[32] and the Registrar has a discretion to refuse an application or insist on modifications, e.g. on grounds of illegality or immorality.[33] If the application is successful, the design is registered and a certificate of registration is issued to the proprietor.[34] The register is open to public inspection and search;[35] but s. 5 provides for secrecy directions in the interests of defence analogous to those contained in ss. 22 and 23 of the Patents Act 1977. In view of the limitation of the 1949 Act to designs which have eye-appeal and are not functional, presumably the secrecy is needed because of the nature of the article to which the design is to be applied; e.g. in the case of an attractive pattern to be painted on a missile!

A design is normally registered as of the date of the application, but no action can be brought in respect of infringements committed before the issue of the certificate.[36] Registration now confers protection for a period of twenty-five years from the date of registration, provided that the four necessary applications for renewal are made.[37] But a registered design which corresponded to an artistic work, and which was only registrable because prior non-industrial uses of the work were disregarded under s. 6(4), expires when copyright in the work expires, if earlier than the registered design would otherwise expire.[38]

An opponent cannot intervene in the pre-registration procedure, but after registration he may apply for cancellation for lack of novelty or some other ground for refusal of registration. The application may be made to the Registrar, with appeal to the Registered Designs Appeal Tribunal, which consists of one or more nominated High Court judges, or directly to the High Court.[39]

Infringement and remedies
By s. 7 (as amended by s. 268),[40] the following acts, if done in the United Kingdom without the licence of the registered proprietor, constitute infringement of a registered design:

(a) Making or importing, for sale or hire or for use for the purposes of a trade or business: (i) an infringing article – i.e. an article of a type for which the design is registered, and to which the design, or a design not substantially different (as regards the registrable features)[41] from it, has been applied;[42] or (ii) a kit – i.e. an entirely or substantially complete set of components, intended to be assembled into an infringing article.[43]
(b) Selling, hiring, or offering or exposing for sale or hire, an infringing article[44] or kit.[45]
(c) Making anything for enabling an infringing article or kit to be made or assembled (in the United Kingdom or elsewhere), for sale, hire or use for the purposes of a trade or business.[46]

As regards 'not substantially different', it was said in *Holdsworth v. McCrea*[47] that if the plaintiff has registered a pattern, without verbal description, his protection is limited to the pattern as a whole. Now, however, except in the case of textiles, wallpaper or lace, r. 15 of the Registered Designs Rules 1989[48] requires the application to state the features for which novelty is claimed. In *Dean's Rag Book v. Pomerantz*,[49] which involved a toy Mickey Mouse, it was emphasized that the better known the subject of the design is, the narrower will be the scope of protection conferred; and in the case of a well-known subject-matter, such as Mickey Mouse, small differences from the registered design may prevent infringement. In *Valor v. Main*,[50] which involved gas-fires, Whitford J. explained that, by and large, the tests for anticipation and for infringement are the same; and added that the question of resemblance must be considered not merely by looking at the articles standing side-by-side, but also by looking at the registered design, going away and then looking at the defendant's article and considering whether you would take it for the plaintiff's. Similarly in *Benchairs Ltd. v. Chair Centre Ltd..,*[51] which involved stacking chairs, Russell L.J. emphasized the need to consider the parties' designs as a whole and through the eyes of a potential customer.

As regards remedies, s. 9 exempts from liability for damages (but not injunctions) a defendant who proves that he was not aware, and had no reasonable ground for supposing, that the design was registered; and this defence is not affected by the plaintiff's marking of his products with words such as 'registered' unless the number of the design registration also appears.[52] Section 26 provides a remedy against unjustified threats of proceedings for infringement of a registered design, similar to that provided in the case of patents by s. 70 of the Patents Act 1977.

Compulsory licences, licences of right, and Crown use

Section 10 enables the Registrar to grant compulsory licences where the design is not being applied industrially to the specified article to the extent reasonable in the circumstances.

Section 11A, added by s. 270 of the 1988 Act, enables the Registrar, on application by a Minister who has received a report from the Monopolies and Mergers Commission indicating that restrictive conditions in licences granted in respect of a registered design, or a refusal by the proprietor of a registered design to grant licences on reasonable terms, have operated or may be expected to operate against the public interest, to make an order cancelling or modifying such conditions and/or an entry in the register that licences under the design are to be available as of right. In default of agreement, the terms of a licence of right will be settled by the Registrar on application by the intending licensee, and will enable the licensee to perform all acts which are covered by the design registration. The licence will operate from the date of the application to the Registrar.

By s. 11B, similarly added, where licences are available of right and the defendant in an infringement action undertakes to accept such a licence, no injunction can be granted against him, and damages or profits awarded against him in respect of infringements committed after licences became available of right cannot exceed double the amount which would have been payable in respect of the acts in question under such a licence. A defendant may give the undertaking at any time before final order in the infringement action, and need not admit liability.

Section 12 and Schedule 1 enable a government department to use or authorize the use of a registered design for the services of the Crown, usually in return for compensation. The Schedule is now amended by s. 271(1) of the new Act to ensure that in appropriate cases compensation is assessed by reference to the proprietor's loss of the profit which he would have made if he had been awarded a contract to supply the articles in question.[53]

ORDINARY COPYRIGHT IN INDUSTRIAL DESIGNS

After the decision of the Court of Appeal in *Dorling v. Honnor Marine*[54] and the enactment of the Design Copyright Act 1968, ordinary copyright under the 1956 Act came to play an important role in the sphere of industrial design. It was capable of protecting both designs which have eye-appeal and thus were registrable under the 1949 Act, and designs which were purely functional and thus were not registrable. Prior to the decision of the House of Lords in *British Leyland Motor Corp. v. Armstrong Patents Co. Ltd.*[55] it appeared to be capable of conferring on a manufacturer of a complex mechanical product, such as a motor-car, an effective monopoly in the supply of spare parts, such as exhaust systems, for his products. But that decision invoked the principle of non-derogation from grant to prevent the use of copyright to maintain such a monopoly. Outside the sphere of spare parts, however, copyright continued to provide substantial, albeit rather arbitrary, protection for industrial designs until it was excluded from this sphere, and replaced by a new unregistered design right, by the 1988 Act.

It seems useful, however, to sketch briefly the operation of ordinary copyright in this sphere prior to the 1988 Act, especially as under transitional provisions it will continue to have practical importance for ten years from the commencement of the new Act.[56]

The copyright work

The basis of ordinary copyright in an industrial design was usually a (two-dimensional) drawing, for, as we have noted in Chapter 2, drawings have long qualified as artistic works irrespective of their artistic quality,[57] and 'drawing' was defined as including a diagram, map, chart or plan.[58] A three-dimensional prototype, on the other hand, would seldom, if ever, qualify for protection as a work of artistic craftsmanship or a sculpture,[59] and copyright in a literary work, such as a set of verbal instructions as to how to manufacture a product, would not be infringed by making the product in accordance with the instructions, for there was no visual similarity between the instructions and the product.[60]

It was well established that a drawing would attract copyright despite its simplicity, and despite the fact that it was a technical drawing without aesthetic appeal.[61] The drawing had, of course, to be original, but in *LB (Plastics) v. Swish Products*[62] Whitford J. said *obiter* that an engineering drawing would be original even if it were copied from a three-dimensional prototype, in view of the skill and labour involved in making such drawings. One qualification was, however, suggested in *Catnic Components v. Hill & Smith*,[63] where Whitford J. took the view that an applicant for a patent must be treated, on publication of the specification, as abandoning his copyright in drawings equivalent to those contained in the specification.

Recently, in *Interlego v. Tyco Industries*,[64] the Privy Council recognized that engineering drawings were artistic works within the meaning of the 1956 Act, despite the fact that they were essentially no more than manufacturing instructions for a three-dimensional article. It proceeded to hold, however, that a drawing is not original if it is simply copied from an earlier drawing, without some, qualitatively significant, element of material alteration or embellishment. Moreover, even in the case of an engineering drawing, the alteration or embellishment necessary to establish originality must exist in the new drawing itself, as a visual image, and not in the explanatory words and figures which accompanied it and constituted manufacturing instructions. Lord Oliver admitted that explanatory words and figures could be taken into account in determining infringement, but distinguished the issues of originality and infringement.

Infringement

Usually, in cases of industrial design, the defendant would not have had access to the plaintiff's drawings, but would have produced his three-dimensional product by copying the plaintiff's three-dimensional product. Such copying could amount to infringement, since s. 48(1) of the 1956 Act defined 'reproduction' as including, in the case of a two-dimensional artistic work, a version produced by conversion into a three-dimensional form,[65] and it was well established that indirect copying sufficed for infringement.[66] But s. 9(8) of the 1956 Act introduced a test of lay recognition, by providing that the making of a three-dimensional object did not infringe copyright in a two-dimensional artistic work, if the object would not have appeared, to persons who were not experts in relation to objects of that description, to be a reproduction of the work.[67]

As regards derivation, in the leading case of *LB (Plastics) v. Swish Products*,[68] which involved plastic knock-down drawers, i.e. furniture drawers made of components, usually delivered unassembled, which the customer puts together and can dismantle, Lord Wilberforce inferred copying from the striking general similarity between the parties' drawers, coupled with the defendants' opportunity to copy the plaintiff's drawer. This established a *prima facie* case of copying, which the defendant had failed satisfactorily to answer. In particular, the need for interchangeability, i.e. that the defendants' drawers needed to fit into the customer's furniture, which was designed to accomodate the plaintiffs' drawer (rather than vice versa), indicated causal connection via the furniture. Moreover in *Solar Thomson v. Barton*,[69] which involved rubber rings for pulleys, the Court of Appeal had held that a sufficient causal link was created by the defendant's sending a blank steel-ring to an independent designer, with detailed instructions to design a suitable rubber ring. On the other hand in *Gleeson v. Denne*,[70] which involved clerical shirts, the attempt to found a causal link on a description of the plaintiff's shirt given by a traveller employed by the defendants, who had been shown such a shirt by a customer, to the defendant's designer, failed because the description was insufficiently detailed.

As regards objective similarity and lay recognition, in *LB Plastics* Lord Wilberforce also explained that s. 9(8) created a defence, to be established by the defendant after the issue of copying had been decided in the plaintiff's favour. For this purpose the judge had to place himself in the position of a non-expert in relation to extruded or moulded components, and to compare the object with the drawing, taking account of any written matter on the drawing. He had also to be credited with some ability to interpret design drawings; otherwise the comparison could not be made; but the comparison had to be a visual comparison. On s. 9(8), Lord Hailsham was puzzled by the concept of the notional non-expert and the policy underlying the provision, and Lord Scarman described it as a curious provision for which he could discover no sensible rationale. He conjured up a bizarre picture of witnesses stating that they had no knowledge or experience of the subject, and proceeding to state whether it appeared to them that the object was reproduced from the drawing. Similarly in *Temple Instruments v. Hollis Heels*,[71] which involved divan legs, Graham J. had held that several drawings on the same sheet and obviously relating to the same article could be considered together, and account had to be taken of wording indicating that a drawing was of a section of the article. Again, in *Solar Thomson v. Barton*,[72] the Court of Appeal had also held that, for the purpose of s. 9(8), in the case of a sectional drawing the notional unskilled observer should be treated as having a sectioned check piece in his hand, and would be entitled to interpret the sectional drawing in the light of the contemporary associated drawings.[73] On the other hand in *Merlet v. Mothercare*,[74] which involved a baby's cape, Walton J. distinguished *Solar Thomson* and held that a three-dimensional garment could not reproduce or appear to reproduce a cutting-plan, and that one could not notionally dissect the garment into its component parts so as to match the pieces shown on the cutting-plan.

In *British Leyland Motor Corp. v. Armstrong Patents Co. Ltd.*,[75] the Court of Appeal rejected an argument that the defendant had not infringed because he had only copied the dimensions of the exhaust pipe, which were shown in words, figures and lines on the plaintiff's drawing. But the decision was reversed by the House of Lords on other grounds.[76] In that case Leyland were seeking to prevent another company from manufacturing exhaust pipes as spare parts for the Marina car, and the decision of the House in the defendant's favour effectively eliminated the operation of ordinary copyright in the case of spare parts for complex products, such as motor-cars. The House reasoned that the manufacturer of such a product granted to his ultimate customers the right to repair the product, and therefore could not derogate from this grant by invoking copyright so as to prevent other manufacturers from producing and marketing the necessary spare parts, and thereby to establish a monopoly in the supply of such parts. This determined decision overrode the Copyright Act by main force rather than interpretation, but left the established law undisturbed outside the sphere of spare parts.

Overlap and term

Prior to the 1988 Act the overlap between ordinary copyright and design registration was dealt with by s. 10 of the Copyright Act 1956, as amended by the Design Copyright Act 1968. The following definitions applied for the purposes of s. 10:

(a) 'Corresponding design', in relation to an artistic work, meant a design which, when applied to an article, resulted in a reproduction of the relevant work.[77]

(b) A design was 'applied industrially' if it was applied to more than fifty articles, other than a single 'set' of articles within the meaning of s. 44(1) of the Registered Designs Act 1949, or to goods manufactured in lengths or pieces, other than hand-made goods. The application could be by printing or embossing or by any other process, including reproduction of the design on or in the articles or goods in the course of their production.[78]

(c) But no account was taken of articles, such as printed matter primarily of a literary or artistic character, which were excluded from design registration by s. 1(4) of the 1949 Act and r. 26 of the Design Rules 1949.[79]

(d) 'The scope of the copyright in a registered design' referred to the aggregate of the things which s. 7 of the Registered Designs Act conferred on the registered proprietor the exclusive right to do.[80]

(e) 'The scope of the copyright in a registered design as extended to all associated designs and articles' referred to the aggregate of the things which s. 7 would have conferred the exclusive right to do if there had also been registered, along with the design, every possible modificaton or variation of the design not altering its character or substantially affecting its identity, and the design, and such modifications and variations thereof, had been registered in respect of all articles to which they were capable of being applied.[81]

The substantive enactments were contained in s. 10(2) and (3), as amended by the 1968 Act. These applied where: (i) a corresponding design to an artistic work in which copyright subsisted was applied industrially by or with the consent of the copyright owner; and (ii) articles to which the design had been so applied were sold, hired out, or offered for sale or hire, whether in the United Kingdom or elsewhere. After the 1968 amendment, it was no longer material whether at the time of the marketing the 'corresponding design' was actually registered under the 1949 Act.

Where these conditions were fulfilled, then, after the end of a period of fifteen years beginning with the date of such first marketing, it was not infringement of the ordinary copyright in the artistic work to do anything which would, if a corresponding design had been registered under the 1949 Act immediately before the otherwise infringing act, have been within the scope of the copyright in the design, as extended to all associated designs and articles. Thus in substance, in the case of a registrable design, an industrial producer could obtain a full monopoly for fifteen years by registration under the 1949 Act. But, regardless of whether he obtained a design registration, if he marketed a product incorporating the design, he could invoke ordinary copyright in a corresponding artistic work against competing industrial products for fifteen years from his first marketing of his product, but not beyond the fifteen-year period.[82]

However, even after the 1968 amendment, s. 10 only applied where the 'corresponding design' was registrable under the 1949 Act. If it was not registrable, e.g. because it was purely functional, ordinary copyright in a drawing could be enforced, despite its industrial application and the marketing of resulting industrial products by the copyright owner, and even against competing industrial products, for the normal copyright period of the author's life plus fifty years.[83] On the other hand, registrability referred to the nature of the design in relation to factors such as eye-appeal and functionality, and not to its novelty or originality.[84]

Abolition by the 1988 Act

In accordance with the proposals of the 1986 White Paper, s. 51 of the 1988 Act effectively abolishes the use of ordinary copyright in the sphere of industrial designs by excluding certain acts from constituting infringement of copyright in a work which is a design document or model recording or embodying a design for an article which is not itself an artistic work or a typeface.[85] 'Design' is defined as the design of any aspect of the shape or configuration (whether internal or external) of the whole or part of an article, other than surface decoration, and 'design document' as any record of a design, whether in the form of a drawing, a written description, a photograph, data stored in a computer or otherwise.[86] The acts covered by the section are: (a) making an article to the design;[87] (b) copying an article made to the design;[88] and (c) issuing to the public, or including in a film, broadcast or cable transmission, an article whose making was authorized by the section.[89]

Transitionally, by para. 19 of Sch. 1 of the new Act, s. 51 does not apply for ten years after the commencement of the new Act in relation to a design recorded or embodied in a design document or model before such commencement. During those ten years the copyright is effectively treated, as regards acts which would be permitted by s. 51, in the same way as a design right under Part III of the Act. Thus licences of right are available, on terms settled (in default of agreement) by the Comptroller-General of Patents, Designs and Trade Marks, in the last five of the ten years, or earlier in pursuance of an order made in consequence of a report of the Monopolies and Mergers Commission. The remedies of the copyright owner are limited by analogy with s. 239 where a licence of right is available and the defendant undertakes to accept such a licence. The holder of a voluntary licence granted before the commencement of the new Act is enabled to apply to the comptroller for an order adjusting its terms; and the right to seize infringing copies under s. 100 is excluded.

In addition, s. 52, drawing inspiration from s. 10(2) and (3) of the 1956 Act as amended, applies where an artistic work has been exploited, by or with the licence of the copyright owner, by the making by an industrial process[90] of articles (other than films) which are regarded as copies of the work, and the marketing[91] of such articles, in the United Kingdom or elsewhere, after the commencement of the new Act.[92] In such a case, after the end of a period of twenty-five years from the end of the calendar year in which the articles were first marketed, the work may be copied by making articles of any description (other than films), or doing anything for the purpose of making such articles, and anything may be done in relation to articles so made, without infringing copyright in the work. The same result applies where s. 10 of the 1956 Act applied to the work at any time before the commencement of the new Act, except that in that case the period of protection is limited to fifteen years in accordance with s. 10(3) of the 1956 Act.[93] Section 52 seems of most significance in relation to three-dimensional artistic works, such as engravings or sculptures. Thus if an engraving of a person's head has been used by the copyright owner for twenty-five years as a design for industrially-produced medallions, it can thereafter be copied as a design for printing on shirts.

By s. 53, copyright in an artistic work is not infringed by anything which is done in pursuance of an assignment or licence made or granted by the proprietor of a registered design corresponding to the work,[94] if it is done in good faith in reliance on the registration and without notice of any proceedings for cancellation or rectification, even if the design was registered in favour of the wrong person as proprietor.

THE NEW UNREGISTERED DESIGN RIGHT

In accordance with proposals contained in the 1986 White Paper,[95] Part III (ss. 213–64) of the 1988 Act introduces an unregistered design right to protect original designs for the shape or configuration of articles which are not artistic works in their own right, with the object of giving the designer a market lead over the copyist. The new right applies to both functional and aesthetic designs. Spare parts are not excluded altogether, but features of spare parts which are essential to enable them to operate as such are not protected. Ordinary copyright protection is, however, retained, subject to s. 52,[96] for articles which qualify as artistic works in their own right, and the new right is effectively excluded as regards such articles.

The effective term of the new right is ten years from first marketing of an article to which the design has been applied, but licences are available as of right, on terms settled by the Comptroller-General of Patents, during the second five years of the term. Moreover, the Secretary of State may order that licences should be available as of right even earlier in a particular case if the

Monopolies and Mergers Commission has found that the right has been exercised contrary to the public interest. The new right is also subject to Crown use provisions analogous to those applicable to patents and registered designs. Jurisdiction over disputes relating to the subsistence, term or first ownership of design right, as well as the terms of a licence as of right, is given to the Comptroller-General of Patents, though infringement actions are brought before the court.

It is primarily infringement of design right to reproduce the design for commercial purposes, by copying it so as to make articles (including kits) exactly or substantially embodying the design, or by making a design document recording the design for the purpose of enabling such articles to be made, or to authorize such reproduction. It is secondary infringement to import an infringing article, have such an article in one's possession for commercial purposes, or to sell, hire out, or offer or expose for sale or hire such an article in the course of a business, knowing or having reasonable cause to believe that the article is an infringing article.

Nature and subsistence

By s. 213(1), the new design right is a property right which subsists in accordance with Part III in an original design. 'Design' refers to any aspect of the shape or configuration (whether internal or external) of the whole or part of an article, but design right does not subsist in any of the following: (i) a method or principle of construction; (ii) features of shape or configuration which enable an article to be connected to or placed in, around or against another article so that either article may perform its function; (iii) features of shape or configuration which are dependent upon the appearance of another article of which the article in question is intended by the designer to form an integral part; (iv) surface decoration.[97] A design is not 'original' if it is commonplace in the design field in question at the time of its creation.[98] Moreover design right does not subsist unless and until the design has been recorded in a design document or an article has been made to the design, nor in a design which had been so recorded or applied before the commencement of Part III of the Act.[99] Moreover if the article to which a design right relates is an artistic work in its own right (as an engraving or a sculpture, or possibly a work of artistic craftsmanship), design right is in effect excluded by s. 236, which provides that, where copyright subsists in a work which consists of or includes a design in which design right subsists, it is not an infringement of the design right to do anything which is an infringement in the copyright.

The first owner of a design right is (i) normally the designer, i.e. the person who created the design or, in the case of a computer-created design, the person who undertook the arrangements necessary for its creation;[100] but (ii) if it was created in pursuance of a commission for money or money's worth, the commissioner;[101] or (iii) if it was created (otherwise than under commission) in the course of the designer's employment, his employer.[102] Design right (or future design right) may be assigned or licensed in the same way as copyright under Part I;[103] and where a person who is both the proprietor of a registered design, and the owner of unregistered design right in the same design, assigns the registered design, the assignment extends to the unregistered design right unless a contrary intention appears.[104]

For design right to exist in a design there must be an appropriate connecting factor. A design qualifies for protection if the designer (if the design is not created in pursuance of a commission nor in the course of employment), or the commissioner or employer, is a qualifying person.[105] A 'qualifying person' is an individual who is a citizen or subject of, or habitually resident in, a qualifying country; or a corporation which is formed under the law of, or has a place of business at which substantially business activity (other than by way of dealings with goods located elsewhere) is carried on in, a qualifying country;[106] or the government of a qualifying country.[107]

The qualifying countries are: (a) the United Kingdom (including its territorial waters and also including structures or vessels present on its continental shelf for purposes of exploration of the sea bed or subsoil or exploitation of their natural resources);[108] (b) if Part III is extended thereto by Order in Council, any of the Channel Islands, the Isle of Man, and any British colony;[109] (c) the other EEC Member States; and (d) reciprocating countries designated by Order in Council.[110] It is alternatively sufficient if the first marketing of articles made to the design is effected by a qualifying person who has an exclusive licence to market in the United Kingdom from the person who would (but for not being a qualifying person) have been the owner of the design right,

163

and takes place in the United Kingdom, a relevant dependent territory, or another EEC Member State. In such a case the exclusive licensee who carries out the marketing is the first owner of the design right.[111]

Design right expires fifteen years from the end of the calendar year in which the design was first recorded in a design document or implemented by the making of an article to the design; or if articles made to the design are made available for sale or hire, anywhere in the world, by or with the licence of the design right owner, within five years from the end of the calendar year of the first recording or implementation, then the right expires ten years from the end of the calendar year of the first such marketing.[112]

Infringement

It is primary infringement of design right, without the licence of the owner, in the United Kingdom to reproduce the design for commercial purposes [113] by making articles to the design, or by making a design document recording the design for the purpose of enabling such articles to be made, or to authorize another person to perform such reproduction.[114] Reproduction by making articles means copying the design so as to produce articles exactly or substantially to the design.[115] Reproduction may be direct or indirect, and it is immaterial whether any intervening acts themselves infringe the design right.[116] For purposes of infringement, 'article' includes a kit, i.e. a complete or substantially-complete set of components intended to be assembled into an article, as well as the assembled article.[117]

By s. 227 it is secondary infringement, without the licence of the owner, to: (a) import into the United Kingdom for commercial purposes an article which is, and which one knows or has reason to believe is, an infringing article; or (b) have such an article in one's possession for commercial purposes; or (c) sell, hire out, or offer or expose for sale or hire such an article in the course of a business.

An infringing article is an article (other than a design document) of which (a) the making constituted primary infringement of the design right; or (b) in the case of an article (other than a design document) which has been or is proposed to be imported in the United Kingdom, the making in the United Kingdom would have infringed the design right or an exclusive licence agreement relating to the design.[118] But the definition gives way to directly effective rules of European Community law, e.g. under the doctrine of exhaustion.[119] Where an article is made to a design in which design right subsists or has subsisted, it is presumed, unless the contrary is proved, that the article was made at a time when the design right subsisted.[120]

Section 245 enables the Secretary of State by statutory instrument, for the purpose of complying with international obligations or securing or maintaining reciprocal protection for British designs abroad, to provide that acts of a specified description, in relation to a specified or any description of design or article, do not infringe design right.

As regards civil remedies for infringement, Part III makes similar provision in relation to design right as Part I makes in relation to copyright, including provision for additional damages, delivery up and disposal, and exclusive licences.[121] As with copyright, a primary infringer of design right has a defence to a claim for damages, but not as to other remedies, if he shows that at the time of the infringement he did not know, and had no reason to believe, that design right subsisted in the design,[122] but in addition a secondary infringer of design right who shows that the infringing article was acquired by him or a predecessor in title of his without knowledge, and without reason to believe, that it was an infringing article, is liable only for damages not exceeding a reasonable royalty in respect of the infringing act, to the exclusion of other remedies.[123]

By s. 239, in the case of infringements committed while a licence is available as of right under ss. 237 or 238, if the defendant undertakes to take a licence on terms to be agreed or, in default of agreement, settled by the comptroller, then no injunction is to be granted against him, no order for delivery up is to be made under s. 230, and an award against him of damages or profits is limited to double the amount which would have been payable under a licence of right. Such an undertaking may be given at any time before final order in the infringement proceedings, and without any admission of liability.[124]

Licences of right

By s. 237, in the last five years of the term of a design right anyone is entitled as of right to a licence to do any act which would otherwise infringe the design right on terms to be settled, in default of agreement, by the Comptroller-General of Patents, Designs and Trade Marks.[125] In addition, by s. 238, where a report of the Monopolies and Mergers Commission specifies restrictive conditions in licences granted by a design right owner, or a refusal by a design right owner to grant licences on reasonable terms, as matters which operate, may be expected to operate, or have operated against the public interest, the powers conferred by the Secretary of State by Part I of Schedule 8 to the Fair Trading Act 1973 to make orders by statutory instrument for the purpose of remedying or preventing such adverse effects, include power to cancel or modify such conditions and/or to provide that licences in respect of the design right shall be available as of right. Again, in default of agreement, the terms of such a licence will be settled by the comptroller.

An application for settlement of the terms of a licence of right under ss. 237 or 238 is made by the licensee to the comptroller, in the case of a licence under s. 237 not earlier than a year before the earliest date on which the licence may take effect.[126] In the case of a licence under s. 237, the terms fixed by the comptroller must not prevent the licensee from doing anything within the design right; and in the case of a licence under s. 238, they must not prevent him from doing anything for which the licence is available.[127] Otherwise in settling the terms the comptroller must have regard to factors prescribed by statutory instrument.[128] If the identity of the owner cannot be discovered on reasonable inquiry, the comptroller may order that the licence should be free of payment, subject to the right of the owner to apply to the comptroller to vary the terms as from his application for variation.[129] Where the terms are settled by the comptroller, the licence has effect from the earliest date on which licences of right become available under s. 237, in the case of an application for a licence under s. 237 made before that date; and in other cases from the date on which the application to the comptroller was made.[130] An appeal lies from any decision of the comptroller settling the terms of a licence of right to the Appeal Tribunal established under the Registered Designs Act 1949.[131]

By s. 254, it is a wrong, actionable by the design right owner, for the holder of a licence of right, without the owner's consent, to apply to goods which he markets in reliance on that licence a trade description indicating that he is a licensee of the owner, or to use any such trade description in an advertisement in relation to such goods.

Crown use
Sections 240–44 create elaborate powers of Crown use of designs analogous to those applicable to patents. Section 240 permits a government department, or a person authorized[132] in writing by a government department, without the licence of the design right owner, to do anything for the purpose of supplying articles for the services of the Crown in relation to the defence of the realm, foreign defence purposes, or health service purposes, and to dispose of articles no longer required for the services of the Crown,[133] without infringing the design right. During a period of emergency, declared by Order in Council, the Crown use powers become virtually unlimited.[134]

Where Crown use is made of a design, the government department concerned must notify the design owner as soon as practicable, and give him such information as to the extent of the use as he may from time to time require, unless it appears that it would be contrary to the public interest to do so or his identity cannot be ascertained by reasonable inquiry.[135] Crown use is on terms agreed (before or after the use) with Treasury approval between the department concerned and the owner, or in default of agreement on terms determined (on a reference by a party to the dispute) by the High Court or the Court of Session.[136] As now with registered designs and patents, payment for Crown use includes compensation for loss of the manufacturing profit which the owner would have made if he had been awarded a contract to supply the articles.[137]

The Crown-use provisions override the terms of licences, assignments and agreements between private parties, as well as copyrights in models and documents, but do not protect disclosures in breach of confidence.[138] Complex provisions are made to protect the interest of exclusive licensees, assignors for royalties, and others involved in agreements, in the payments to be made for the Crown use.[139]

Wrongful threats
Section 253 creates a civil wrong, analogous to those created by s. 70 of the Patents Act 1977 and s. 26 of the Registered Designs

Act 1949 (as amended), of groundlessly threatening proceedings for infringement of design right, otherwise than in respect of the making or importing of an article. Where a person (not necessarily the owner of the design right) threatens another person with such proceedings, a person aggrieved by the threats (not necessarily the person threatened; but perhaps a supplier whose customers were threatened) may bring an action against the threatener claiming a declaration that the threats are unjustifiable, an injunction against their continuance, and damages in respect of any loss which he has sustained from them. If the plaintiff proves that the threats were made and that he is a person aggrieved by them, the action will succeed unless the defendant shows that the acts in respect of which proceedings were threatened did constitute, or would if done have constituted, an infringement of the design right. But mere notification that a design is protected by design right does not constitute a threat of proceedings for this purpose.

Jurisdiction of the comptroller and the court

As has been seen, the comptroller has jurisdiction to determine the terms of licences of right.[140] In addition s. 246 empowers the comptroller to give a binding decision, on a reference by a party to a dispute, as to the subsistence, term or first ownership of a design right, and no other court or tribunal may decide such a matter except on appeal or reference from the comptroller, or incidentally in infringement or other proceedings, or in proceedings brought with the agreement of the parties or the leave of the comptroller.[141] The comptroller has jurisdiction to decide any incidental question of fact or law arising in the course of such a reference,[142] but in such proceedings he may at any time refer the whole of the proceedings or any question or issue of fact or law to the High Court or the Court of Session, and must so refer if the parties agree to such a reference.[143] On such a reference the court may exercise any power available to the comptroller relating to the matter referred, and after giving its decision may refer any matter back to the comptroller.[144] In addition an appeal lies from a decision of the comptroller in proceedings under s. 246 to the High Court or the Court of Session.[145] On the other hand, actions for infringement or groundless threats, and disputes relating to Crown use, are brought in the court.[146]

SEMICONDUCTOR TOPOGRAPHIES

Implementing EC Directive 87/54 on the Legal Protection of Topographies of Semiconductor Products,[147] and replacing the Semiconductor Products (Protection of Topography) Regulations 1987,[148] the Design Right (Semiconductor Topographies) Regulations 1989 (hereafter 'the 1989 Regulations')[149] apply Part III of the 1988 Act (on unregistered design right), subject to certain modifications, to semiconductor topographies.

Regulation 1 of the 1989 Regulations elaborately defines 'semiconductor topography' as a design of a pattern to be fixed in or on a layer of a semiconductor product, or in or on a layer of material in the manufacture of a semiconductor product, or a design of the arrangement of the patterns to be fixed in or on the layers of a semiconductor product in relation to one another; and 'semiconductor product' as an article whose purpose is the performance of an electronic function and which consists of two or more layers, at least one of which is composed of semiconducting material, and in or on one or more of which is fixed a pattern relating to a function. More simply, this legislation is concerned with designs for patterns of electronic circuitry to be applied to silicon or similar chips for use in computers.

The 1989 Regulations contain their own provisions as to the connecting factors necessary for the existence of design right in semiconductor topographies, which implement EC Decisions 87/532[150] and 88/311[151] and replace ss. 217 and 220(1) of the 1988 Act. Under reg. 4 of and the Schedule to the 1989 Regulations, the designer, commissioner or employer to whom the design right initially belongs must be:

(i) a British citizen, a British Dependent Territory citizen, a citizen of another Member State of the European Community, or a citizen of Japan, Switzerland, the United States, Austria, Finland, a French overseas territory,[152] Iceland, Norway, or Sweden; or

(ii) an individual habitually resident in the United Kingdom, another EC Member State, the Isle of Man, the Channel Islands, any British colony, Japan, Switzerland, the United States, Austria, Finland, a French overseas territory, Iceland, Norway, or Sweden;

or

(iii) the government of the United Kingdom or another EC Member State; or

(iv) a corporation which has in the United Kingdom, another EC Member State, or Gibraltar a place of business at which substantial business activity is carried on; or

(v) a corporation which is formed under the law of the United Kingdom, another EC Member State, Gibraltar, Japan, Switzerland or the United States, and which has a place of business in Japan, Switzerland or the United States at which substantial business activity is carried on.

If the designer, commissioner or employer does not qualify under these tests, design right will still exist if

(a) the first marketer of articles made to the design is a British citizen, a citizen of another EC Member State, an individual habitually resident in the United Kingdom or another EC Member State, the government of the United Kingdom or another EC Member State, or a corporation which has in the United Kingdom, another EC Member State or Gibraltar a place of business at which substantial business activity is carried on; and

(b) the first marketer has an exclusive licence covering the whole of the European Community;

(c) the first marketing takes place within the European Community.

As regards ownership, reg. 5 of the 1989 Regulations enables first ownership of the design right in a semiconductor topography created in pursuance of a commission or in the course of employment to be vested in the designer by means of a written agreement with the commissioner or employer. As regards duration, the period of protection for a semiconductor topography is similar to that for other types of design,[153] but the provision in Part III of the Act for the automatic availability of licences of right in the last five years of the term is made inapplicable to semiconductor topographies.[154]

As regards primary infringement, the test of substantial similarity under Part III of the Act is replaced by one of copying a substantial part of the topography, but it is declared permissible to copy a topography for purposes of analysis or evaluation, or of teaching concepts, processes, systems or techniques.[155] As regards secondary infringement, 'infringing article' is made to include a design document, but an extended doctrine of exhaustion covers articles previously sold or hired out in another EC Member State or Gibraltar by or with the consent of the person then having marketing rights there.[156]

Notes

CHAPTER 1: INTRODUCTION

1 International Convention for the Protection of Literary and Artistic Works, signed at Berne on 9 September 1886, last revised at Paris in 1971; see Cmnd. 5002 (1972). All the EEC countries are also parties to the Universal Copyright Convention, signed at Geneva on 6 September 1952, revised at Paris in 1971; see Cmnd. 4905. Since the requirements of the Universal Copyright Convention are less demanding than those of the Berne Convention, it is the Berne Convention which is of major importance in the European context.

2 Art. 2(3).

3 Art. 2(5).

4 See Cmnd. 2425.

5 See Cmnd. 5275.

6 Convention on the Grant of European Patents, signed at Munich on 5 October 1973. See [1974] I.L.M. 270.

7 See the Berne Convention, Art. 7(1); the 1988 Act, s. 12(1); and pp. 35–9, below.

8 See the Berne Convention, Art. 5(2). Cf. the Universal Copyright Convention, Art. III(1), permitting a Contracting State to the Universal (but not the Berne) Convention (such as, until recently, the United States) to insist that published copies of foreign works should bear the symbol ©, accompanied by the name of the copyright owner and the year of first publication.

9 See s. 46(5) of the 1956 Act.

10 With minor exceptions, the 1988 Act came into operation on 1 August 1989; see s. 305 and the Copyright, Designs and Patents Act 1988 (Commencement No. 1) Order 1989, S.I. 1989/816. See also the Copyright, Designs and Patents Act 1988 (Commencement No. 2) Order 1989, S.I. 1989/955, and the Copyright, Designs and Patents Act 1988 (Commencement No. 3) Order 1989, S.I. 1989/1032.

11 Sch. 8 of the 1988 Act repeals in their entirety the Copyright Act 1956, the Design Copyright Act 1968, the Copyright (Amendment) Act 1971, the Copyright Act 1956 (Amendment) Act 1982, the Copyright (Amendment) Act 1983, and the Copyright (Computer Software) Amendment Act 1985.

12 See the Whitford Report on *Copyright and Designs Law*, Cmnd. 6732 (1977); the Green Paper on *Reform of the Law relating to Copyright, Designs and Performers' Protection*, Cmnd. 8302 (1981); the Green Paper on *Intellectual Property Rights and Innovation*, Cmnd. 9117 (1983); and the Green Paper on *The Recording and Rental of Audio and Video Copyright Material*, Cmnd. 9445 (1985).

13 Cmnd. 9712 (1986). Hereafter 'the 1986 White Paper'.

14 See chap. 2, below.

15 See chap. 3, below.

16 See chap. 6, below.

17 See chap. 5, pp. 103–4, below.

18 See chap. 4, below.

19 See chap. 5, pp. 104–15, below.

20 See chap. 2, pp. 30–4, below.

21 These are repealed by Sch. 8.

22 See chap. 7, below.

23 On industrial designs, see chap. 8 below.

24 Exceptions made by the Schedule are referred to in their context in subsequent chapters.

25 Sch. 1, paras. 1(3) and 3.

26 Sch. 1, para. 4.

27 Sch. 1, para. 5(1).

28 Sch. 1, paras. 10 and 11(1).

29 Sch. 1, paras. 14(1), 31(1) and 33(1).

30 COM (88) 172 final, released on 7 June 1988.

31 The Commission's views on the protection of computer programs are considered at relevant points in chaps. 2 and 3 below. In January 1989 the Commission filed with the Council a proposal for a directive under Article 100A of the EEC Treaty (as amended), designed to harmonize the laws of the Member States in relation to the protection of computer programs within the framework of copyright; see [1989] O.J.E.C. C91/13.

32 Reg. 3842/86, [1986] O.J. L357/1.

33 With regard to digital sound recordings, the Commission contemplates the adoption and enforcement of technical measures to limit the copying facility of digital audio tape recorders which may be made available to the public. Non-brain-damaged digital recorders would be available only to holders of special licences, such as companies which issue legitimate recordings.

34 [1984] O.J. L252/1.

35 See a press-release, P–88, 6 July 1988.

36 Art. 7 of the Directive proposed by the Commission in January 1989 (see n. 31 above) specifies a duration of fifty years from the creation of the program.

CHAPTER 2: SUBSISTENCE

1 Sch. 1, paras. 1(3) and 3.

2 Sch. 1, para. 5(1).

3 Sch. 1, paras. 10 and 11(1).

4 Replacing ss. 2 and 3 of the 1956 Act.

5 S. 48(1) defined 'writing' as including any form of notation, whether by hand or by printing, typewriting or any similar process.

6 E.g. by recording on tape or on a computer chip or disk; see per Mason and Walsh JJ., dissenting in the High Court of Australia, in *Computer Edge Pty. Ltd. v. Apple Computer Inc.* [1986] F.S.R. 537 at 556.

7 See para. 9.4.

8 Cf. s. 17(6), under which the making of transient copies amounts to infringement by copying; see pp. 43–5, below.

9 See chap. 7, below.

10 In the United States, which has long been a party to the Universal Copyright Convention, a work normally had to be registered with the Copyright Office before an action for infringement was brought, and a notice claiming copyright normally had to be placed on copies distributed to the public; see 17 U.S. Code, ss. 401–11. But the United States has recently acceded to the Berne Convention.

11 See *Libraco v. Shaw Walker* (1913) 30 T.L.R. 22.

12 See *Cramp v. Smythson* [1944] A.C. 329.

13 See *Leslie v. Young* [1894] A.C. 335.

14 See *Francis Day v. 20th Century Fox* [1940] A.C. 112, involving 'The man who broke the bank at Monte Carlo', and *Ladbroke v. Hill* [1964] 1 W.L.R. 273 at 286.

15 See *Exxon Corp. v. Exxon Insurance Consultants International Ltd.* [1982] Ch. 119, where, however, the Court of Appeal emphasized that the word lacked meaning except as a trade mark, and afforded neither information, instruction nor literary enjoyment. This test was derived from *Hollinrake v. Truswell* [1894] 3 Ch. 420, which held that a cardboard sleeve chart, with certain scales of measurements on it, for use in dressmaking, was not a literary work. The test was, however, declared not to be an exhaustive definition of a literary work by Mason and Walsh JJ.,

dissenting, in the High Court of Australia in *Computer Edge Pty. Ltd. v. Apple Computer Inc.* [1986] F.S.R. 537 at 553–54, and their view is now confirmed in the United Kingdom by the statutory definition of 'literary work' as including a computer program (see pp. 12–19, below).

16 See s. 11, considered on pp. 26–30, below.

17 See s. 12, considered on pp. 35–8, below.

18 See Phillips, *Introduction to Intellectual Property Law*, at para. 11.12.

19 See s. 178.

20 This departs from the proposals of the 1986 White Paper, which rejected suggestions for the enactment of specific provisions to determine the authorship of computer-aided works, and envisaged leaving the question to the general principle referring to the person (if any) who provided the essential skill and labour in the creation of the work, and to the existing provisions concerning joint authorship; see paras. 9.6–9.8.

21 See the Green Paper, n. 70 below, at paras. 5.6.24–25.

22 [1916] 2 Ch. 601.

23 (1923) 93 L.J.P.C. 113.

24 See *Macmillan v. Cooper* (1923) 93 L.J.P.C. 113, which involved a selection from North's translation of Plutarch's *Life of Alexander*, but which admitted an exception in the case of closely-reasoned scientific works.

25 See *Byrne v. Statist* [1914] 1 K.B. 622 and *Cummins v. Bond* [1927] 1 Ch. 167. See also s. 21(4) of the 1988 Act (replacing s. 1(2) of the Copyright (Computer Software) Amendment Act 1985), defining 'translation', in relation to a computer program, as including a version converted into a different computer language or code.

26 See *Graves' Case* (1869) L.R. 4 Q.B. 715.

27 See *Martin v. Polyplas* [1969] N.Z.L.R. 1046.

28 See *Arnold v. Miafern* [1980] R.P.C. 397.

29 See per Whitford J. in *LB (Plastics) v. Swish Products* [1979] R.P.C. 551. But in the sphere of industrial designs, copyright is now excluded in favour of a special unregistered design right, governed by Part III of the new Act; see chap. 8 below.

30 [1988] 3 W.L.R. 678.

31 Formerly s. 48(1) of the 1956 Act defined 'literary work' as including any written table or compilation, and 'writing' as including any form of notation, whether by hand or by printing, typewriting or any similar process.

32 Formerly the Copyright (Computer Software) Amendment Act 1985 provided in effect that a computer program should be treated as a literary work for the purposes of copyright (see s. 1(1)), and that the storage of a work in a computer should constitute a fixation of the work (see s. 2).

33 Formerly s. 48(1) of the 1956 Act defined 'dramatic work' as including a choreographic work or an entertainment in dumb show, if reduced to writing in the form in which it is to be presented, but not a cinematograph film, as distinct from a scenario or script for a cinematograph film.

34 Cf. *Waterlow Publishers Ltd v. Rose, The Times*, 8 December 1989, where C.A. seem to accept that a company may be an author of a compilation. There was no definition of musical work in the 1956 Act.

35 See, however, *Green v. Broadcasting Corp. of New Zealand, The Times* of 24 July 1989, where the Privy Council held that a dramatic work must have sufficient unity to be capable of performance, and thus that the so-called 'format' of a television series of talent, quiz or game shows (in casu, *Opportunity Knocks*), comprising a title, the use of certain catch phrases, the use of a 'clapometer' to measure audience reaction, and the use of sponsors to introduce competitors, amounted only to accessories to be used in the presentation of some other performance, and thus did not attract copyright.

36 Now 17 U.S. Code, ss. 101–810.

37 Cf. *Exxon Corp. v. Exxon Insurance Consultants* [1981] 3 All E.R. 241, where C.A. rejected the single invented word, 'Exxon', as affording neither meaning (except when used as a trade mark), nor information, instruction, or literary enjoyment.

38 [1916] 2 Ch. 601.

39 See *University of London Press v. University Tutorial Press* [1916] 2 Ch. 601.

40 See *Blacklock v. Pearson* [1915] 2 Ch. 376.

41 See *Collis v. Cater* (1898) 78 L.T. 613.

42 See *Purefoy v. Sykes Boxall* (1955) 72 R.P.C. 89.

43 See *Kelly v. Morris* (1866) L.R. 1 Eq. 697.

44 See *Football League v. Littlewoods Pools* [1959] Ch. 637.

45 See *Ladbroke v. Hill* [1964] 1 W.L.R. 273.

46 See *Portway Press v. Hague* [1957] R.P.C. 426.

47 See *Byrne v. Statist* [1914] 1 K.B. 622 and *Cummins v. Bond* [1927] 1 Ch. 167.

48 Cf. s. 21(4) of the 1988 Act, replacing s. 1(2) of the Copyright (Computer Software) Amendment Act 1985.

49 See *Warwick Film Productions v. Eisinger* [1969] 1 Ch. 508, which involved selection from and editing of a trial transcript.

50 See *Macmillan v. Cooper* (1923) 93 L.J.P.C. 113.

51 See *Macmillan v. Suresh Chunder Deb*, approved in *Macmillan v. Cooper*, n. 50 above, at 119–20.

52 See *Football League v. Littlewoods Pools*, n. 44 above.

53 See *Ladbroke v. Hill*, n. 45 above.

54 See *Sweet v. Benning* (1855) 139 E.R. 838, involving headnotes to law reports; cf. *Macmillan v. Cooper*, n. 50, rejecting a mere selection of verbatim passages from a biographical work with notes linking them.

55 See *Wood v. Boosey* (1868) L.R. 3 Q.B. 223.

56 See *Football League v. Littlewoods Pools*, n. 44 above, and *Ladbroke v. Hill*, n. 45 above.

57 See pp. 5–8, above.

58 S. 1(1) of the 1985 Act applied to programs created before as well as after the commencement of the 1985 Act on 16 September 1985, and applied whether or not copyright would otherwise have subsisted, but did not affect infringements or offences committed before that date; see ss. 1(1) and 4(3) & (4) of the 1985 Act.

59 S. 1(2) of the (British) Patents Act 1977, and Art. 52(2) of the European Patent Convention (1973), exclude an invention from patentability to the extent that it relates to a computer program as such. The scope of this exclusion has recently been clarified by the Technical Board of Appeal of the European Patent Office in *Vicom System Inc.'s Patent Application*, [1987] 1 EPO Journal 14, approved in the European Commission's *Green Paper on Copyright* (at paras. 5.3.3 and 5.5.2), and by the English Court of Appeal in *Genentech Inc.'s Patent*, [1989] R.P.C. 147, and *Re Merrill Lynch, Pierce, Fenner & Smith Inc.'s Application, The Times* of 27 April 1989, affirming on different grounds the decision of Falconer J., [1988] R.P.C. 1, to the effect that the exclusion catches not only a claim for a new computer program *simpliciter*, but also a claim for a floppy disk or other conventional medium containing a new program, or (subject to what follows) a claim for a conventional computer containing or running a new program. But a combination of elements which includes a computer program may be patentable if it amounts to a technical advance over the prior art in the form of a new result, such as an increase in processing speed or a change in a physical entity (whether a material object or an image stored as an electric signal). In such a case the combination will be patentable even though the only feature of the combination which is new and inventive is the program, but it will be fatal if the new result itself falls into another category excluded from patentability, such as a method of doing business or a presentation of information. See also *Diamond v Diehr*, 450 U.S. 175 (1981).

60 See pp. 23–5, below.

61 17 U.S. Code, s. 101 (as amended in 1980).

62 The exclusion of an incidental conversion is an addition by the 1988 Act.

63 [1983] F.S.R. 73.

64 [1983] F.S.R. 502.

65 [1986] F.S.R. 537. The majority holding in that case, denying that an object-code version is an adaptation of the source-code version from which it is derived, is in any event now overruled in the United Kingdom

by s. 21(4) of the 1988 Act, replacing the similar provision of s. 1(2) of the 1985 Act. See also (from Canada and South Africa) *I.B.M. Corp. v. Ordinateurs Spirales Inc.* (1984) 80 C.P.R. (2d) 187; *La Société d'Informatique R.D.G. Inc. v. Dynabec Ltd.* (14 August 1984, unrep.); and *Northern Micro Computers v. Rosenstein* [1982] F.S.R. 124.

66 See *Babolat–Maillot–With v. Pachot*, Paris C.A., 2 November 1982; *Apple Computer v. Segimex* [1985] F.S.R. 608, Paris Trib., 21 September 1983; and *Atari v. Sidam*, Cass., 7 March 1986.

67 See *Visicorp v. Basis Software GmbH*, LG Munich, 1983; and *Sudwestdeutsche Inkasso KG v. Bappert & Burker Computer GmbH*, Fed. Sup. Court, 1985.

68 See *Atari Inc. and Bertolini v. Didam Srl.*, Turin Trib., 14 July 1983; and *Unicomp Srl. v. Italcomputers and General Informatics*, Pisa Trib., 14 April 1984.

69 See *The 'Logboekprogram' Case*, Hertogenbosch Dist. Court, 14 May 1982.

70 COM (88) 172 final, issued on 7 June 1988. Chapter 5, pp. 170–204, of the Green Paper deals specifically with computer programs.

72 See especially at para. 5.3.9.

72 See [1989] O.J.E.C. C91/13, [1989] 2 C.M.L.R. 180.

73 See pp. 9–11, above.

74 This replaces, without change of substance, s. 49(4) of the Copyright Act 1956, by which a literary work was regarded as made when it was first reduced to writing or some other material form, and s. 2 of the Copyright (Computer Software) Amendment Act 1985, by which the storage of a work in a computer was treated as its reduction to a material form.

75 See n. 70 above, at para. 5.6.8.

76 See n. 72 above.

77 See *Sudwestdeutsche Inkasso KG v. Bappert & Burker Computer GmbH*, (1985).

78 See *Atari v. Sidam*, Cass., 7 March 1986.

79 See the Green Paper, n. 70, at para. 5.6.7.

80 See n. 72 above.

81 See s. 4(3) of the 1985 Act. By s. 4(4), the 1985 Act did not affect infringements or offences committed before its commencement.

82 See s. 1(1) of the 1985 Act.

83 The case-law prior to the 1985 Act recognized the existence of copyright at least in a source-code version of a program; see text to nn. 63–5, above.

84 For recognition of copyright in object code under similar legislation in the United States, see *Apple Computer Inc. v. Franklin Computer Corp.*, 714 F.2d 1240 (C3, 1983), and *Apple Computer Inc. v. Formula*

International Inc., 725 F.2d 521 (C9, 1984); both involving the operating system for the APPLE II computer.

85 See s. 21(3) & (4). No doubt for a document or an electronic file expressed in a human language to amount to a computer program, and not merely an ordinary literary work, it would have to specify the structure and logic of the program in such detail that the writing of source code would be a task analogous to translating an ordinary document from one human language into another.

86 Such a distinction has been rejected in the United States (see the cases cited in n. 84, above), and there is nothing in the British legislation to support any such distinction.

87 See n. 70 above.

88 See [1989] O.J.E.C. C91/13.

89 Formerly s. 3(1)(a) of the 1956 Act referred to paintings, sculptures, drawings, engravings and photographs. It should be noted that, except for sculptures and engravings, these were all two-dimensional.

90 S. 4(1)(a).

91 S. 4(2).

92 S. 4(2).

93 See *Kenrick v. Lawrence* (1890) 25 Q.B.D. 99.

94 See *Taverner Rutledge v. Specters* [1959] R.P.C. 355.

95 See *Walker v. British Picker* [1961] R.P.C. 57.

96 [1977] R.P.C. 537 at 558.

97 See also *Lerose v. Hawick Jersey* [1974] R.P.C. 42, holding that 'drawing' includes a point-pattern giving instructions for setting a knitting-machine so as to reproduce the pattern in knitted fabric.

98 [1965] Ch. 1.

99 See Chap. 8, below.

100 S. 4(1)(b). By s. 4(2), 'building' includes any fixed structure, and a part of a building or fixed structure.

101 S. 4(1)(c).

102 [1976] A.C. 64.

103 [1984] F.S.R. 358.

104 See [1986] R.P.C. 115, where an appeal on other points was dismissed by the Court of Appeal.

105 By Sch. 1, paras. 2(2) and 7, of the new Act, there is no copyright in a film as such if the film was made before the commencement of the 1956 Act (on 1 June 1957), though such a film may continue to receive protection as an original dramatic work or as a series of photographs.

106 By Sch. 1, para. 9, of the new Act, no copyright subsists in a broadcast made before the commencement of the 1956 Act (on 1 June 1957), or in a cable programme transmitted before 1 January 1985, and

such a broadcast or transmission is ignored for the purpose of the duration of copyright in repeats under s. 14(2) of the new Act.

107 Formerly s. 12(8) & (9) of the 1956 Act defined 'sound recording' as the aggregate of the sounds embodied in, and capable of being reproduced by means of, a record of any type, but with the exclusion of a sound-track associated with a cinematograph film, and accorded copyright to the first record embodying the recording, i.e. the master tape.

108 Formerly s. 13(10) of the 1956 Act defined a 'cinematograph film' as a sequence of visual images recorded on any material so as to be capable, by the use of that material, of being shown as a moving picture, or of being recorded on other material by the use of which it could be so shown.

109 By Sch. 1, para. 8(1), of the new Act, a sound-track created before the commencement date is thereafter no longer treated as part of the film, but separately as a sound recording. However, by para. 8(2), the authorship of, and the duration and first ownership of copyright in, such a recording will follow those of the film.

110 669 F.2d 852 (C2, 1982). See also *Williams Electronics Inc. v. Artic International Inc.*, 685 F.2d 870 (C3, 1982); *Midway Manufacturing Co. v. Strohan*, 564 F.Supp. 741 (N.D. Ill., 1983); and *M. Kramer Manufacturing Co. v. Andrews*, 783 F.2d 421 (C4, 1986).

111 See *WGN Continental Broadcasting Co. v. United Video*, 693 F.2d 622 (C7, 1982).

112 659 F. Supp. 449 (N.D. Ga., 1987). For an excellent review, see A.L. Middleton, *A Thousand Clones: the Scope of Copyright Protection in the 'Look and Feel' of Computer Programs*, 63 Washington Law Review 195 (1988).

113 648 F. Supp. 1127 (N.D. Cal., 1986).

114 [1987] F.S.R. 1, 797 F.2d 1222 (C3, 1986).

115 Under the 1956 Act, 'broadcast' meant by wireless telegraphy; 'television broadcast' referred to visual images broadcast by way of television, together with any sounds broadcast for reception along with such images; and 'sound broadcast' referred to sounds broadcast otherwise than as part of a television broadcast (see ss. 14(10) and 48(2)).

116 'Wireless telegraphy' is defined by s. 178 as the sending of electro-magnetic energy over paths not provided by a material substance constructed or arranged for the purpose.

117 By s. 6(2), an encrypted transmission is not regarded as capable of being lawfully received by members of the public unless decoding equipment has been made available to members of the public by or with the authority of the person making the transmission or the person providing its contents.

118 S. 6(6).

119 Defined by s. 178 as a system for conveying visual images, sounds or other information by electronic means.

120 Defined by s. 7(2)(a) as a service of which it is an essential feature that, while visual images, sounds or other information are being conveyed by the person providing the service, there will or may be sent from each place of reception, by means of the same system or part of system, information (other than signals sent for the operation or control of the service) for reception by the person providing the service or other persons receiving it.

121 Defined by s. 7(2)(b) as a service where (i) the service is run for the purpose of a business, and (ii) no person except the person carrying on the business is concerned in the control of the apparatus comprised in the system, and (iii) the visual images, sounds or other information are conveyed by the system solely for purposes internal to the running of the business and not by way of rendering a service or providing amenities for others, and (iv) the system is not connected to any other telecommunications system.

122 Defined by s. 7(2)(c) as a service where (i) the service is run by a single individual, and (ii) all the apparatus comprised in the system is under his control, and (iii) the visual images, sounds or other information conveyed by the service are conveyed solely for domestic purposes of the individual running it, and (iv) the system is not connected to any other telecommunications system.

123 Defined by s. 7(2)(d) as services where (i) all the apparatus comprised in the system is situated in, or connects, premises which are in single occupation, (ii) the system is not connected to any other telecommunications system, and (iii) the services are not operated as part of the amenities provided for residents or inmates of premises run as a business.

124 Defined by s. 7(2)(e) as services run for persons providing broadcasting or cable programme services or providing programmes for such services.

125 S. 7(3) and (4). Such an order may contain transitional provisions.

126 S. 7(6).

127 See s. 14(2) and (3) of the new Act, following s. 14(3) of the 1956 Act.

128 See s. 8(1).

129 See s. 17(6) of the new Act. S. 178 specifies that 'facsimile copy' includes a copy which is reduced or enlarged in scale. Under s. 15(3) of the 1956 Act, it was infringement to copy the typographical arrangement of the edition by means of a photographic or similar process.

130 See s. 8(2) of the new Act, replacing s. 15(1) of the 1956 Act.

131 The 1956 Act spoke of the 'author' of an original literary, dramatic,

musical or artistic work, and of the 'maker' of a sound recording, cinematograph film or broadcast. By Sch. 1, para. 10, of the new Act, the authorship of a work created before its commencement is determined in accordance with the law in force at its creation.

132 See *Walter v. Lane* [1900] A.C. 539 and *Donoghue v. Allied Newspapers* [1938] Ch. 106.

133 See *Donoghue v. Allied Newspapers*, n. 132 above.

134 See *Cummins v. Bond* [1927] 1 Ch. 167 and *Leah v. Two Worlds* [1951] Ch. 393.

135 [1921] 1 Ch. 503.

136 [1900] A.C. 539.

137 [1976] R.P.C. 169.

138 Admittedly s. 3(3) also, rather puzzlingly, saves the question whether copyright subsists in a record made without the author's permission, as distinct from in the work itself.

139 S. 9(2)(a). Under the 1956 Act, initial ownership of copyright in a sound recording or a film normally belonged to the 'maker', defined as the owner of the first record embodying the recording or the person who arranged for the making of the film (i.e. the production company); see ss. 12(4) & (8) and 13(4) & (10).

140 Ss. 6(3), 9(2)(b) and 10(2).

141 Ss. 7(5) and 9(2)(c).

142 S. 9(2)(d), replacing s. 15(2) of the 1956 Act.

143 On the assignment or licensing of copyright, see pp. 103–4, below.

144 See ss. 10 and 11(1) of the new Act.

145 A work is of unknown authorship if the identity of the author, or all the joint authors, is unknown in the sense that it is not, and has not previously been, possible to ascertain the identity of the author, or any of the joint authors, by reasonable inquiry (see s. 9(4) & (5) of the new Act).

146 See s. 104(1) & (4), and pp. 38–40, below.

147 Ss. 11(2) and 178; replacing ss. 4(4) & (5) of the 1956 Act. The former rule (under s. 4(2) of the 1956 Act) whereby an author employed as a journalist was entitled to the copyright in his work except as regards publication in a newspaper, magazine or similar periodical is no longer retained.

148 See ss. 11(3) and 163, replacing s. 39 of the 1956 Act, under which the Crown was also entitled to copyright in an original work which was first published by or under the direction of the Crown. S. 163 of the new Act applies to a work (other than an Act of Parliament, a Measure of the General Synod, or a work to which Parliamentary copyright applies) created before its commencement if s. 39 of the 1956 Act applied to the

work immediately before such commencement, but the Crown's title in such a case is subject to any agreement entered into before commencement under s. 39(6) of the 1956 Act; see Sch. 1, para. 40, of the 1988 Act. Somewhat puzzlingly, in view of the provisions of s. 163(3) on the duration of Crown copyright, s. 163(4) provides that, in the case of a work of joint authorship where one or more, but not all, of the authors are officers or servants of the Crown acting in the course of their duties, s. 163 applies only in relation to the former authors and the copyright arising by virtue of their contribution to the work.

149 See ss. 157, 158 and 178. But the provisions on Crown and Parliamentary copyright do not apply to formerly dependent territories, even where they continue to be treated as extended territories for other purposes; see s. 158(2)(b).

150 S. 164; which extends to existing Acts of Parliament and Measures of the General Synod or the Church Assembly (see Sch. 1, para. 42).

151 See ss. 11(3) and 165, which (by Sch. 1, para. 43(1)) extends to existing unpublished literary, dramatic, musical or artistic works, but not to other works created before commencement. For this purpose the Speaker (in the case of the Commons) or the Clerk of the Parliaments (in the case of the Lords) will act on behalf of the House; see s. 167.

152 S. 165(4). As regards works of joint authorship, s. 165(5) makes a similar provision to that made for Crown copyright by s. 163(4), as to which see n. 148 above.

153 S. 165(7) and (8). As to formerly dependent territories, see n. 149 above.

154 S. 166. For transitional provisions, see Sch. 1, para. 43(2).

155 I.e. an organization whose members include one or more States (s. 178).

156 As to connecting factors, see pp. 30–4, below.

157 See ss. 11(3) and 168, replacing s. 33 of the 1956 Act. By Sch. 1, para. 44(1), of the new Act, any work in which immediately before its commencement copyright subsisted by virtue of s. 33 of the 1956 Act is treated as satisfying s. 168, but otherwise s. 168 does not apply if the relevant creation or publication took place before such commencement. By the Copyright (International Organizations) Order 1957, S.I. 1957/ 1524, as amended by S.I. 1958/1052, the following organizations were designated under s. 33 of the 1956 Act: the United Nations Organization; the Specialized Agencies of the United Nations Organization; the Organization of American States; the Council of Europe; the Organization for European Economic Co-operation; the Baghdad Pact Organization; and the Western European Union.

158 See the Copyright (International Organizations) Order 1989, S.I. 1989/989.

159 [1988] 3 A11 E.R. 545.

160 COM (88) 172 final, issued on 7 June 1988, at paras. 5.6.24–5.6.25.

161 It by no means follows that a British court cannot entertain an action for infringement abroad of a copyright granted by the law of the place of the infringing act. Indications to the contrary in *Def Lepp Music v. Stuart-Brown* [1986] R.P.C. 273 and *James Burrough Distillers v. Speymalt Whisky Distributors, The Times* of 30 January 1989, are open to the gravest doubt, as ignoring *Boys v Chaplin* [1971] A.C. 356 and Title II of the EEC Convention of 27 September 1968 on Jurisdiction and the Enforcement of Judgments in Civil and Commercial Matters (as amended), now implemented in the United Kingdom by the Civil Jurisdiction and Judgments Act 1982.

162 See Cmnd. 5002 (1972); and pp. 1–3, above.

163 See Cmnd. 4905; and pp. 1–3, above.

164 Collecting, without important alteration, provisions scattered about the 1956 Act, including ss. 1(5), 2(1) & (2), 3(2) & (3), 12(1) & (2), 13(1) & (2), 15(1), 31, 32 and 49(2)(d). By Sch. 1, para. 35, of the new Act, every work in which copyright subsisted under the 1956 Act immediately before the commencement of the new Act is deemed to satisfy the connecting-factor requirements of the new Act.

165 See ss. 157(1), 161 and 162; replacing s. 51(3) of the 1956 Act. The extension to territorial waters, the continental shelf, ships, hovercraft and aircraft does not apply in relation to things done before commencement; see Sch. 1, paras. 38 and 39.

166 The following are the territories, currently or formerly dependent on the United Kingdom, to which the 1956 Act has been extended by Order under s. 31 thereof: Bermuda (S.I.1962/1642 and 1985/1985); British Indian Ocean Territory (S.I. 1984/541); British Virgin Islands (S.I. 1962/2185 and 1985/1988); Cayman Islands (S.I. 1965/2010); Falkland Islands and Dependencies (S.I. 1963/1037); Gibraltar (S.I. 1960/847 and 1985/1986); Hong Kong (S.I. 1972/1724); Isle of Man (S.I. 1986/1299); Montserrat (S.I. 1965/1858 and 1985/1987); and St Helena and its Dependencies (Ascension, Tristan da Cunha) (S.I. 1963/1038). The Copyright, Designs and Patents Act 1988 (Isle of Man) Order 1989, S.I. 1989/981, extends provisions of the 1988 Act relating to registered designs, trade marks and patents, but not those relating to copyright, rights in performances or unregistered design right, to the Isle of Man. See also the Registered Designs Act 1949 (Isle of Man) Order 1989 (S.I. 1989/982), and the Patents, Designs and Marks Act 1986 (Amendments to the Registered Designs Act 1949 and the Patents Act 1977) (Isle of Man) Order 1989 (S.I. 1989/493).

167 See ss. 25(1) and 37(2)(c) of the 1911 Act; Sch. 7, para. 41, of the 1956 Act; and Sch. 1, para. 36(1) and (4), of the 1988 Act.

Notes

168 By Sch. 1, para. 5, a work created before the commencement of
the new Act may obtain copyright by virtue of a connection of the author
or the place of first publication with a country which is designated as a
reciprocating country by an Order made under the new Act.
169 All EEC countries are now parties to the Berne Copyright
Convention, and also to the Universal Copyright Convention.
170 Sch. 1 to the Copyright (Application to Other Countries) Order
1989, S.I. 1989/988, lists the following countries as reciprocating countries
for most purposes: Algeria; Andorra; Argentina; Australia (including
Norfolk Island); Austria; Bahamas; Bangladesh; Barbados; Belgium;
Belize; Benin; Brazil; Bulgaria; Burkina; Cameroon; Canada; Central
African Republic; Chad; Chile; Colombia; People's Republic of Congo;
Costa Rica; Côte d'Ivoire; Cuba; Republic of Cyprus; Czechoslovakia;
Denmark (including the Faeroe Islands); Dominican Republic; Ecuador;
Egypt; El Salvador; Fiji; Finland; France (including all Overseas
Departments and Territories); Gabon; German Democratic Republic
(and East Berlin); Federal Republic of Germany (and West Berlin);
Ghana; Greece; Guatemala; Republic of Guinea; Haiti; Holy See;
Hungary; Iceland; India; Republic of Ireland; Israel; Italy; Japan;
Kampuchea; Kenya; Republic of Korea; Laos; Lebanon; Libya;
Liechtenstein; Luxembourg; Madagascar; Malawi; Mali; Malta;
Mauritania; Mauritius; Mexico; Monaco; Morocco; Netherlands
(including Aruba and the Netherlands Antilles); New Zealand;
Nicaragua; Niger; Nigeria; Norway; Pakistan; Panama; Paraguay; Peru;
Philippines; Poland; Portugal; Romania; Rwanda; St. Vincent and the
Grenadines; Senegal; Singapore; South Africa; Soviet Union; Spain; Sri
Lanka; Surinam; Sweden; Switzerland; Taiwan; Thailand; Togo;
Trinidad and Tobago; Tunisia; Turkey; United States of America
(including Puerto Rico and all territories and possessions); Uruguay;
Venezuela; Yugoslavia; Zaire; Zambia; and Zimbabwe. All except
Singapore and Taiwan are listed as being parties to the Berne Copyright
Convention, or the Universal Copyright Convention, or both. In addition
Indonesia counts as a reciprocating country in relation to sound
recordings only; see S.I. 1989/988, Art. 3(b). The list given in Sch. 1 does
not, however, apply in relation to performing or broadcasting rights in
sound recordings (other than sound-tracks of films), nor in relation to the
protection of broadcasts or cable programmes, see nn. 171 and 172,
below. Nor does it apply to typefaces; see S.I. 1989/988, Art. 2(3).
171 Sch. 2 to the Copyright (Application to Other Countries) Order
1989 lists the following countries as reciprocating countries for this
purpose: Australia (including Norfolk Island); Austria; Barbados; Brazil;
Burkina; Chile; Colombia; People's Republic of Congo; Costa Rica;
Czechoslovakia; Denmark (including the Faeroe Islands); Dominican

185

Republic; Ecuador; El Salvador; Fiji; Finland; France (including all Overseas Departments and Territories); Federal Republic of Germany (and West Berlin); Guatemala; Indonesia; Republic of Ireland; Italy; Luxembourg; Mexico; Monaco; New Zealand; Niger; Norway; Pakistan; Panama; Paraguay; Peru; Philippines; Sweden; Taiwan; and Uruguay. All these countries, except Australia, Indonesia, New Zealand and Pakistan, are listed by virtue of being parties to the Rome Convention for the Protection of Performers, Producers of Phonograms and Broadcasting Organizations. It will be noted that only six EEC countries (other than the United Kingdom) qualify for this purpose.

172 By Sch. 3 to S.I. 988/1989, the following countries are designated as reciprocating (mainly as parties to the Rome Convention for the Protection of Performers, Producers of Phonograms and Broadcasting Organizations and/or the European Agreement on the Protection of Television Broadcasts): in relation to the protection of both sound and television broadcasts – Austria; Barbados; Brazil; Burkina; Chile; Colombia; People's Republic of Congo; Costa Rica; Czechoslovakia; Denmark (including the Faeroe Islands); Dominican Republic; Ecuador; El Salvador; Fiji; Finland; France (including all Overseas Departments and Territories); Federal Republic of Germany (and West Berlin); Guatemala; Republic of Ireland; Italy; Luxembourg; Mexico; Monaco; Niger; Norway; Panama; Paraguay; Peru; Philippines; Singapore; Sweden; and Uruguay; in relation to television (but not sound) broadcasts – Belgium; Republic of Cyprus; and Spain. Only Singapore is designated as reciprocating in relation to cable programmes; see S.I. 1989/988, Art. 4(6). It will be noted that only eight EEC countries (apart from the United Kingdom) qualify even in relation to television broadcasts.

173 See at paras. 5.6.28–29.

174 See n. 88 above.

175 S. 154(1)(a). It is noteworthy that Commonwealth citizens and Irish citizens are no longer included as such; cf. s. 1(5) of the 1956 Act and *Milltronics v. Hycontrol, The Times* of 2 March 1989.

176 Ss. 154(2) and 159(1)(a).

177 Ss. 154(1)(b) & (2) and 159(1)(a).

178 Ss. 154(1)(c) & (2) and 159(1)(b).

179 S. 154(3).

180 S. 155(3), replacing s. 49(2)(d) of the 1956 Act. By Sch. 1, para 5, of the new Act, the new rules enable a work created before the commencement date to obtain copyright by virtue of its first publication in a qualifying country after that date.

181 S. 154(4)(a).

182 S. 154(4)(b). On joint authorship, see n. 179 above.

183 Ss. 155(1) & (2) and 159(1)(c).

184 Ss. 154(5)(d) and 155.

185 S. 154(5)(a).

186 S. 155.

187 See n. 171 above.

188 Ss. 154(5)(b) & (c), 156 and 159(1)(d). Cf. s. 32 of the 1956 Act.

189 See n. 172, above.

190 See ss. 153(1) & (2), 157, 158, 163–67 and 178.

191 Ss. 153(2) and 168.

192 See ss. 2(5)(b) and 3(5)(b) of the 1956 Act; *Infabrics Ltd. v. Jaytex Ltd.* [1982] A.C. 1; and pp. 45–7, below.

193 For exceptions, see s. 12(2) and (5), which takes into account the first 'making available to the public' in connection with works of unknown authorship; s. 13(2), on the 'release' of sound recordings and films; and s. 15, on published editions.

194 See s. 18, and pp. 45–7, below.

195 Replacing with alterations ss. 49, 12(9) and 13(10) of the 1956 Act.

196 S. 175(1)(a), largely following ss. 49(2)(c), 12(9) and 13(10) of the 1956 Act. In the case of a literary, dramatic, musical or artistic work, an issue is also regarded as a 'commerical publication' if it takes place at a time when copies made in advance of the receipt of orders are generally available to the public; see s. 175(2)(a).

197 I.e. acts not authorized by the actual or prospective owner of the copyright; see ss. 175(6) and 178, largely following s. 49(3) of the 1956 Act. For a transitional provision, see Sch. 1, para. 46, of the new Act.

198 See s. 175(5), following s. 49(2)(b) of the 1956 Act, and *Francis Day & Hunter v. Feldman* [1914] 2 Ch. 728.

199 See *Francis Day & Hunter v. Feldman*, n. 198 above.

200 See *British Northrop v. Texteam* [1974] R.P.C. 57.

201 [1972] 1 W.L.R. 680.

202 Cf. the last clause of s. 49(2), and s. 12(9), of the 1956 Act.

203 S. 175(1)(b), which also applies to artistic works. Such publication is also regarded as 'commercial publication'; see s. 175(2)(b).

204 S. 175(4)(a). It should be noted that the issue of copies of a sound recording (as well as copies of a film) of a literary, dramatic or musical work now publishes the work; cf. s. 49(2)(a) of the 1956 Act.

205 S. 175(4)(b), largely following s. 49(2)(a).

206 S. 175(3), not following s. 49(2)(a) of the 1956 Act. The new rule does not apply if the construction of the building began before the commencement of the new Act; see Sch. 1, para. 45.

207 S. 175(4)(c).

208 For sentimental reasons, Parliament chose to extend indefinitely, but subject to licences of right at royalties fixed by the Copyright Tribunal, in favour of the Hospital for Sick Children, Great Ormond

Street, the performing rights in Sir James Barrie's play, *Peter Pan*, of which copyright had expired at the end of 1987; see s. 289 and Sch. 6 of the new Act.

209 See paras. 15.1 & 15.2. In the case of existing unpublished works of deceased authors, copyright will expire fifty years after the end of the calendar year in which Part I of the new Act comes into force; see Sch. 1, para. 10(2) & (3), implementing para. 15.8 of the 1986 White Paper.

210 See Sch. 1, para. 13(1).

211 S. 12(3).

212 See ss. 2(1)–(3) and 3(2)–(4) of the 1956 Act.

213 See Sch. 1, para. 12(2)(a) & (b), of the new Act.

214 See s. 3(4)(b) of the 1956 Act, and Sch. 1, para. 12(2)(c), of the 1988 Act. The former rules also continue to apply to photographs taken before the commencement of the 1956 Act; see para. 12(2)(c). The 1986 White Paper proposed to make copyright in a photograph expire fifty years after the end of the calendar year in which the photograph was taken (see para. 15.4), but this proposal was rejected by Parliament.

215 See Sch. 1, para. 12(4), of the new Act.

216 A work of joint authorship is one produced by the collaboration of two or more authors in which the contribution of each author is not distinct from the contribution of the other author(s); see s. 10(1).

217 S. 12(4)(a)(i).

218 S. 12(4)(a)(ii).

219 A work is of unknown authorship if the identity of the author, or all of the joint authors, is unknown, and the identity of an author is regarded as unknown if it is not, and has not previously been, possible to ascertain his identity by reasonable inquiry (s. 9(4) & (5)).

220 It is sufficient to make a literary, dramatic or musical work available to the public for it to be performed in public, broadcast or included in a cable service; or in the case of an artistic work for it to be exhibited in public or included in a film shown in public, a broadcast or a cable transmission; but unauthorized acts are disregarded; see s. 12(2).

221 S. 12(2) & (4)(b). For transitional provisions relating to works created before the new Act, see Sch. 1, para. 12(3).

222 See s. 57, which is based on the Paris Act to the Berne Convention, and implements a proposal of the 1986 White Paper (see para. 15.3). The section does not apply to works in which Crown copyright subsists, nor to works in which copyright originally vested in an international organization under s. 168 and in respect of which a longer duration than fifty years is specified by order; see s. 57(2). Formerly, by s. 11(1) and Sch. 2 of the 1956 Act, where an original work, other than a photograph, was published anonymously or pseudonymously, copyright subsisted until the end of the fiftieth calendar year after that of the first publication, and then expired;

but this did not apply if, at any time before the end of that period, it was possible for a person without previous knowledge of the facts to ascertain the identity of the author by reasonable inquiry. For transitional provisions in respect of works created before the commencement of the new Act, see Sch. 1, para. 15.

223 See n. 70, above, at paras. 5.6.19–23.

224 See n. 88 above.

225 S. 13(1).

226 S. 13(2).

227 S. 13(2).

228 Under the 1956 Act copyright in a sound recording subsisted from its making until the end of the fiftieth calendar year after that of its first publication (s. 12(1)–(3)); and copyright in a film subsisted from its making until the end of the fiftieth calendar year after its registration, if it was registrable, or its publication, if it was not registrable (s. 13(1)–(3)). The former rules continue to apply to sound recordings and films which were published before the commencement of the new Act, to sound recordings which were made before the commencement of the 1956 Act, and to films registered under former enactments before the commencement of the new Act; see Sch. 1, para. 12(2)(d) & (e) of the new Act. As regards sound recordings made after the commencement of the 1956 Act but not published before the commencement of the 1988 Act, and films made but not registered before the commencement of the 1988 Act, copyright subsists until the end of the fiftieth calendar year after that of the commencement of the new Act, unless the recording or film is published during that period, in which case copyright continues until the end of the fiftieth calendar year after that of the publication.

229 See para. 15.5 of the 1986 White Paper.

230 S. 14(1) of the new Act. See similarly, as regards broadcasts, s. 14(1)–(3) of the 1956 Act.

231 S. 14(2). An original broadcast or cable programme 'anticipates' a repeat in either of these forms (s. 14(3)).

232 See s. 15 of the new Act, following s. 15(1) & (2) of the 1956 Act.

233 Ss. 12(5) and 163(3), implementing para. 15.6 of the 1986 White Paper. Cf. s. 39(3) and (4) of the 1956 Act. For the concept of 'commercial publication', see s. 175 and pp. 33–4, above.

234 Ss. 12(5) and 165(3).

235 Ss. 164(2) and 166(5).

236 Ss. 163(5) and 165(6); replacing s. 39(5) of the 1956 Act.

237 Ss. 12(5) and 168(3).

238 See Sch. 1, para. 44, to the new Act.

239 Replacing s. 20 of the 1956 Act, which continues to apply in

proceedings brought by virtue of the 1956 Act; see Sch. 1, para. 31(4), of the 1988 Act.

240 S. 104(1) & (2). The position is similar where joint authors are so named; see s. 104(3).

241 S. 104(1) & (4), replacing s. 20(4) of the 1956 Act.

242 [1969] 1 Ch. 508. See also *Waterlow Publishers Ltd. v. Rose, The Times*, 8 December 1989.

243 S. 104(5).

244 S. 106.

245 S. 105(1) & (4).

246 S. 105(2) & (4).

247 S. 105(5).

248 S. 105(3) & (4).

CHAPTER 3: INFRINGEMENT

1 These sections replace ss. 1, 2(5), 3(5), 12(5), 13(5), 14(4) and 15(3) of the 1956 Act.

2 Replacing ss. 5 and 16 of the 1956 Act.

3 Sch. 1, paras. 1(3) and 3.

4 Sch. 1, para. 14(1), of the 1988 Act. For some special savings in relation to certain works (dramatic or musical works, and articles first published in periodicals) created before the commencement of the 1911 Act on 1 July 1912, see Sch. 1, paras. 17 and 18, of the 1988 Act.

5 On dependent territories, see p. 30, above.

6 These provisions follow s. 1 of the 1956 Act.

7 See s. 49(1) of the 1956 Act.

8 Cf. the proposal in the 1986 White Paper that it should be made clear that the rights over reproduction extend to copying by fixing a work on any medium from which the work can in principle be reproduced; see para. 9.5.

9 See pp. 57–61, below.

10 S. 87(1), replacing s. 17(2) of the 1956 Act.

11 See *Mansell v Valley Printing* [1908] 2 Ch. 441, and *Byrne v. Statist* [1914] 1 K.B. 622. Cf. s. 18(2) of the 1956 Act, relating to the now abolished claim for conversion damages.

12 See ss. 5 and 16 of the 1956 Act.

13 See ss. 22 and 23 of the new Act.

14 Ss. 25 (replacing s. 5(5)) and 26(3).

15 S. 26(2).

16 Replacing ss. 2(5)(a), 3(5)(a), 12(5)(a), 13(5)(a), 14(4)(a) & (b), and 15(3) of the 1956 Act.

17 This follows ss. 2(5)(a), 3(5)(a) and 48(1) of the 1956 Act, which

defined 'reproduction' as including, in the case of a literary, dramatic or musical work, a reproduction in the form of a record or film, and s. 2 of the Copyright (Computer Software) Act 1985, which provided that the 'storage' of a work in a computer constituted reproduction of the work.

18 17 U.S. Code, s. 117.

19 See further pp. 77–80, below.

20 S. 17(3), following s. 48(1) of the 1956 Act.

21 Defined by s. 51(3) as any record of a design, whether in the form of a drawing, a written description, a photograph, data stored in a computer or otherwise.

22 Defined by s. 51(3) as the design of any aspect of the shape or configuration of an article.

23 See chap. 8, below.

24 S. 17(4), confirming and widening the ruling in *Spelling Goldberg Productions v. BPC Publishing* [1981] R.P.C. 283 that under s. 13(10) of the 1956 Act copyright in a film was infringed by printing enlarged copies of a single frame as a poster.

25 See s. 70.

26 See s. 71.

27 Ss. 17(5) and 178. Cf. s. 15(3) of the 1956 Act, which referred to the making, by any photographic or similar process, of a reproduction of the typographical arrangement of the edition.

28 See ss. 2(5)(b) and 3(5)(b).

29 [1982] A.C. 1. The case involved a drawing of a horse-race, known as 'Past the Post', which had been used as a decorative design printed on shirts in Hong Kong. The House held that, in view of the statutory history and context, s. 49(2)(c) – 'issue of reproductions to the public' – did not apply for the purpose of defining 'publication' in ss. 2(5)(b) and 3(5)(b). For the latter purpose, 'publication' meant making public for the first time in the United Kingdom and the relevant British dependent territories a work which had not previously been made public in such territories. Thus sales of copies would rarely constitute primary infringement by way of publication, and would normally only constitute secondary infringement by way of dealing, which required some degree of knowledge of the illicit character of the copies on the part of the defendant.

30 Ss. 16(1)(b) and 18.

31 See n. 29 above.

32 On such dependent territories, see p. 30, above.

33 By Sch. 1, para. 14(2), the extension to cover rental does not apply in relation to a copy of a sound recording, film or computer program which before the commencement of the new Act had been acquired by anyone for the purpose of renting it to the public.

34 By s. 178, 'electronic' means actuated by electric, magnetic,

electro-magnetic, electro-chemical or electro-mechanical energy, and 'in electronic form' means in a form usable only by electronic means.

35 See, as regards the consequences for trade between Member States, the recent decision of the European Court in Case 158/86: *Warner Bros. v. Christiansen*, 17 May 1988, *The Times* of 1 June 1988, and pp. 85–89, below.

36 In determining the royalty, the Tribunal will take into account any reasonable payments which the owner of the copyright in the sound recording, film or program is liable to make in consequence of the granting of the licence, or of the acts authorized by the licence, to owners of copyright in works included in the sound recording, film or program; see s. 133(1). A subsequent application for variation of the Tribunal's order fixing the royalty rate may be made by one of the parties, but usually only after at least twelve months have elapsed since the previous order; see s. 142(3) & (4). An order varying a previous order takes effect on the date on which it is made or on a later date specified by the Tribunal; see s. 142(5).

37 See ss. 16(1)(e) and 21(1) and (2); replacing s. 2(5)(f) & (g) and (6) of the 1956 Act.

38 S. 21(1).

39 S. 21(2).

40 S. 21(3)(a)(i).

41 S. 21(3)(a)(ii).

42 S. 21(3)(a)(ii).

43 S. 21(3)(a)(iii).

44 S. 21(3)(b).

45 S. 21(4).

46 See *Bauman v. Fussell* [1978] R.P.C. 485.

47 See *Lerose v. Hawick Jersey* [1974] R.P.C. 42.

48 See *Bradbury Agnew v. Day* (1916) 32 T.L.R. 349.

49 Replacing with modifications ss. 5 and 16 of the 1956 Act.

50 S. 27(2) and (3). By Sch. 1, para. 14(3), in the case of an article made before the commencement of the new Act, whether its making did or would have constituted an infringement of copyright must be determined in accordance with the previous law.

51 [1980] 2 A11 E.R. 807.

52 S. 27(5). See pp. 85–89, above.

53 S. 27(4).

54 See ss. 32(5), 35(3), 36(5), 63(2) and 141(5). In the case of s. 63, 'dealing' also includes exhibiting in public or distributing. In the case of copies made under a statutory licence ordered by the Secretary of State in accordance with s. 141, 'dealing' also includes exhibiting in public, but the extended definition of 'infringing copies' applies only insofar as the

Ministerial order granting the statutory licence so provides. On ss. 32, 35, 36, 63 and 141 generally, see pp. 67–69, 76 and 112–15, below.

55 See ss. 27(6) and 37(3). The provisions of the Act relating to librarians and archivists are considered on pp. 70–2, below.

56 See s. 68(4); and p. 75, below.

57 See s. 56; and pp. 77–80, below.

58 S. 22, following ss. 5(2) and 16(2) of the 1956 Act.

59 S. 23(b). Under ss. 5(3)(a) and 16(3)(a) of the 1956 Act, offering or exposing for sale or hire only infringed if done 'by way of trade'.

60 S. 23(c). Ss. 5(3)(b) & (4) and 16(3)(b) & (4) of the 1956 Act referred to exhibiting 'by way of trade' and distributing 'for purposes of trade'.

61 S. 23(d), following ss. 5(4)(b) and 16(4)(b) of the 1956 Act.

62 S. 23(a). Mere possession, even for purposes of trade, was not infringement under the 1956 Act.

63 Cf. Patents Act 1977, s. 60(1) and (5), under which it is infringement of a patent to use the patented product otherwise than privately and for non-commercial purposes.

64 See *Van Dusen v. Kritz* [1936] 2 K.B. 176, and per Whitford J. at first instance in *Infabrics v. Jaytex* [1978] F.S.R. 451 at 463–67.

65 See p. 30, above.

66 See s. 27(2) & (3).

67 By ss. 178 and 296(5), 'electronic' means actuated by electric, magnetic, electro–magnetic, electro–chemical or electro–mechanical energy, and 'in electronic form' means in a form usable only by electronic means.

68 See s. 296(1) & (4).

69 See ss. 18(2) and 296(5).

70 S. 296(2).

71 S. 296(3) and (6). On ss. 99, 100 and 114, see pp. 94–6, below.

72 See pp. 38–40, above.

73 See chap. 4, p. 92, below.

74 Ss. 16(2)(c), 19(1) and 21(2); following s. 2(5)(c) & (g) of the 1956 Act.

75 S. 19(2).

76 Ss. 16(1)(c) and 19(3); following ss. 12(5)(b) and 13(5)(b) of the 1956 Act.

77 Ss. 16(1)(c), 19(3) and 72(1)(a) of the new Act, following, as regards television broadcasts, s. 14(4)(c) of the 1956 Act.

78 See s. 72(2) & (3), replacing s. 14(8) of the 1956 Act.

79 S. 72(1), replacing (as regards sound recordings and films) s. 40(1), (2) & (4) of the 1956 Act.

80 Ss. 16(1)(d), 20 and 21; following ss. 2(5)(d), (e) & (g), 3(5)(c) & (d), 12(5)(c), 13(5)(c) & (d) and 14(4)(d) of the 1956 Act.

81 S. 19(4), replacing s. 48(5) of the 1956 Act. By s. 178, 'electronic' means actuated by electric, magnetic, electro-magnetic, electro-chemical or electro-mechanical energy.

82 S. 65, replacing s. 40(3)–(5) of the 1956 Act.

83 S. 25(1), replacing s. 5(5) of the 1956 Act. The former exemption for one who gave permission gratuitously, or for a nominal consideration, or for not more than a reasonable estimate of his expenses, is not retained.

84 S. 25(2), replacing s. 5(6) of the 1956 Act.

85 See pp. 56–7, below.

86 On the meaning of 'electronic', see n. 81 above. S. 26 replaces s. 48(6) of the 1956 Act, by which, where a work was performed, or visual images or sounds were caused to be seen or heard, by the operation of a television or radio receiver, or, in the case of sounds, a record-player or tape-player, and such equipment was provided by or with the consent of the occupier of the premises in which it was situated, it was the occupier, and not the operator of the equipment, who was regarded as performing or causing to be seen or heard and thus was liable for infringement. On s. 48(6) see *Phonographic Performances v. Lion Breweries* [1980] F.S.R. 1, which involved a disc-jockey in a bar; but note that the New Zealand Act contained a special defence not contained in the British Act. In any event s. 48(6) did not extend to film-projection equipment or video-cassette-players.

87 S. 26(2). Cf. paras. 13.3–4 of the 1986 White Paper, which envisaged a stricter rule in the latter case.

88 See paras. 13.3–4.

89 S. 26(3).

90 S. 26(4).

91 (1884) 13 Q.B.D. 843.

92 *PRS v. Hawthorns Hotel* [1933] Ch. 855.

93 *Harms v. Martens Club* [1927] 1 Ch. 526.

94 *PRS v. Rangers Supporters Club* [1975] R.P.C. 626.

95 *Jennings v. Stephens* [1936] Ch. 469.

96 *Turner v. PRS* [1943] Ch. 167.

97 *PRS v. Harlequin Record Shops* [1979] F.S.R. 233.

98 Replacing s. 41(3) & (4) of the 1956 Act.

99 See s. 174; and p. 67, below.

100 Following s. 12(7)(b) of the 1956 Act. In accordance with proposals in the 1986 White Paper (at para. 13.2), the new Act does not retain the former exception (contained in s. 12(7)(a) of the 1956 Act) in favour of premises where persons reside or sleep.

101 See s. 299. See also *BBC Enterprises Ltd. v. Hi-Tech Xtravision Ltd., The Times*, 2 January 1990, where C.A. held that, for the purpose of s. 298, a person is not entitled to receive broadcasts unless he is authorized by the broadcaster to do so.

102 Replacing s. 1(1)–(4) of the 1956 Act.

103 See text to and nn. 83–90 above.

104 [1924] 1 K.B. 1.

105 [1926] 2 K.B. 474.

106 [1976] R.P.C. 151.

107 [1988] 1 A.C. 1013, agreeing with the Court of Appeal in *Amstrad Consumer Electronics v. British Phonographic Industry* [1986] F.S.R. 159.

108 See n. 105, above.

109 See *Falcon v. Famous Players*, n. 105 above.

110 *Australasian PRA v. Koolman* [1969] N.Z.L.R. 273. Cf. *PRS v. Ciryl*, n. 104 above, where the *managing director* of a theatre company was held not liable for infringement by the band. The rule whereby the occupier of premises is taken to authorize the conduct of those whom he engages to perform there is convenient for the PRS, whose policy is to grant licences for premises rather than performers.

111 See n. 106, above.

112 See n. 107, above.

113 See *CBS Songs v. Amstrad Consumer Electronics*, n. 107 above, which involved Amstrad's audio-machines with twin cassette-decks capable of recording between cassettes at double the playback speed, a feature emphasized in Amstrad's advertisements. See also *Vigneux v. Canadian PRS* [1945] A.C. 108, which involved the hiring out of a juke-box with records.

114 See *CBS Songs v. Amstrad Consumer Electronics*, n. 107 above.

115 [1963] Ch. 587.

116 Similarly, in its Green Paper (see pp. 5–8, above) at para. 5.6.31, the EC Commission proposed that difficulties of proving infringement in the case of computer programs should be alleviated by a presumption of infringement where the copyright owner shows that the defendant's program achieves the same results as, and by a very similar method to, the plaintiff's program, and that the defendant had had access to the plaintiff's program. However, its proposed Directive of January 1989, [1989] O.J.E.C. C91/13, is silent on this point.

117 (1913) 29 T.L.R. 570. See also per Evershed M.R. in *Purefoy v. Sykes Boxall* (1955) 72 R.P.C. 89 at 99–100.

118 See *Brigid Foley v. Ellott* [1982] R.P.C. 433, which involved a knitting guide comprising, in words and numerals, instructions to producers of knitwear as to how to produce a garment; and *Cuisenaire v. Reed* [1963] V.R. 719, where Pape J. held that a set of coloured rods did not infringe copyright in a book which described a method of teaching mathematics with the aid of such rods. See also per Gibbs C.J. in *Computer Edge Pty. Ltd. v. Apple Computer Inc.* [1986] F.S.R. 537 at 549, holding that the object code of a computer program does not

reproduce the source code from which it is derived, for there was 'not the slightest resemblance' between them, though they gave effect to the same idea. Cf. *Purefoy v. Sykes Boxall*, n. 117 above, which turned on the chain of derivation. But *Boosey v. Wright* [1900] 1 Ch. 122, holding that perforated rolls used to produce melodies did not infringe copyright in sheet music, must be regarded as obsolete.

119 Following s. 49(1) of the 1956 Act.

120 See W.R. Cornish, *Intellectual Property: Patents, Copyright, Trade Marks and Allied Rights*, 2nd ed. (1989), at p. 290.

121 [1964] 1 W.L.R. 273.

122 [1969] 1 Ch. 508.

123 Similarly s. 103 of the American Copyright Act limits the protection of compilations to the extent of the author's contribution to the work.

124 (1868) L.R. 3 Q.B. 387.

125 See also *Hansfstaengl v. Empire Palace* [1984] 3 Ch. 109; *King Features v. Kleeman* [1941] A.C. 417, the 'Popeye' case, where the defendant's dolls and brooches were copied from the plaintiff's dolls and brooches, which had been copied from the plaintiff's strip-cartoon; and *Dorling v. Honnor Marine* [1965] Ch. 1, where the defendant's photographs of a boat and its parts were indirectly copied from the plaintiff's plans.

126 (1955) 72 R.P.C. 89.

127 See *Sinanide v. Kosmeo* (1928) 44 T.L.R. 371, *Francis Day & Hunter v. Bron* [1963] Ch. 587 and *Industrial Furnaces v. Reaves* [1970] R.P.C. 605.

128 See *Weatherby v. International Horse Agency* [1910] 2 Ch. 297, and *Ravenscroft v. Herbert* [1980] R.P.C. 193.

129 Following s. 9(9) of the 1956 Act.

130 See Cornish, n. 120 above, pp. 293–4.

131 See, e.g., *Donoghue v. Allied Newspapers* [1938] Ch. 106. In the United States this principle is explicitly enacted by s. 102(b) of the Copyright Act: 'In no case does copyright protection for an original work of authorship extend to any idea, procedure, process, system, method of operation, concept, principle, or discovery, regardless of the form in which it is described, explained, illustrated, or embodied in such work.'

132 (1913) 30 T.L.R. 116.

133 [1928–35] Mac.C.C. 362. See, similarly, in America, *Twentieth-Century Fox Film Corp. v. MCA Inc.*, 715 F.2d 1327 (C9, 1983).

134 [1975] F.S.R. 499. See also *Moffat & Paige v. Gill* (1902) 86 L.T. 465, where it was held infringement to copy a selection of quotations in an annotation of a Shakespeare play.

135 See *Glyn v. Weston* [1916] 1 Ch. 261, and *Joy Music v. Sunday Pictorial* [1960] 2 Q.B. 60.

136 See *Kenrick v. Lawrence* (1890) 25 Q.B.D. 99.

137 See per Whitford J. in *Krisarts v. Briarfine* [1977] F.S.R. 557.

138 *Bauman v. Fussell* [1978] R.P.C. 485.

139 See *Jarrold v. Houlston* (1857) 69 E.R. 1294, *Pike v. Nicholas* (1869) 5 Ch. App. 251, *Kelly v. Morris* (1866) L.R. 1 Eq. 697, *Morris v. Ashbee* (1868) L.R. 7 Eq. 34, *Hogg v. Scott* (1874) L.R. 18 Eq. 444, and *Waterlow Publishers Ltd. v. Rose, The Times*, 8 December 1989.

140 [1980] R.P.C. 213.

141 See *Sweet v. Benning* (1855) 139 E.R. 838, per Jervis C.J.

142 [1983] F.S.R. 502.

143 [1988] F.S.R. 242.

144 [1987] F.S.R. 1, 797 F.2d. 1222 (C3, 1986).

145 797 F.2d. 1222 (C3, 1986).

146 605 F.Supp. 816 (M.D. Tenn., 1985).

147 2 Copyright L. Rev. (CCH) P26,062 at 20,912 (S.D.N.Y., 1987).

148 807 F.2d 1256 (C5, 1987).

149 462 F.Supp. 1003 (N.D. Texas, 1978).

150 See T.M. Gage, *Whelan Associates v. Jaslow Dental Laboratories: Copyright Protection for Computer Software Structure – What's the Purpose?* [1987] Wisconsin Law Review 859.

151 See text to and nn. 132 and 133 above.

152 [1989] O.J.E.C. C91/13.

153 See s. 28(1). Most of the provisions of Chapter III of the Act are considered in this part of this chapter. See, however, on ss. 51–53 (industrial designs), chap. 8 below; on s. 57 (assumed expiry of copyright in anonymous or pseudonymous works), see p. 36, above; on s. 64 (copying of artistic work by the same author), p. 59; on s. 66 (rental of sound recordings, films and computer programs), pp. 45–7, above; on s. 67 (playing of sound recordings by non-profit-making clubs), p. 55, above; and on ss. 70–72 (various acts in relation to broadcasts or cable transmissions), pp. 44–5 and 52–3, above.

154 See s. 28(2).

155 See Sch. 1, para. 21, of the new Act.

156 See pp. 105–8, below.

157 Cf. s. 41(7) of the 1956 Act, which simply defined 'school' by reference to the Education Act 1944.

158 See the Copyright (Application of Provisions relating to Educational Establishments to Teachers) (No. 2) Order 1989 (S.I. 1989/ 1067), so extending ss. 35, 36 and 137–41 of the 1988 Act.

159 See paras. 8.11–8.13.

160 See *University of London Press v. University Tutorial Press* [1916] 2 Ch. 601.

161 Replacing s. 6(6) of the 1956 Act.

162 See s. 178.

163 Defined by s. 178 as a process for making facsimile copies, or a process involving the use of an appliance for making multiple copies, and including any copying by electronic means of a work held in electronic form, but excluding the making of a film or sound recording. Cf. s. 41(1)(a) of the 1956 Act, which referred to a duplicating process. The changes implement para. 8.19 of the 1986 White Paper, which proposed to make absolutely clear that this exception does not permit the use of a photocopier or any other process for making facsimile copies; but not to preclude the making of films or sound recordings of works performed during instruction.

164 Cf. s. 41(1)(a) of the 1956 Act, which referred to copying 'in the course of instruction, whether at a school or elsewhere . . . by a teacher or pupil'.

165 Replacing s. 41(1)(b) of the 1956 Act.

166 S. 34(1) and (3), replacing s. 41(3) & (4) of the 1956 Act.

167 S. 34(2), replacing s. 41(5) of the 1956 Act.

168 On certified schemes, see pp. 114–15, below.

169 See paras. 8.1–8.9.

170 See pp. 112–14, below.

171 Replacing s. 7 of the 1956 Act. In relation to works created before the commencement of the new Act, Sch. 1, para. 16, continues the operation of s. 7(6)–(8) of the 1956 Act concerning works not published within 100 years of their creation.

172 S.I. 1989/1009.

173 See S.I. 1989/1009, regs. 4(2)(a) and 7(2)(a), and Sch. 2. A person who makes a false declaration is liable for infringement as if he had made the copy himself, and the copy is treated as an infringing copy; see s. 37(3).

174 See ss. 37(2), 38(2), 39(2) and 43(3); and S.I. 1989/1009, regs. 4 and 7. Somewhat different restrictions apply to copying under ss. 41 or 42; see S.I. 1989/1009, regs. 6 and 7.

175 I.e. the librarian of a prescribed library, defined (for the purposes of ss. 38 and 39) as any library administered by a statutory library authority; the British Library, the National Library of Wales, the National Library of Scotland, the Bodleian Library, Oxford and the University Library, Cambridge; any library of a school within the meaning of, or other type of educational establishment designated under, s. 174 of the Act; any parliamentary library, or library administered as part of a government department, or by an agency administered by a Minister; any

library administered by a local authority; and any other library conducted for the purpose of facilitating or encouraging the study of bibliography, education, fine arts, history, languages, law, literature, medicine, music, philosophy, religion, science (including natural and social science) or technology, or administered by any establishment or organization which is conducted wholly or mainly for such a purpose. But a library does not qualify as prescribed for the purpose of ss. 38 and 39 if it is established or conducted for profit, or forms part of, or is administered by, a body established or conducted for profit. See S.I. 1989/1009, regs. 2 and 3(1) & (5), and Sch. 1, Part A.

176 See s. 178.

177 See ss. 7(3) and 15(4) of the 1956 Act and S.I. 1957/868, rr. 6 and 7.

178 See para. 8.10 of the 1986 White Paper.

179 Implementing para. 8.17 of the 1986 White Paper. All libraries and archives in the United Kingdom are prescribed for the purpose of s. 43; see S.I. 1989/1009, reg. 3(2) & (4).

180 See S.I. 1989/1009, reg. 6(2).

181 See S.I. 1989/1009, reg. 3(2)–(5); see also Sch. 1, Parts A and B.

182 Implementing para. 8.18 of the 1986 White Paper.

183 See the Copyright (Recordings of Folksongs for Archives) (Designated Bodies) Order 1989 (S.I. 1989/1012), which designates: the Archive of Traditional Welsh Music, University College of North Wales; the Centre for English Cultural Tradition and Language; the Charles Parker Archive Trust (1982); the European Centre for Traditional and Regional Cultures; the Folklore Society; the Institute of Folklore Studies in Britain and Canada; the National Museum of Wales, Welsh Folk Museum; the National Sound Archive, the British Library; the North West Sound Archive; the Sound Archives, British Broadcasting Corporation; the Ulster Folk and Transport Museum; and the Vaughan Williams Memorial Library, English Folk Dance and Song Society.

184 See the Copyright (Recording for Archives of Designated Class of Broadcasts and Cable Programmes) (Designated Bodies) Order 1989, S.I. 1989/1011.

185 Replacing s. 6(3) & (10) of the 1956 Act, which was limited to dealings with literary, dramatic and musical works, and to reports in newspapers, magazines, similar periodicals, broadcasts and films.

186 Replacing ss. 6(2) & (10) and 9(2) of the 1956 Act, which only permitted dealing with literary, dramatic, musical or artistic works.

187 [1972] 2 Q.B. 84.

188 [1973] 1 All E.R. 241.

189 S. 31(1). Cf. s. 9(5) of the 1956 Act, which permitted the incidental inclusion of an artistic work in a film or broadcast.

190 S. 31(2). This extends to copies made before the commencement of the new Act; see Sch. 1, para. 14(4).

191 S. 31(3).

192 Replacing ss. 6(4), 9(7), 13(6), and 14(9) of the 1956 Act. On the extension of the exception allowing copying for the purpose of judicial proceedings to cover copyright in published editions and sound recordings, see para. 8.14 of the 1986 White Paper.

193 By s. 178, 'judicial proceedings' includes proceedings before any court, tribunal or person having authority to decide any matter affecting a person's legal rights or liabilities, and 'parliamentary proceedings' includes proceedings of the European Parliament.

194 See para. 8.15 of the 1986 White Paper.

195 S. 47(5) & (7).

196 See para. 8.16 of the 1986 White Paper.

197 Replacing the narrower provisions of s. 6(7)–(9) of the 1956 Act, which were confined to literary, dramatic and musical works, and adaptations; and implementing para. 8.20 of the 1956 White Paper.

198 See the Copyright (Sub-titling of Broadcasts and Cable Programmes) (Designated Body) Order 1989, S.I. 1989/1013.

199 Replacing s. 6(5) of the 1956 Act.

200 Replacing s. 9(3), (4) & (11) of the 1956 Act.

201 S. 62(3). This extends to copies made before the commencement of the new Act; see Sch. 1, para. 14(4).

202 Replacing s. 9(10) of the 1956 Act.

203 See Sch. 1, para. 14(7).

204 See s. 178.

205 S. 55. 'Marketed' means sold, hired out, or offered or exposed for sale or hire (s. 55(3)). If such marketing had occurred before the commencement of the new Act, protection expires at the end of the twenty-fifth calendar year after commencement; see Sch. 1, para. 14(5).

206 S. 54(1).

207 S. 54(2).

208 See Sch. 1, para. 14(6).

209 See s. 56(3) and (4).

210 [1986] A.C. 577.

211 COM (88) 172 final, issued on 7 June 1988.

212 [1989] O.J.E.C. C91/13.

213 See *Glyn v. Weston* [1916] 1 Ch. 261, where Elinor Glyn's novel, *Three Weeks,* was described as 'a glittering record of adulterous sensuality masquerading as superior virtue'.

214 See *Wright v. Tallis* (1845) 135 E.R. 794. See also *Slingsby v. Bradford Patent Truck & Trolley Co.* [1905] W.N. 122, [1906] W.N. 51.

215 See *Attorney-General v. Guardian Newspapers* [1988] 3 A11 E.R. 545, H.L.

216 [1973] 1 A11 E.R. 241.

217 Cf. *Woodward v. Hutchins* [1977] 2 A11 E.R. 751, where, in the context of confidence alone, the Court of Appeal were inclined to recognize a public interest in the correction of false favourable publicity about pop-singers.

218 Following Art. 29(a) & (c) of the Community Patent Convention, signed in 1975 but not yet in force. See s. 130(7) of the Act and *Smith Kline & French v. Harbottle* [1979] F.S.R. 555.

219 See *Betts v. Willmott* (1871) L.R. 6 Ch. App. 239.

220 See *Dunlop Rubber v. Longlife Battery* [1958] R.P.C. 473.

221 See *Betts v. Willmott*, n. 219 above; *De Glaces v. Tilghman* (1883) 25 Ch.D. 1; *Beecham v. International Products* [1968] R.P.C. 129; and *Minnesota Mining v. Geerpres* [1973] F.S.R. 133.

222 [1980] F.S.R. 85. See also *Champagne Heidsieck v. Buxton* (1930) 47 R.P.C. 28.

223 Cases of this kind are: *Wilkinson Sword v. Cripps & Lee* [1982] F.S.R. 16, where Falconer J. held the importer liable for passing off; *Castrol v. Automotive Oil Supplies* [1983] R.P.C. 315, where Price Q.C. held him liable for infringement of the registered mark; and *Colgate Palmolive v. Markwell Finance* [1988] R.P.C. 283, where Falconer J. held him liable for both. Use of the 1938 Act in the latter two cases is difficult to reconcile with the decision of the Court of Appeal in *Revlon*, which seems to indicate that the consent to use referred to in s. 4(3)(a) need not be to use in the United Kingdom.

224 See pp. 48–50, above.

225 Replacing ss. 5 and 16 of the Copyright Act 1956.

226 Otherwise than for his own private and domestic use.

227 I.e. sell, hire out, offer or expose for sale or hire, exhibit in public in the course of a business, or distribute either in the course of a business or to such an extent as prejudicially to affect the copyright owner (s. 23(b)–(d)). It is also secondary infringement to *possess* in the course of a business (s. 23(a)). Thus, unlike under the 1956 Act, which referred to 'trade' rather than 'business' and did not make possession as such an infringing act, it is now effectively secondary infringement merely to *use* an infringing copy in one's business. Non-commercial possession or use do not, however, infringe.

228 Replacing ss. 5(2) & (3), 16(2) & (3) and 18(3) of the 1956 Act.

229 [1980] 2 A11 E.R. 807.

230 S. 27(5).

231 See *CBS v. Charmdale* [1980] 2 A11 E.R. 807.

232 See s. 27(3)(b) of the 1988 Act.

233 See *Polydor v. Harlequin* [1980] 2 C.M.L.R. 413, distinguishing *Revlon v. Cripps & Lee* [1980] F.S.R. 85 (on trade marks).

234 S. 227 makes reference also to possessing for commercial purposes, but omits references to exhibiting or distributing.

235 See Case 78/70: *Deutsche Grammophon GmbH v. Metro-SB-Grossmarkte GmbH* [1971] E.C.R. 487, [1971] C.M.L.R. 631. Signs of the direction in which the Court was likely to move had already appeared in Case 24/67: *Parke, Davis v. Probel* [1968] E.C.R. 55, [1968] C.M.L.R. 47.

236 See Case 15/74: *Centrafarm v. Sterling Drug* [1984] E.C.R. 1147, [1974] 2 C.M.L.R. 480; and Case 187/80: *Merck v. Stepfar* [1981] E.C.R. 2063, [1981] 3 C.M.L.R. 463, [1982] F.S.R. 57. See also the Community Patent Convention, [1976] O.J. L17, not yet in force, Arts. 32 & 81, and the (British) Patents Act 1977, s. 60(4).

237 See Case 16/74: *Centrafarm v. Winthrop* [1974] E.C.R. 1183, [1974] 2 C.M.L.R. 480, [1975] F.S.R. 161.

238 See Case 78/70: *Deutsche Grammophon GmbH v. Metro-SB-Grossmarkte GmbH* [1971] E.C.R. 487, [1971] C.M.L.R. 631; and Joined Cases 55 & 57/80: *Musik-Vertrieb v. GEMA* [1981] E.C.R. 147, [1981] 2 C.M.L.R. 44, [1981] F.S.R. 433.

239 See Case 58/80: *Dansk Supermarked v. Imerco* [1981] E.C.R. 181, [1981] 3 C.M.L.R. 590.

240 As in *Centrafarm v. Sterling Drug*, n. 236 above.

241 As in *Merck v. Stepfar*, n. 236 above.

242 See Cases 51, 86 & 96/75: *EMI v. CBS* [1976] E.C.R. 811, 871 and 913, [1976] 2 C.M.L.R. 235, [1976] F.S.R. 457; and Case 270/80: *Polydor Ltd. and RSO Records v. Harlequin Record Shops Ltd.* [1982] E.C.R. 329, [1982] 1 C.M.L.R. 677.

243 See Case 19/84: *Pharmon v. Hoechst* [1985] 3 C.M.L.R. 775.

244 Case 434/85, [1988] 1 C.M.L.R. 701.

245 See pp. 165–7, below.

246 Case 102/77, [1978] E.C.R. 1139, [1978] 3 C.M.L.R. 217.

247 Case 1/81, [1981] E.C.R. 2913, [1982] 1 C.M.L.R. 406, [1982] F.S.R. 269.

248 See n. 246 above.

249 Case 3/78, [1978] E.C.R. 1823.

250 Case 158/86, 17 May 1988, *The Times* of 1 June 1988. See also Cases 60–61/84: *Cinéthèque v. Fédération Nationale des Cinémas Français* [1986] 1 C.M.L.R. 365, holding that Community law does not prevent a Member State from prohibiting the release of films on video until a year after they have been shown in cinemas.

251 See Case 62/79: *Coditel v. Cine Vog Films* (No. 1) [1980] E.C.R. 881, [1981] 2 C.M.L.R. 362.

252 See Case 262/81: *Coditel v. Cine Vog Films* (No. 2) [1982] E.C.R. 3381, [1983] 1 C.M.L.R. 49, [1983] F.S.R. 148.

253 See Case 402/85: *Basset v. SACEM* [1987] 3 C.M.L.R. 173.

254 See Case 192/73: *Van Zuylen v. Hag* [1974] E.C.R. 731, [1974] 2 C.M.L.R. 127.

255 See Case 119/75: *Terrapin v. Terranova* [1976] E.C.R. 1039, [1976] 2 C.M.L.R. 482.

256 Now replaced by the Patents Act 1977, which contains no provision similar to the former s. 50(1). The latter continues, however, to apply to patents granted under the 1949 Act.

257 See Case 35/87: *Thetford Corporation v. Fiamma SpA* [1988] 3 C.M.L.R. 549.

258 See Case 341/87: *EMI Electrola v. Patricia* [1989] 2 C.M.L.R. 413.

259 See Case 53/87: *CICRA v. Renault,* and Case 238/87: *Volvo v. Veng,* both decided on 5 October 1988 and reported in *The Times* of 15 November 1988.

CHAPTER 4: REMEDIES

1 Replacing s. 17(1) of the 1956 Act. Ss. 96 and 97 of the new Act apply only to infringements committed after the commencement of the new Act, and s. 17 of the 1956 Act continues to apply to infringements committed earlier; see Sch. 1, para. 31(1), of the new Act.

2 See *CBS Songs v. Amstrad Consumer Electronics* [1988] 1 A.C. 1013.

3 S. 92(1) defines 'exclusive licence' as a licence in writing signed by or on behalf of the copyright owner, authorizing the licensee, to the exclusion of all other persons (including the owner himself), to exercise a right which would otherwise be exercisable exclusively by the owner. By s. 92(2), an exclusive licensee has the same rights against a successor in title who is bound by the licence as he has against the grantor.

4 S. 102(1)–(3).

5 S. 102(4).

6 [1980] 2 A11 E.R. 807.

7 See Sch. 1, paras. 31(3) and 32, of the 1988 Act.

8 [1975] A.C. 396.

9 See *Anton Piller v. Manufacturing Processes* [1976] Ch. 55, where the Court of Appeal first gave its approval to such orders.

10 [1982] A.C. 380.

11 [1936] Ch. 323 at 336.

12 Replacing s. 17(2) of the 1956 Act.

13 See *Byrne v. Statist* [1914] 1 K.B. 622. Cf. s. 18(2) of the 1956 Act, under which a plaintiff was not entitled on the basis of conversion (now

abolished) to any damages or other pecuniary remedy, except costs, if it was proved that, at the time of the conversion or detention, the defendant was not aware, and had no reasonable grounds for suspecting, that copyright subsisted in the work or matter, or that he believed, and had reasonable grounds for believing, that the articles were not infringing copies.

14 See per Lord Scarman in *Infabrics v. Jaytex* [1981] 1 A11 E.R. 1057 at 1068.

15 See pp. 43, 50 and 53–4, above.

16 See *Penn v. Jack* (1867) L.R. 5 Eq. 81, *Meters Ltd. v. Metropolitan Gas Meters Ltd.* (1911) 28 R.P.C. 157, *Watson, Laidlaw v. Pott, Cassels & Williamson* (1914) 31 R.P.C. 104, *General Tire v. Firestone* [1976] R.P.C. 197, and *Catnic Components v. Hill & Smith* (No. 2) [1983] F.S.R. 512.

17 See per Lord Wright M.R. in *Sutherland v. Caxton* [1936] Ch. at 336–37. See also, as regards registered designs, *Khawam v. Chellaram* [1964] R.P.C. 337, permitting loss of goodwill to be taken into account.

18 'Copyright and Designs Law', Cmnd. 6732 (1977), at paras. 698 and 704.

19 'Reform of the Law relating to Copyright, Designs and Performers' Protection', Cmnd. 8302 (1981), chap. 14(3).

20 'Intellectual Property and Innovation', Cmnd. 9712 (1986), at paras. 12.2 & 12.3.

21 [1980] R.P.C. 193.

22 [1960] 2 A11 E.R. 806.

23 [1964] A.C. 1129 at 1225–29.

24 [1972] A.C. 1027 at 1134.

25 [1973] 1 A11 E.R. 241.

26 See n.18 above.

27 See *Infabrics v. Jaytex* [1982] A.C. 1.

28 See per Whitford J. and Lords Wilberforce and Scarman in *Infabrics v. Jaytex,* n. 27 above, and Lawton and Dillon L.JJ. in *Lewis Trusts v. Bambers Stores* [1983] F.S.R. 453.

29 At para. 702.

30 At paras. 12.2–3.

31 See Sch. 1, para. 31(2).

32 After the grant of an exclusive licence the copyright owner and the exclusive licensee have concurrent rights and remedies under ss. 99 and 100, but the owner must notify the licensee before applying for an order under s. 99 or making a seizure under s. 100, and the court may at the instance of the licensee make an order under s. 99 or prohibit the owner from making a seizure under s. 100 – see ss. 101 and 102(5).

33 If the value of the copies or articles is within the county-court limit

for tort actions, an application under s. 99 may be made to a county court; see s. 115.

34 As defined in s. 27; see pp. 48–50, above. Ss. 99 and 100 extend to infringing copies and articles made before the commencement of the new Act; see Sch. 1, para. 31(2).

35 S. 99 is without prejudice to any other powers of the court; see s. 99(4).

36 Cf. *CBS Songs v. Amstrad Consumer Electronics* [1988] 1 A.C. 1013, where H.L. held that only a master recording, and not an ordinary record or pre-recorded tape, was a 'plate' within the meaning of s. 21(3) of the 1956 Act.

37 S. 296(3); see pp. 51–2, above.

38 Ss. 99(2) and 113(1)–(3).

39 See s. 99(2).

40 S. 99(3).

41 S. 114(2).

42 See s. 114(3)–(6).

43 See the Copyright and Rights in Performances (Notice of Seizure) Order 1989, S.I. 1989/1006.

44 For offences under the 1988 Act, see pp. 96–7, below. S. 108 does not prejudice other powers of criminal courts to order forfeiture of property; see s. 108(6).

45 See ss. 108(3)(a) and 113(4).

46 Replacing s. 21 of the 1956 Act (as amended). S. 107 applies only to offences committed after the commencement of the new Act, and s. 21 of the 1956 Act continues to apply to offences committed earlier; see Sch. 1, para. 33(1), of the 1988 Act.

47 S. 107(4) and (5).

48 S. 109. The constable must satisfy the magistrate by information on oath that there are reasonable grounds for believing that a more serious offence has been or is about to be committed in the relevant premises, and that evidence thereof (other than personal or confidential material within s. 9(2) of the Police and Criminal Evidence Act 1984) is in the premises. The warrant enables a constable to enter and search the premises, using reasonable force. It may authorize persons to accompany the constable making the search, and will remain in force for twenty-eight days. In executing the warrant, a constable may seize articles reasonably believed to be evidence that any offence under s. 107 has been or is about to be committed. For transitional provisions, see Sch. 1, para. 33(2).

49 S. 107(1) and (4).

50 S. 107(1) and (5).

51 S. 107(2) and (5).

52 S. 107(3) and (5).

53 S. 107(6).
54 S. 110.
55 Replacing s. 22 of the 1956 Act.
56 See chap. 1, pp. 5–8, above.
57 [1987] 1 A11 E.R. 679.
58 See chap. 7 below.
59 [1986] O.J. L357/1.
60 [1981] O.J. L144/1.
61 [1988] 1 A.C. 1013.

CHAPTER 5: LICENCES

1 Sch. 1, para. 25, of the new Act preserves the operation in accordance with the former law of documents made and events occurring before its commencement which affected the ownership of, or created, transferred or terminated an interest, right or licence in respect of, copyright in a work created before such commencement. For some special provisions relating to dealings before the commencement of the 1956 Act, see Sch. 1, paras. 27 and 28, of the new Act. On ss. 94 and 95 of the new Act, which regulate dealings with 'moral' rights, see chap. 6 below.

2 S. 90(1), replacing s. 36(1) of the 1956 Act. By s. 93, replacing the narrower s. 38 of the 1956 Act, unless the will otherwise indicates, a bequest of an original document or other material thing which records, embodies or contains an unpublished literary, dramatic, musical or artistic work, sound recording or film carries with it the copyright in the work insofar as owned by the testator. For transitional provisions on bequests, see Sch. 1, para. 30, of the new Act.

3 S. 90(2), replacing s. 36(2) of the 1956 Act, which mentioned also the possibility of a territorially limited assignment.

4 S. 173(1).

5 S. 90(3), replacing s. 36(3). In the case of a corporation, the affixing of its seal suffices by way of signature; see s. 176(1).

6 Replacing s. 37 of the 1956 Act. S. 91(1) does not apply to agreements made before the commencement of the 1956 Act; see Sch. 1, para. 26(1), of the new Act.

7 On qualifying authors and countries, see chap. 2, pp. 30–5, above.

8 Ss. 90(4) and 91(3), replacing ss. 36(4) and 37(3) of the 1956 Act.

9 S. 92(1).

10 S. 92(2), which does not apply to exclusive licences granted before the commencement of the new Act (see Sch. 1, para. 29).

11 See ss. 27(3) and 101–02; and pp. 48–49 and 90–1, above.

12 S. 173(2).

13 See the 1986 White Paper, esp. Chapters 8 and 18.

14 S. 145(1). As regards proceedings pending before the Tribunal at the commencement of the new Act, see Sch. 1, para. 34.

15 S. 145(2) & (3).

16 S. 148(1).

17 S. 148(2).

18 On s. 142, which provides for statutory licences for the rental of sound recordings, films and computer programs, see chap. 3, pp. 45–7, above.

19 On s. 190, which relates to rights of performers under Part II of the Act, see chap. 7, p. 145, below.

20 On Sch. 6, which deals with the play, *Peter Pan,* by Sir James Barrie, see chap. 2, n. 208, above.

21 S. 150.

22 S. 151(1).

23 S. 152.

24 'Licensing scheme' is defined by s. 116(1) & (3) as a scheme (including anything in the nature of a scheme, however described) setting out (a) the classes of case in which the operator of the scheme, or the person on whose behalf he acts, is willing to grant licences to do (or authorize) any acts restricted by copyright, and (b) the terms on which licences would be granted in those classes of case.

25 'Licensing body' is defined as a society or other organization whose main objects include the negotiation or granting of licences to do (or authorize) acts restricted by copyright, either as copyright owner or prospective owner or as agent for such owner, and whose objects include the granting of licences covering works of more than one author (see s. 116(2) & (3)). In other words, 'licensing body' refers to what is usually known as a collecting society.

26 This excludes a scheme which is confined to a single collective work (defined as a work of joint authorship, or a work in which there are distinct contributions by different authors, or in which works or parts of works of different authors are incorporated), or to several collective works of which the authors are the same, or to works made by, or made by employees of, or commissioned by, a single individual, firm, company or group of companies; see ss. 116(4) and 178.

27 S. 117(1)(a).

28 S. 117(1)(b) & (c).

29 S. 119(1).

30 S. 119(2).

31 S. 119(3).

32 S. 119(4). An order made under s. 119 reducing fees for licences

under a scheme certified under s. 143 is retroactive to the date of the reference; otherwise an order under s. 119 varying the amount of charges payable may contain a provision making it operative from a date earlier than its making, but not earlier than that of the reference or the coming into operation of the scheme, whichever is later; see s. 123(3) & (4).

33 S. 123(1).
34 S. 123(2).
35 S. 120(2). These are hereafter referred to as 'the usual time-limits'.
36 Ss. 120(3) & (4) and 123.
37 S. 120(1) & (2).
38 S. 121(1).
39 S. 121(4).
40 S. 121(5).
41 S. 123(5).
42 S. 122.
43 S. 121(3).
44 S. 121(2).
45 S. 121(4).
46 See ss. 121(5), 122 and 123(5).
47 S. 128(1).
48 S. 128(2).
49 See s. 128(3).
50 I.e. copying by a process for making facsimile copies, or by a process involving the use of an appliance for making multiple copies, or in the case of a work held in electronic form, any copying by electronic means (see s. 178).
51 I.e. any school (within the meaning of the Education Act 1944), and any other description of educational establishment specified by statutory instrument (s. 174).
52 S. 132.
53 S. 133(2).
54 Implementing a proposal of the 1986 White Paper at para. 8.7.
55 S. 136(1).
56 S. 136(2) & (3).
57 S. 136(4).
58 S. 136(5).
59 See pp. 67–69, above.
60 Implementing a proposal of the 1986 White Paper at para. 8.8.
61 See the 1986 White Paper at para. 8.9, which is now implemented by ss. 137–41 of the new Act.
62 S. 139.
63 S. 138.
64 S. 139(2).

65 For present purposes 'general licence' means a licence granted by a licensing body which covers all works of the description to which it applies; see s. 140(7).

66 S. 141(1), (6) & (8).

67 Ss. 140(7) and 141(2) & (9).

68 S. 141(3).

69 S. 141(4) & (5).

70 S. 141(7).

71 S. 143(1)–(3).

72 S. 143(3).

73 S. 143(4).

74 S. 143(5).

75 S. 144(3).

76 Reg. 2349/84 entered into force on 1 January 1985, and will expire on 31 December 1994 (see Art. 14). For its text, see [1984] O.J. L219/15. For a commentary, see P.A. Stone, *The EEC Block Exemption for Patent Licences,* [1985] 6 European Intellectual Property Review 173 and [1985] 7 European Intellectual Property Review 199.

77 [1989] O.J. L61/1. The Know-how Regulation entered into force on 1 April 1989, and will expire on 31 December 1999 (see Art. 12).

78 See Case 258/78: *Nungesser and Eisele v. Commission* [1982] E.C.R. 2015, [1983] 1 C.M.L.R. 278.

79 Patent Reg., Art. 1(1); Know-how Reg., Art. 1(1).

80 On industrial designs under British law, see chap. 8, below.

81 Art. 1(1).

82 [1987] O.J. L50/30.

83 See Art. 1(1), which also indicates that the inclusion of ancillary provisions relating to trade marks or other intellectual–property right does not exclude its application. See also Art. 1(7)(5) & (6), which define 'pure' know-how agreements as ones for the communication of know-how, with or without an obligation by the licensor to disclose subsequent improvements, and 'mixed' agreements as ones for the licensing of a technology which contains both non-patented elements and elements which are patented in one or more Member States, but excluding agreements which are exempted by the Patent Regulation.

84 Art. 1(7)(2).

85 Art. 1(7)(3).

86 Art. 1(7)(4).

87 Art. 1(3).

88 See Art. 5 of the Patent Reg.; Art. 5 of the Know-how Reg.; and *Re Agreements on Video Cassette Recorders* [1978] F.S.R. 376.

89 See *Raymond/Nagoya* [1972] C.M.L.R. D45; *Davidson Rubber* [1972] C.M.L.R. D52; *Burroughs/Delplanque and Geha-Werke* [1972]

C.M.L.R. D67 and D72; *Kabelmetal/Luchaire* [1975] 2 C.M.L.R. D40; *Bronbemaling v. Heidemaatschappij* [1975] 2 C.M.L.R. D67; *AOIP v. Beyrard* [1976] 1 C.M.L.R. D14; *Davide Campari-Milano* [1978] 2 C.M.L.R. 397; and *Eisele/INRA* [1978] 3 C.M.L.R. 434.

90 Case 258/78, [1982] E.C.R. 2015, [1983] 1 C.M.L.R. 278.

91 See n. 89 above.

92 See n. 90 above.

93 Exclusive licences for territories outside the common market are ignored, presumably because normally they would not infringe Art. 85(1). See also, similarly, Art. 1(7)(11) of the Know-how Regulation.

94 Arts. 1(1)(1)–(5) and 1(2)(i) & (ii).

95 Art. 1(4).

96 Art. 1(3).

97 Arts. 1(1)(1)–(3) and 1(2)(i).

98 Arts. 1(1)(6) and 1(2)(iii).

99 See Arts. 3(11) and 9(5).

100 Arts. 3(12) and 7(5).

101 Arts. 1(1)(7) and 2(1)(6). See, similarly, the Know-how Reg., Arts. 1(1)(7) and 2(1)(11).

102 See Case 193/83: *Windsurfing International v. Commission* [1986] E.C.R. 611, [1986] 3 C.M.L.R. 489, [1988] F.S.R. 139; discussed by P.A. Stone, [1986] 8 E.I.P.R. 242.

103 Art. 4(2).

104 Patent Reg., Art. 2(1)(1) and (1)(9); Know-how Reg., Art. 2(1)(5). See also *Raymond/Nagoya and Campari*, n. 89 above.

105 See also *Vaessen v. Moris* [1979] F.S.R. 259.

106 See n. 102 above.

107 *In casu*, unpatented hulls on which the patented rigs were to be mounted to form a complete sailboard.

108 Patent Reg., Art. 2(1)(2); Know-how Reg., Art. 2(1)(9).

109 Patent Reg., Art. 3(5); Know-how Reg., Art. 3(7) – but subject to Arts. 1(1)(8) and 4(2). See also *Eisele/INRA*, n. 89 above, objecting to a clause requiring the licensee to import a proportion of his requirements of the licensed product.

110 Patent Reg., Art. 2(1)(3); Know-how Reg., Art. 2(1)(8), which also allows restriction of the licensee to particular 'product markets'.

111 Patent Reg., Art. 3(7); Know-how Reg., Art. 3(6).

112 Art. 1(1)(8).

113 Patent Reg., Art. 2(1)(5) & (1)(11); Know-how Reg., Art. 2(1)(2) & (10). Cf. the more severe attitude to most-favoured-licensee clauses adopted earlier in *Kabelmetal/Luchaire*, n. 89 above. Art. 2(1)(12) of the Know-how Reg. also permits clauses forbidding the licensee to use the know-how to construct facilities for third parties.

114 Art. 2(1)(4).

115 Art. 3(2).

116 Art. 3(2).

117 Art. 3(4).

118 Art. 3(4).

119 See Case 193/83: *Windsurfing International v. Commission*, n. 102 above.

120 Art. 2(1)(1) & (1)(3). Cf. case 320/87: *Ottung v. Klee & Weilbach*, 12 May 1989.

121 Art. 2(1)(7). But the benefit of the 'block exemption' may be withdrawn by an individual decision of the Commission if royalties continue payable after publication by third parties for a period substantially exceeding the lead-time acquired because of the licensee's head-start in production and marketing to the detriment of competition in the market; see Art. 7(7).

122 Art. 3(1).

123 Art. 3(5).

124 Art. 3(10).

125 Arts. 2(1)(10) and 3(8). See also *Raymond/Nagoya, Davidson Rubber* and *Kabelmetal/Luchaire*, n. 89 above; *Spitzer/Van Hool* (1982) 12 R.C.P. 72; and *Neilson-Hordell/Richmark* (1982) 12 R.C.P. 73.

126 Arts. 2(1)(4) and 3(2).

127 Patent Reg., Art. 2(1)(8); Know-how Reg., Art. 2(1)(6).

128 Patent Reg., Art. 3(1); Know-how., Reg., Art. 3(4). See also the Commission's decisions in *Davidson Rubber, Kabelmetal/Luchaire, AOIP v. Beyrard* (n. 89 above), *Vaessen v. Moris* (n. 105 above), *IMA v. Windsurfing International* [1983] O.J. L229/1, [1984] 1 C.M.L.R. 1, [1984] F.S.R. 146, and *Neilson-Hordell* (n. 125 above); and the Court's decision in *Windsurfing International v. Commission* (n. 102 above).

129 Patent Reg., Art. 3(1); Know-how Reg., Art. 3(4).

130 Case 65/86, decided on 27 September 1988.

131 Patent Reg., Art. 3(6); Know-how Reg., Art. 3(8). See also *Eisele/ INRA*, n. 89 above.

132 Patent Reg., Art. 3(3); Know-how Reg., Art. 3(9) – which however permits the licensor to terminate the licensee's exclusivity and cease communicating improvements if the licensee engages in competing activities, and to require the licensee to prove that the licensed know-how is not used for unlicensed production. See also *AOIP v. Beyrard* and *Eisele/INRA* (n. 89 above); cf. *Campari* (n. 89 above), which involved a trade mark and know-how licence.

133 Patent Reg., Art. 9(1); Know-how Reg., Art. 7(1).

134 See *Davidson Rubber* and *Campari* (n. 89 above).

135 See pp. 104–15, above.

136 *(No. 1)* [1971] C.M.L.R. D35, and *(No. 2)* [1972] C.M.L.R. D115.

137 In the United Kingdom performing rights in musical works are administered by the Performing Right Society, and physical rights to record musical works by the Mechanical Right Protection Society.

138 Case 127/73, [1974] E.C.R. 313. See also Case 22/79: *Greenwich Film Production v. SACEM* [1980] 1 C.M.L.R. 629, holding that arrangements which are made between a collecting society and authors who belong to the same Member State and which relate to copyrights for non-member States may nonetheless infringe Art. 86, since the activities of the collecting society as a whole may restrict the freedom to provide services within the Community and thus affect the competitive structure therein.

139 See *Re GEMA (No. 1)*, n. 136 above, at D46.

140 See n. 136 above.

141 See n. 138 above.

142 Cf. the concern of Chapter VII of Part I of the 1988 Act for users rather than members. English law may, however, protect authors from unfair contracts by use of the common-law doctrine invalidating contractual provisions which constitute unreasonable restraint of trade; see *Schroeder v. Macaulay* [1974] 3 All E.R. 616 and *Clifford Davis v. WEA Records* [1975] 1 All E.R. 237.

143 [1982] 1 C.M.L.R. 221.

144 Especially *No. 2*, which amends *No. 1* on the points now considered.

145 See n. 138 above.

146 Joined Cases 55 & 57/80, [1981] E.C.R. 147, [1981] 2 C.M.L.R. 44, [1981] F.S.R. 433; see pp. 85–89, above.

147 [1982] 2 C.M.L.R. 482.

148 Case 395/87, decided on 13 July 1989.

CHAPTER 6: MORAL RIGHTS

1 See paras. 19.2–19.3.

2 Cmnd. 5002 (1972). The first two, but not the latter two, of the moral rights provided for in the 1988 Act are derived from the Berne Convention.

3 S. 103(1).

4 See Sch. 1, para. 22, of the 1988 Act.

5 See Sch. 1, para. 10.

6 S. 94.

7 S. 87(1) & (4).

8 S. 87(2). See also s. 176(2).

9 S. 87(3).

10 S. 79(2).

11 Ss. 77(1) and 89(1). In the case of a work of joint authorship or a film of joint direction (i.e. one made by the collaboration of two or more directors whose contributions are not distinct), each author or director has a right to identification as a joint author, which he must assert in relation to himself, and a waiver by one of the joint authors or directors does not affect the rights of others (s. 88(1), (3) & (5)).

12 S. 86(1).

13 S. 95(1). If the author divides the copyright by bequest, the right to identification is similarly divided (s. 95(2)). If on the author's death several persons become entitled to the right, each may assert it, and a waiver by one does not affect the rights of the others (s. 95(3)(a) & (c)). Any damages recovered by personal representatives become part of the estate (s. 95(6)). A consent or waiver given by the author or director binds his successors (s. 95(4)).

14 S. 103(1).

15 See Sch. 1, para. 23(1) and (2).

16 See Sch. 1, para. 23(3). See also para. 23(4), on acts done in relation to records made under the statutory recording licence granted by s. 8 of the 1956 Act.

17 S. 79(3).

18 S. 79(7).

19 S. 79(5).

20 S. 79(6)(a); see also s. 81(4)(a), which makes the same exception to the right to object to derogatory treatment. Possibly a purposive construction, viewing these provisions as designed to assist those who have rigid deadlines to meet, may limit the concept of a 'similar' periodical so as exclude a publication which, though appearing regularly, does not purport to provide 'up-to-the-minute' information. On this basis, the exclusion would cover, e.g. the *New Law Journal*, but not the *International and Comparative Law Quarterly*.

21 S. 79(6)(b); see also s. 81(4)(b), which makes the same exception to the right to object to derogatory treatment. The rationale of this exclusion appears to be to enable the editor of a collective work to ensure a consistent viewpoint throughout, overriding the idiosyncratic views of contributors.

22 S. 79(4). These relate to: (a) fair dealing for the purpose of reporting current events by means of a sound recording, film, broadcast or cable programme (under s. 30); incidental inclusion in an artistic work, sound recording, film, broadcast or cable programme (s. 31); examination questions (s. 32(3)); parliamentary or judicial proceedings, Royal Commissions and statutory inquiries (ss. 45 and 46(1) & (2)); industrial designs (ss. 51 & 52); and acts permitted on assumptions that copyright has expired (s. 57). See pp. 35, 68, 72–3 and 159–16.

23 Ss. 77(1) and 78(1).
24 S. 78(2).
25 S. 78(2)(a) & (4)(a).
26 S. 78(2)(b) & (4)(b). In addition, by s. 78(3) and (4)(c) & (d), as regards the public exhibition of an artistic work, an assertion may be effected: (i) by securing that when the author or other first owner of copyright parts with possession of the original or of a copy made by him or under his direction or control, that the author is identified on the original or copy, or on a frame, mount or other thing to which it is attached, in which case the assertion binds anyone into whose hands that original or copy comes, even if the identification is not visible; (ii) by including in a licence granted by the author or other first owner of the copyright to make copies a statement signed by or on behalf of the licensor that the author asserts his right to be identified in the event of the public exhibition of a copy made in pursuance of the licence, in which case the assertion binds the licensee and anyone into whose hands such a copy comes, regardless of notice of the assertion. On assertion by a corporation, see s. 176.
27 S. 78(5).
28 S. 77(2).
29 S. 77(3).
30 S. 77(4)(a) & (b).
31 S. 77(4)(c).
32 S. 77(5).
33 S. 77(6).
34 S. 89(2).
35 S. 79(2)(a).
36 S. 79(2)(b).
37 S. 86(1).
38 S. 95. See n. 13, above.
39 S. 103.
40 See Sch. 1, paras. 22 and 23; and text to nn. 4, 15 and 16, above.
41 See s. 87 and text to nn. 7–9 above. In the case of joint authorship (or direction), each author (or director) has a right to object to derogatory treatment, and his right is satisfied if he consents to the treatment in question, but a waiver by one author (or director) does not affect the others (s. 88(2), (3) & (5)).
42 S. 81(2) & (3).
43 S. 81(5).
44 S. 81(4). For comment on concepts involved in these exclusions, see nn. 20 and 21 above.
45 Ss. 81(6) and 178.
46 Ss. 82 and 178.
47 S. 79(3); which is similar to s. 77(2) on the right to identification in the case of a literary or dramatic work, other than a lyric.

214

48 S. 79(4)(a) & (b); similar to s. 77(4)(a) & (b), on the right to identification in respect of any artistic work.

49 S. 79(4)(c); similar to s. 77(4)(c) on the right to identification, which, however, extends to buildings.

50 S. 79(5).

51 S. 80(6); similar to s. 77(6) on the right to identification.

52 S. 79(6).

53 S. 84 replaces s. 43 of the 1956 Act, which did not extend to films.

54 S. 84(1).

55 S. 89(2).

56 S. 84(8).

57 S. 88(4). The same applies as regards joint directorship of a film (s. 88(5)).

58 S. 87. See p. 131, above.

59 S. 86(2).

60 S. 94.

61 S. 95(5) & (6).

62 S. 84(2)(a).

63 S. 84(2)(b).

64 S. 84(3)(a).

65 S. 84(3)(b).

66 S. 84(4).

67 S. 84(5)(a) and (7).

68 S. 84(5)(b) and (7).

69 S. 84(6) and (7).

70 S. 85(2).

71 See Sch. 1, para. 24.

72 [1960] 2 A11 E.R. 806.

73 On damages for copyright infringement, see pp. 92–4, above.

74 S. 89(1).

75 S. 86(1). On the death of the commissioner, this right devolves and becomes exercisable in the same way as in the case of the right of an author to object to derogatory treatment (s. 95).

76 S. 87.

77 S. 88(6).

78 S. 103(1).

CHAPTER 7: PERFORMERS' RIGHTS

1 See esp. pp. 9–11, above.

2 (1930) 46 T.L.R. 485.

3 [1977] F.S.R. 345.

4 [1978] Ch. 122.

5 [1982] A.C. 173.

6 [1983] Ch. 135.

7 [1987] 1 A11 E.R. 679; according with dicta of Lord Diplock in *Lonrho,* and of Vinelott J. at first instance and Lawton and Slade L.JJ in *RCA,* and with the decision of Peter Gibson J. in *Ekland v. Scripglow* [1982] F.S.R. 431. Cf. the contrary decision of Harman J. in *Shelley v. Cunane* [1983] F.S.R. 390.

8 They are repealed by s. 303(2) and Sch. 8.

9 S. 194.

10 See ss. 207, 209 and 210.

11 In this one case, it seems that the work performed must previously have been embodied in a fixation, so as to attract copyright protection.

12 S. 180(2).

13 S. 180(2).

14 S. 180(3).

15 S. 180(4).

16 S. 185(1).

17 S. 185(1) and (2)(a).

18 S. 185(2)(b).

19 See ss. 181, 206 and 208.

20 See ss. 185(2), 206 and 208.

21 S. 185(3).

22 S. 191.

23 S. 192(1) and (2). If a performer's rights are specifically bequeathed to several persons, they become exercisable by each of them independently of the others; see s. 192(3). Damages recovered by a performer's personal representatives become part of his estate; see s. 192(5).

24 S. 185(2) and (3), and s. 192(1) and (4).

25 See s. 193(2) and (3).

26 Consent may be given in relation to a specific performance, a specified description of performances, or performances generally, and may relate to past performances; see s. 193(1).

27 S. 182(1)(a). It is a defence to a claim for damages (but not any other remedy) for such infringement to show that at the time of the infringement one believed on reasonable grounds that the performer's consent had been given; see s. 182(2).

28 S. 182(1)(b). The partial defence under s. 182(2), mentioned in n. 27 above, also applies to this type of infringement.

29 S. 183.

30 See ss. 184(1) and 197(2). But s. 184(2) and (3) limits the remedies

for such an infringement to damages not exceeding a reasonable payment in respect of the act complained of, if it is shown that the defendant or a predecessor in title of his acquired the recording without knowing, and with no reason to believe, that it was an illicit recording.

31 The person having recording rights has no protection corresponding to s. 182(1)(b).

32 See s. 186, corresponding to s. 182(1)(a) and (2).

33 I.e. a performance given by a qualifying individual or in a qualifying country; see ss. 181 and 206.

34 See s. 187, corresponding to s. 183; s. 188, corresponding to s. 184; and s. 197(3), corresponding to s. 197(2). Similarly as regards the partial defence of innocent acquisition, see ss. 184(2) and (3), 188 (2) and (3) and 197.

35 See s. 197(5) and Sch. 2, paras. 4(3), 6(2), and 16(3). See also Sch. 2, para. 12(2), on copies of electronic recordings wrongfully retained when the original is transferred.

CHAPTER 8: INDUSTRIAL DESIGNS

1 Cmnd. 6732, (1977).

2 Cmnd. 8302, (1981).

3 Cmnd. 9117, (1983).

4 Cmnd. 9712, (1986), pp. 18–23.

5 See ss. 51–53. For a further exclusion of copyright in industrial designs which were capable of registration under the 1949 Act and were created before the 1956 Act, see Sch. 1, para. 6, of the 1988 Act.

6 S. 8 of the 1949 Act (as amended). Formerly the maximum period was fifteen years.

7 S. 1(1).

8 S. 1(1).

9 S. 1(3). This is a new provision, implementing para. 3.37 of the 1986 White Paper, but it probably only elaborates the established understanding of the requirement of eye-appeal.

10 S. 1(1)(a).

11 S. 1(1)(b)(i).

12 S. 1(1)(b)(ii). This is a new provision.

13 See the 1986 White Paper, para. 3.37, which envisaged the exclusion of an article which is an integral or working part of a further article, unless their appearances are substantially independent. Cf. the rejection by the House of Lords of attempts to use ordinary copyright in this way in *British Leyland Motor Corp. v. Armstrong Patents Co. Ltd.* [1986] A.C. 577. For transitional provisions relating to applications made

before the commencement of Part IV of the new Act, see ss. 265(2) and 266.

14 [1972] R.P.C. 103.

15 [1988] 3 W.L.R. 678.

16 S.I. 1989/1105.

17 As to ordinary trade variants, see per Lord Moulton in *Phillips v. Harbro Rubber* (1920) 37 R.P.C. 233 at 240, who refers to putting spikes into the soles of an old type of running shoes.

18 See *Rosedale v. Airfix* [1957] R.P.C. 239.

19 See *Bissell's Design* [1964] R.P.C. 125, where the product was marketed abroad and an illustration advertising it was published in this country.

20 S. 6(1)(a) & (b).

21 S. 6(1)(c).

22 S. 6(2).

23 S. 6(3).

24 Paris Convention for the Protection of Industrial Property (1883), last revised at Stockholm in 1967. See Cmnd. 4431 (1970).

25 S. 1(2), as amended.

26 See s. 44(1).

27 See the Registered Designs Rules 1989, r. 13.

28 See s. 1(2), as amended.

29 S. 2(2), as amended.

30 See pp. 161–8, below.

31 S. 3(1A) of the 1949 Act, as amended.

32 See s. 3(2).

33 See ss. 3(3) and 43(1).

34 See ss. 17(1) and 18(1).

35 See ss. 17(4)–(7), 22 and 23.

36 See s. 3(5).

37 See ss. 8–8B, as amended in accordance with para. 3.38 of the 1986 White Paper. Before the 1988 Act the maximum duration was fifteen years. These amendments do not apply to applications made before the commencement of Part IV of the 1988 Act; see s. 269(2).

38 S. 8(4), as amended.

39 See ss. 11(2) and 28.

40 The amendments to s. 7 do not apply to designs registered in pursuance of applications made before the commencement of Part IV of the 1988 Act; see s. 268(2).

41 See s. 7(6), a new provision added by s. 268(1).

42 S. 7(1)(a) and (2), as amended.

43 S. 7(4), as amended. The provisions on kits are new, and are designed to overrule *Dorling v. Honnor Marine* [1965] Ch. 1, where

Harman L.J. took the view that making something for enabling the making of an infringing article did not extend to making parts of the article, such as kits of parts for making a boat, and Danckwerts L.J. added that the provision on enabling was not intended to cover purely functional articles.

44 S. 7(1)(b) and (2), as amended.

45 S. 7(4), as amended.

46 S. 7(3) and (4), as amended.

47 (1867) L.R. 2 H.L. 380.

48 Replacing r. 14(2) of the Design Rules 1949.

49 (1930) 47 R.P.C. 485.

50 [1972] F.S.R. 497.

51 [1973] F.S.R. 123.

52 See, similarly, s. 62(1) of the Patents Act 1977.

53 Similar provision in the case of patents is made by Sch. 5, para. 16(1), of the new Act, adding s. 57A to the Patents Act 1977, and overruling *Patchett's Patent* [1967] R.P.C. 237.

54 [1965] Ch. 1.

55 [1986] A.C. 577.

56 See pp. 159–61, below.

57 See s. 3(1)(a) of the 1956 Act, and s. 4(1)(a) and (2) of the 1988 Act.

58 By s. 48(1) of the 1956 Act. Now, to similar effect, s. 4(2) of the 1988 Act defines 'graphic work' as including any drawing, diagram, map, chart or plan.

59 See *George Hensher Ltd. v. Restawhile Upholstery (Lancs.) Ltd.* [1976] A.C. 64.

60 See *Brigid Foley v. Ellott* [1982] R.P.C. 433.

61 See per Megarry J. in *British Northrop v. Texteam* [1974] R.P.C. 57, which involved spare parts for looms, such as a rivet, a screw, a stud, a bolt, a metal bar, a length of wire with a thread cut at one end, a length of cable with nipples at each end, a block of leather, a washer and a collar; and per Whitford J. at first instance in *LB (Plastics) v. Swish Products* [1979] R.P.C. 551, which involved plastic knock-down drawers. See also *Gleeson v. Denne* [1975] R.P.C. 471; and *Solar Thomson v. Barton* [1977] R.P.C. 537.

62 See n. 61 above.

63 [1978] F.S.R. 405.

64 [1988] 3 W.L.R. 678.

65 This provision is substantially repeated by s. 17(3) of the 1988 Act.

66 See *King Features v. Kleeman* [1941] A.C. 417, where the defendant's dolls and brooches were copied directly from the plaintiff's dolls and brooches, which had been copied from the plaintiff's strip cartoon. The principle is now made explicit in s. 16(3) of the new Act.

67 No such provision is contained in the 1988 Act.

68 [1979] R.P.C. 551.

69 [1977] R.P.C. 537.

70 [1975] R.P.C. 471.

71 [1973] R.P.C. 15. See also *Lerose v. Hawick Jersey* [1974] R.P.C. 42. which involved point-patterns for setting knitting machines to produce a particular pattern. The point-patterns were composed of lines drawn on paper showing a pattern, accompanied by hieroglyphics, figures and words giving instructions to the machine operator.

72 [1977] R.P.C. 537.

73 See also on the latter point *Merchant Adventurers v. Grew* [1971] 2 All E.R. 657.

74 [1984] F.S.R. 358.

75 [1984] 3 C.M.L.R. 102.

76 [1986] A.C. 577.

77 See s. 10(7).

78 See s. 10(5) and the Copyright (Industrial Designs) Rules 1957, S.I. 1957/867.

79 Now s. 1(5) of the 1949 Act as amended, and r. 26 of the Registered Designs Rules 1989, S.I. 1989/1105.

80 See s. 10(6).

81 See s. 10(6).

82 See *Sifam v. Sangamo* [1971] 2 All E.R. 1074.

83 See *Dorling v. Honnor Marine* [1965] Ch. 1, *Vernon v. Universal Pulp Containers* [1980] F.S.R. 179, and *British Leyland v. Armstrong* [1984] 3 C.M.L.R. 102, where C.A. overruled the contrary view of Whitford J. in *Hoover v. Hulme* [1982] F.S.R. 565.

84 See *Interlego v. Tyco Industries,* n. 64 above, construing the transitional but for this purpose analogous provision of Sch. 7, para. 8(2), of the 1956 Act, and not following *Stephenson, Blake & Co. v. Grant, Legros & Co. Ltd.* (1916) 33 R.P.C. 406.

85 S. 51(1).

86 S. 51(3).

87 S. 51(1).

88 S. 51(1).

89 S. 51(2). By Sch. 1, para. 14(4), this extends to articles made before the commencement of the new Act.

90 To be defined by a statutory instrument made by the Secretary of State, which may also exclude articles of a primarily literary or artistic character; see s. 52(4).

91 'Marketing' means selling, hiring out, or offering or exposing for sale or hire; see s. 52(6).

92 See Sch. 1, para. 20(2).

93 See Sch. 1, para. 20(1), of the 1988 Act.

94 I.e. a registered design which, if applied to an article, would produce a copy of the artistic work; see s. 53(2).

95 At pp. 18–23.

96 See pp. 159–61, above.

97 S. 213(2) & (3).

98 S. 213(4).

99 S. 213(6) & (7). By s. 263(1), 'design document' means any record of a design, whether in the form of a drawing, a written description, a photograph, data stored in a computer, or otherwise. On existing designs, see Sch. 1, para. 19; considered on p. 160, above.

100 Ss. 214 and 215(1).

101 S. 215(2).

102 S. 215(3).

103 See ss. 222, 223, 225, 258 and 261, which correspond to ss. 90–92, 173 and 176.

104 S. 224.

105 Ss. 213(5)(a), 218 and 219. As to joint designers, commissioners or employers, see ss. 218(3) & (4), 219(2) & (3), and 259.

106 S. 217(1) & (5).

107 S. 217(2).

108 Ss. 217(3)(a) and 257. For this purpose citizenship or subjecthood refers to British citizenship in the strictest sense; cp. s. 217(4)(a) with s. 154(1)(a).

109 Ss. 217(3)(b) and 255. In relation to a colony, citizenship or subjecthood refers to British Dependent Territories' citizenship by connection with the colony; see s. 217(4)(b). As to the effect of the attainment of independence by a colony to which Part III has been extended, see s. 255(5) and (6).

110 See ss. 217(3)(d) and 256. By the Design Right (Reciprocal Protection) Order 1989, S.I. 1989/990, the following countries are designated as reciprocating countries for this purpose: Anguilla; Bermuda; British Indian Ocean Territory; British Virgin Islands; Cayman Islands; Channel Islands; Falkland Islands; Gibraltar; Hong Kong; Isle of Man; Montserrat; New Zealand; Pitcairn, Henderson, Ducie and Oeno Islands; St Helena and Dependencies; South Georgia and South Sandwich Islands; and the Turks and Caicos Islands.

111 Ss. 213(5)(b), 215(4) and 220. By s. 221, further alternative qualifications may be specified by Order in Council.

112 S. 216.

113 By s. 263(3), an act is done for commercial purposes if it is done with a view to the article in question being sold or hired in the course of a business.

114 S. 226(1) & (3). As to design documents, see s. 263(1) and n. 99 above.

115 S. 226(2).

116 S. 226(4).

117 S. 260.

118 S. 228(1)–(3) & (6).

119 S. 228(5). See pp. 85–89, above.

120 S. 228(4).

121 Ss. 229–32 and 233(1) correspond to ss. 96, 97, 99 and 113–15, and ss. 234 and 235 to ss. 101 and 102. However, there is no provision for seizure of copies infringing design right, corresponding to s. 100 in relation to copyright. See chap. 4 above.

122 S. 233(1), following s. 97(1).

123 S. 233(2) & (3).

124 S. 239(2).

125 This right may be excluded by statutory instrument in relation to a description of designs or articles in order to comply with international obligations or to secure or maintain reciprocal protection for British designs abroad. See s. 237(3) and (4) and s. 263(1), which defines 'British designs' as ones which qualify by reason of a connection of the designer, commissioner or employer with the United Kingdom.

126 S. 247(1) & (2).

127 S. 247(3).

128 S. 247(4) & (5).

129 S. 248(1)–(3). By s. 248(4), if the owner's identity could not be discovered on reasonable inquiry, and after the comptroller has settled the terms it is established that licences of right were not available, the licensee is not liable for damages or profits in respect of things done before he was aware of any claim by the owner that a licence of right was not available.

130 S. 247(6).

131 See s. 249 of the 1988 Act.

132 The authorization may be given before or after the use in question, and regardless of whether the person authorized also has a licence from the design right owner; see s. 240(6).

133 Moreover the buyer and his successors in title may freely deal with an article sold under the Crown use powers; see s. 240(7).

134 See s. 244.

135 S. 241(1). By s. 241(3), if the owner's identity is not ascertainable on reasonable inquiry, the department may apply to the court for an order that Crown use shall be free of payment until he agrees terms or applies to the court.

136 Ss. 241(2) and 252(1). For details relating to such proceedings, see s. 252(2)–(5).

137 See ss. 243, 271 and 295, and Sch. 5, para. 16, of the 1988 Act.
138 S. 242(1) & (2).
139 S. 242(3)–(6).
140 See pp. 165–6, above.
141 S. 246(1) & (2).
142 S. 246(3).
143 S. 251(1) & (2).
144 S. 251(3).
145 S. 251(4).
146 See ss. 229, 234, 235, 246, 252 and 253.
147 [1987] O.J. L24/36.
148 For the replacement, see reg. 10 of the 1989 Regulations, which also contains transitional provisions.
149 S.I. 1989/1100.
150 [1987] O.J. L313/22.
151 [1988] O.J. L140/13.
152 I.e. French Polynesia, French Southern and Antarctic Territories, Mayotte, New Caledonia and its dependencies, St. Pierre and Miquelon, or the Wallis and Fortuna Islands.
153 See reg. 6. But reg. 7 provides for the disregarding of an initial marketing which is subject to a confidence obligation in respect of information about the topography, other than one imposed under governmental pressure for military reasons.
154 See reg. 9.
155 Reg. 8(1) and (5).
156 Reg. 8(2) and (3).

Bibliography

COMMENTARIES

Blanco White, T.A., and Jacob, R., *Patents, Trade Marks, Copyright and Industrial Designs,* 3rd ed., Sweet & Maxwell (1986).

Cornish, W.R., *Intellectual Property: Patents, Copyright, Trade Marks and Allied Rights,* 2nd ed., Sweet & Maxwell (1989).

Dworkin, G., and Taylor, R.D., *Blackstone's Guide to the Copyright, Designs and Patents Act 1988,* Blackstone Press (1989).

Flint, M.F., *A User's Guide to Copyright,* 2nd ed., Butterworths (1985).

Laddie, H., Prescott, P., and Vitoria, M., *Modern Law of Copyright,* Butterworths (1980).

Phillips, J., *Introduction to Intellectual Property Law,* Butterworths (1986).

Skone James, E.P., Mummery, J.F., and Rayner James, J.E., *Copinger and Skone James on Copyright,* 12th ed., Sweet & Maxwell (1980).

McFarlane, G., *Copyright through the Cases,* Waterlow (1986).

OFFICIAL PUBLICATIONS

Whitford Report on *Copyright and Designs Law,* Cmnd. 6732 (1977).

1981 Green Paper, *Reform of the Law relating to Copyright, Designs and Performer's Protection,* Cmnd. 8302 (1981).

1983 Green Paper, *Intellectual Property Rights and Innovation,* Cmnd. 9117 (1983).

1985 Green Paper, *The Recording and Rental of Audio and Video Copyright Material,* Cmnd. 9445 (1985).

1986 White Paper, *Intellectual Property and Innovation,* Cmnd. 9712 (1986).

EC Commission, *Green Paper on Copyright and the Challenge of Technology – Copyright Issues requiring Immediate Action,* COM (88) 172 final, 7 June 1988.

Table of Cases

Index

buildings, 76; of registered designs, 152–3; and similarity, 57–66; by solo readings or recitations, 76; of unregistered design right, 164–5; of typefaces, 76–7

International conventions, 1–3

Legislation (British), 3–5

Licences: general rules, 103–4; licensing schemes, 104–15; Community competition law on, 116–29

Literary works, *see* Original works

Moral rights: against derogatory treatment, 134–6; against false attribution, 136–7; generally, 130–1; to identification, 131–4; in private photographs or films, 138

Musical works, *see* Original works

Original works: artistic works as, 19–22; authorial effort in, 11–12; computer programs as, *see* Computer programs; dramatic works as, 12; duration of copyright in, 34–5; fixation of, 9–11; literary works as, 12–14; musical works as, 12; originality of, 12

Originality, *see* Original works

Ownership, 27–30

Parliamentary copyright, *see* Crown and Parliamentary copyrights

Performers' rights: generally, 139–42; infringement of, 143–4; remedies for, 145–6; subsistence of, 142–3

Presumptions, 38–40

Publication, 33–5, 45–7

Published editions, 25

Registered designs, *see* Industrial designs

Remedies: Community policy on, 98–102; damages, 92–4; delivery up and disposal, 94–6; generally, 90–1; injunctions, 91–2; offences, 96–7; for performers' rights, 145–6; stoppage by Customs, 98

Sound recordings, 22, 36, 45–7

Semiconductor topographies, 169–71

Transitional provisions: generally, 3–4 and *passim*; on industrial designs, 159–61

Typographical arrangements, *see* Published editions

Unregistered design right, *see* Industrial designs